AF506126

The Political Economy of Competitiveness
in an Enlarged Europe

The Political Economy of Competitiveness in an Enlarged Europe

Julie Pellegrin
UNU/INTECH
Maastricht
The Netherlands

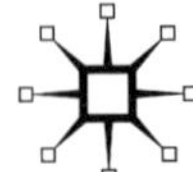

First published 2001 by
PALGRAVE
Houndmills, Basingstoke, Hampshire RG21 6XS and
175 Fifth Avenue, New York, N.Y. 10010
Companies and representatives throughout the world

PALGRAVE is the new global academic imprint of
St. Martin's Press LLC Scholarly and Reference Division and
Palgrave Publishers Ltd (formerly Macmillan Press Ltd).

ISBN 0–333–77572–4

This book is printed on paper suitable for recycling and made from fully managed and sustained forest sources.

A catalogue record for this book is available from the British Library.

Library of Congress Cataloging-in-Publication Data
Pellegrin, Julie, 1969–
    The political economy of competitiveness in an enlarged
    Europe / Julie Pellegrin.
        p. cm. — (Studies in economic transition)
    Includes bibliographical references and index.
    ISBN 0–333–77572–4
    1. European Union—Europe, Eastern. 2. European Union–
    –Europe, Central. 3. Europe, Eastern—Economic policy–
    –1989– 4. Europe, Central—Economic policy. 5. Competition,
    International. I. Title. II. Series.
    HC240.25.E852 P45 2001
    337.1'42—dc21
                                                              2001021883

10   9   8   7   6   5   4   3   2   1
10 09 08 07 06 05 04 03 02 01

Printed and bound in Great Britain by
Antony Rowe Ltd, Chippenham, Wiltshire

In memory of Susan Strange

Contents

List of Tables

List of Figures

Acknowledgements

This book draws its origin from research started at the European University Institute (Florence) for a PhD thesis carried out under the supervision of Professor S. Strange. As such, it is a product of the all-encompassing learning process that working with Susan Strange represents. My debt to her is academic, intellectual, personal and immeasureable. At an early conceptual stage, I greatly benefited from the analytical insight of Professor P. Messerlin (Institut d'Etudes Politiques de Paris), and from thorough discussions engaged in while visiting the Centre d'Etudes et de Recherche sur les Entreprises Multinationales (Université Paris X Nanterre), and the Berkeley Roundtable on the International Economy (University of California). This project has been possible thanks to extensive fieldwork undertaken from Prague (Central European University and CERGE) in the framework of several ACE Research Projects directed by Dr J. Sereghyová. Her support has been decisive, together with the encouragement of Professor V. Benacek. A second round of interviews has been undertaken thanks to a fellowship of the Abgeordnetenhauses of Berlin which enabled me to spend one year at the Wissenschaftszentrum-Berlin in possibly the most stimulating environment. All my thanks go to the managers of the firms I interviewed. By sharing with me their personal experience, they let me follow them through the maze of the historic transition of their countries. This contributed to make 'Central Europe' peculiarly central to my heart. I also would like to thank those civil servants at the European Commission who were genuinely concerned to make more 'transparent' the sometimes arcane Community procedures I was asking them about.

The book itself has been written while doing post-doctoral research at the Institute for German Studies (Birmingham) which has offered all the material support I needed. In particular, grants from the ESRC Programme 'One Europe or Several?' and from the Volkswagen Foundation are gratefully acknowledged.

Finally, my gratitude goes to Lynn K. Mytelka who opened new conceptual perspectives while providing indefatigable moral support, and to Jens Hölscher for his trust and friendly encouragement. Also special thanks to Claire McGrath for her careful corrections, and to Jean Pellegrin for his inalterable and accurate patience.

List of Abbreviations

CAD	Computer Assisted Design
CEEC4	The Czech Republic, Hungary, Poland and Slovakia
CEEC6	Bulgaria, Romania, Estonia, Lithuania, Latvia, and Slovenia
CEEC10	The Czech Republic, Hungary, Poland, Slovakia, Bulgaria, Romania, Estonia, Lithuania, Latvia and Slovenia
CEECs	Central and Eastern European countries
CMEA	Council for Mutual Economic Assistance (COMECON)
CNPN	Cross National Production Networks
COMECON	See CMEA
EC	European Community
ECU	European Currency Unit
EU	European Union
FDI	Foreign Direct Investment
GDP	Gross Domestic Product
HO	Heckscher–Ohlin
IIT	Intra-Industry Trade
IP	International Production
IPN	International Production Networks
ISC	International Sub-Contracting
IT	International Trade
JIT	Just-In-Time
M&A	Mergers and Acquisitions
MFA	Multi-Fibre Agreement
MNCs	Multinational Companies
NFI	New Forms of Investment
NIS	National Systems of Innovation
OEM	Original Equipment Manufacturer
OETH	Observatoire Europe[']en du Textile et de l'Habillement
OPT	Outward Processing Traffic
RCA	Revealed Comparative Advantage
SMEs	Small and Medium Sized Enterprises
T&C	Textile and Clothing

1
The Enlargement Problematic: Heterogeneity, Catching up and Convergence

At first sight, the opening up of Central and Eastern European countries (CEECs) unleashes unprecedented potential for accelerated growth and enhanced competitiveness across Europe. By rendering 'readily' available markets and cheap skilled labour, liberalisation enables Western firms to realise economies of scale and scope as well as providing the opportunity to relocate those segments of the production process which are no longer competitively produced in their domestic economies. At the same time, the process is expected to offer CEECs' firms much needed access to markets, capital and technology. This is a rosy picture of a game where each player apparently has something to gain. But a less optimistic version is equally possible. What if Western firms seize market shares, local firms are locked into low wage specialisation patterns, and no substantial capital and technology, let alone knowledge, is transferred, with the result that local firms are not competitive enough to take advantage of trade liberalisation? Alternatively, how about the possibility of massive imports of 'sensitive goods' and waves of immigration disrupting Western markets with the relocation of Western production to the East potentially causing a significant increase of unemployment in the economies of the European Union (EU)?

These polarisations are exaggerated, but they are quite useful in highlighting two important features characterising the twin processes of CEECs' opening up, and of the Eastern enlargement of the European Union. First, the risks and opportunities mentioned above arise from differentials – of an unprecedented magnitude – between levels of development of CEECs and EU countries. Enlarging the EU by up to 10 new members and possibly more thus has the effect of introducing heterogeneity in a model of integration, based until now on homogeneity. Second, it is not clear exactly who the main beneficiaries of the process are in economic terms. It is generally acknowledged that in the long run enlargement is a positive sum game (Black, 1997). Open and wider markets will obviously benefit EU firms. Moreover, CEEC companies will be able to export freely to the Single European Market and expect, in return, increased levels of foreign direct investments. However, in the short term, there are certain risks that the process could derail, mainly due to the very demanding accession procedures CEECs have to undergo. In this respect, CEECs' positions are broadly favourable even though they have the most to lose, while the EU's reluctance and hesitation appear unjustified if potential costs are compared to the likely benefits (Ellison, 1999).

These interrogations and contradictions can only be explained by the highly political dimension of the rationale driving the whole process of enlargement, as well as by a rather poor assessment of its economic implications. The fact is that the eastward enlargement of the EU has the potential to radically alter the basis of competitiveness in Europe, in the sense that it can make Europe a much more 'attractive place to do business' (Strange, 1998). Whether Western and Eastern firms are able to take advantage of trade liberalisation to foster a dynamic process of regional integration in which differentials are made complementary will have far-reaching consequences for 'European competitiveness' as defined above. However, contrary to what happened in the case of the launch of the Single European Market, there is a surprising lack both of study of the issues and political instrumentalisation of the argument.[1] Political leaders, policy makers and public opinion seem to be either very focused on possible dangers or distracted by the grand political vision that underlies the whole edifice of the enlargement process. As a result, EU enlargement policies continue to be characterised by an exploitative attitude towards CEECs, with little understanding that the best guarantee against the risks associated with CEECs' opening up is if the dynamics of growth in the region take off. It is certainly not the least paradoxical that, while the enlargement process risks establishing new dividing lines in Europe – or at least does nothing to reduce them – it actually posits that accession countries 'converge' towards EU standards. The enlargement process makes necessary structural reforms within the EU in order to cope with the sheer number of candidate countries, and the degree of economic heterogeneity between the latter and current member states (Grabbe and Hughes, 1998). However, in the face of relative uncertainty concerning the EU's ability to undertake such reforms, it is vital that CEECs adopt sound development trajectories so as to catch up with Western levels of development without relying too much on the EU.

What effective strategy could be implemented in order to reach this goal? To assess this, a full understanding of the mutations at work in the world economy is necessary as the opening up of CEECs is taking place at a quite specific time in the history of international competition (Mytelka, 1991; Stopford and Strange with Henley, 1991). The increasing knowledge content of competitiveness has reduced its cost component so that it is no longer sufficient to rely on low costs in order to be successful in world markets. Rather, new requirements – in terms of flexibility, quality and rapidity – are to be fulfilled. These make necessary a special focus on the conditions promoting a process of continuous innovation within firms and economies (Ernst *et al.*, 1998). In short, if they are to catch up, CEECs must establish a 'knowledge-based economy'. International linkages in general, and international production networks in particular, are going to be crucial in this process. As essential channels through which technology and knowledge can be diffused throughout the economies of CEECs, they are expected to help establish new innovation systems following the disintegration of those in place under a command economy (Radosevic, 2000).

Overall, Central and Eastern European countries do not constitute new economic tigers but, rather, they are peculiar latecomers in the race for development. They have to contend simultaneously with a redefinition of the terms of international competition and a quite cumbersome process of accession to the EU. No one exactly knows whether the two sets of factors reinforce their respective difficulties or, on the contrary, whether they ease one another's constraints. However, much depends on this issue. Whether Europe's competitive position in the world economy will be strengthened is conditional upon the capacity of enlargement to provide an appropriate response to the development challenge that CEECs have to face in the context of economic globalisation.

This volume provides insight into whether and how CEECs are able to catch up within the dual context of the enlargement process and a redefinition of the terms of international competition. It does so on the basis of evidence derived from an analysis of outward processing traffic (OPT), an EU measure promoting and/or controlling the relocation of production activity of EU firms to CEECs. Despite the very significant share that OPT occupies in CEECs' foreign trade, the arrangement has gone strangely unnoticed. Yet, beyond its quantitative importance, of critical interest is OPT's contradictory nature – as a policy measure based on the exploitation of wage differentials *and* as an instrument in the hands of local firms to learn and to upgrade their technological capabilities.

The OPT story is thus at the core of the enlargement problematic. By assessing whether an old-fashioned policy measure can be transformed into an instrument to weather the challenges of international competition, the study of OPT offers evidence as to whether and under what conditions – that is, at what speed and at the instigation of whom – increased heterogeneity in Europe is turned into complementarity and convergence. Ultimately, OPT evidence is useful in testing whether the process of enlargement is able to facilitate both reaping the benefits of globalisation as well as avoidance of its pitfalls.

A political hurdle: entrenching asymmetries and preaching convergence

The redefinition of the action framework

The fall of the Berlin Wall in 1989 brought about a drastic redefinition of the framework of opportunities and constraints within which European firms have traditionally designed their strategies. The major feature here is the fact that the opening up of CEEC markets brings together countries which are at very different levels of development. Overall, real GDP per head in CEECs is 32 per cent of the EU's average.[2] What is more, there are considerable disparities *among* CEECs: while incomes in the Czech Republic, Hungary, Poland, Slovakia and Slovenia are between one-third and two-thirds of the EU average, the rest were below one-third of the EU average in 1995 (Grabbe and Hughes, 1997). In fact, besides differences in *levels* of development, the two areas are characterised by different *forms* (or nature) of development determined by very different histories – something which might be as, if not more, important in understanding how firms will adjust their strategies to this new context.[3]

If they are associated with risks, and perceived as a threat to their vested interests by some of the actors who are party to the integration process, these differences are also sources of considerable opportunities. First, the liberalisation of economic transactions between East and West makes new markets available. As sharply noted by Strange, 'the size of the market' is the strongest motivation for the immediate – and unconditional – accession of CEECs to the EU (Strange, 1998: 111). At country level, however, the opening up of CEECs makes available markets whose individual size is rather limited, the only exception being the case of Poland (Table 1.1). Another factor limiting the attractiveness of CEECs as consumer markets is the low level of income of the population. In this respect, potential in terms of *growth* is of interest to would-be investors.

Table 1.1   Growth rates of real GDP/NMP (%)

	94/95	*96/95*	*96/97*	*97/98*
Czech Republic	+6.4	+3.9	+1.0	−2.7
Hungary	+1.4	+1.4	+4.5	+5.0
Poland	+7.0	+6.0	+6.9	+4.8

Source: UNECE (1999).

Second, the opening up of CEECs brings together economies characterised by large wage differentials. This offers EU firms an alternative production base, something which comes at a particularly appropriate moment during a period of heightened world-wide competition. From a Western perspective, CEECs' comparative advantage in labour-intensive goods is associated with proximity, thus enabling Western firms to take advantage of lower production costs in their immediate vicinity. Indeed, in 1997, 'unit labour costs' were half the Austrian level taken as a reference (Lavigne, 1999: 226). The evolution of wages in CEECs, however, appears to follow a generally increasing trend. What is more, despite remarkable increases since 1991, relatively low absolute levels of labour productivity compensate partially for low labour costs. Finally, an acceleration of inflation might also undermine advantages based on low labour costs.

This combination of large markets and lower production costs has – prima facie – tremendous potential for enhanced competitiveness and growth. However, besides some doubt concerning the real economic significance of the potential that is thus apparently unbridled, there is also a relative uncertainty regarding the identity of winners and losers in the process. For example, who will actually benefit from CEECs' comparative advantage in low labour costs is not entirely clear. This might either be Western firms relocating production eastwards or Eastern producers penetrating EU markets, thus posing a competitive threat to the positions of EU producers. Fundamentally, it is this question of the terms of economic interdependence between areas at such different levels of development which is thus posed.

This book examines OPT developments as an indicator in order to determine ways in which Western and Eastern European firms are reorganising their production activities in this new context. How they make use of the arrangement is indeed indicative of the thrust towards regional integration in Europe. Research findings offer a valuable means of assessing the potential for CEECs to catch up with Western standards.

However, before explaining why this is so, it is first necessary to clarify the other factor that renders OPT a good source of evidence as to whether CEECs are gaining from integration. OPT is a measure devised by EU policy-makers, and if there is a fundamental feature characterising the development of economic interdependence between Western and Eastern Europe, it is indeed its high degree of 'institutionalisation'.

The enlargement constraint: convergence

In the face of a fundamental difficulty in predicting the terms under which East–West (inter)dependence will develop, the process of enlargement poses the principle of convergence as an unquestioned and imperative mode of integration.

The level of heterogeneity reached among economies participating in the integration process is a new feature in the story of regional integration in Europe. This renders the European case more akin to other integration experiences in the world economy. Europe is now one of the three areas where a process of integration brings together economies at different levels of development, be they separated by a clear-cut border in the case of NAFTA on the US/Mexican frontier, or clustered in several tiers as in the Asian example. It is however necessary to relativise this heterogeneity, and not to push comparisons too far. Development gaps reached in Europe are surely greater than ever, but there is also a tendency to overemphasise them, a feature that could mask an underlying political intention. Indeed, Grabbe and Hughes (1997) note that disparities presented by CEECs are not considerably greater than those already existing within the EU. What is more, the degree of heterogeneity introduced in Europe by the enlargement process does not seriously compare with that characterising Asia. Each example of regional dynamics is, in fact, governed by a different logic which in turn depends on the different constraints at work in the world economy when the respective integration processes were initiated (the mode of international competition), as well as on intrinsic features. These include the degree of institutionalisation accompanying the establishment and development of economic interdependence, the latter being very specific to the European case.

However great, these levels of heterogeneity are in stark contrast with the mode of operation on which integration in Europe has been based until now. That regional integration brings about the convergence of participating economies is predicted by theories of international trade and production. However, in the European case it is not market forces alone which are responsible for such convergence; this also results from the high degree of institutionalisation noted above. As a matter of fact, the EU is a formidable device that produces homogeneity from gaps and differentials. The integration process of Western European economies has been based on two key notions of *convergence* and *cohesion*: redistributing resources in order to bring about homogeneous living standards across the Union. Two instruments of redistribution in such a system are the structural funds and the Cohesion Fund. Both are expected to narrow economic disparities across EU member states, the former by providing aid at regional level, the latter by making additional funds available at a national level.

The problem is that the funds' mechanisms which have been used until now can hardly offer a solution to help CEECs reach convergence.[4] These mechanisms have indeed been instrumental in previous enlargements to promote the process of adjustment to EU standards that successful candidates to membership were obliged to undergo. However, this happened in the context of starting levels of divergences and differentials which were broadly in line with the capacities of the funds' system to cope with them, especially in the case of individual 'developed' countries such as the UK, or of groups of countries like the European Free Trade Agreement (EFTA). The cases of Ireland, Greece and the Iberian countries are more relevant in offering some lessons to CEECs as these confronted the whole system of redistribution to a higher level of disparity. For example, GDP perhead in Portugal was 31 per cent of the EU/EC average at the time of entry, and GDP per head in Greece and Spain amounted to, respectively, 43 per cent and 54 per cent of the EU average.

In terms of GDP per capita, the political frictions which took place on the occasion of defining Objective One[5] illustrated the first cracks in the system. It was clear that the whole system was very much dependent on the goodwill of net contributors to the EU budget (first, among others, Germany). More importantly from the CEECs' viewpoint, it appeared that benefiting from the system of funds was by no means a sufficient condition to actually being successful in achieving growth and competitiveness. The trajectories of growth followed by countries of the 'Southern tier enlargements' are indeed very differentiated. Whereas Spain could secure rapid growth due to increased industrial productivity, Ireland based its success on an outward policy stance, and an efficient – and lucky – management of foreign direct investment. Greece, however, lags behind in this picture, demonstrating that integration *per se* and extension of benefits associated with the structural funds are far from being able to guarantee automatic convergence. In short, belonging to the club is not enough to secure growth and competitiveness (Ellison, 1999).

Furthermore, even if relativised, the levels of disparity CEECs bring with them render the present system truly unworkable. The challenge, indeed, is even wider ranging as the Eastern enlargement takes place in a context of greater global uncertainties. It concerns not one or two countries but no less than at least two rounds of five countries each round taking place in a far shorter period of time than previously. To leave the system of structural and cohesion funds in place when CEECs access the EU and extending this to applicant countries would simply be impractical in terms of costs.[6] It has been estimated that in present terms, the 10 applicant countries would receive a total of 42.1 bn ECU compared to a total of 28.4 bn ECU for the EU15 in 1999. The problem is that it would not only be difficult to find the matching funds, it would also be difficult for recipient CEECs to absorb inflow of capital which could amount to more than 40 per cent of total GDP (in the case of Lithuania) (Grabbe and Hughes, 1998).[7] In addition, the entry of 10 new members would bring about a shift in recipients of the cohesion and structural funds causing inevitable political frictions and conflicts.[8] In 'Agenda 2000', its blueprint for enlargement published in July 1997, the Commission started to explore ways of stretching the EU budget so as to cover the costs of enlargement. However, it is necessary to go beyond this to undertake deep structural reforms.[9] What is at stake is the redefinition of some of the fundamental working principles that have underpinned the integration process until now, such as equality of treatment between member states.[10] Whether, how, and how long this will take is not clear as yet.

Far from helping reduce divergences, the accession procedures of CEECs to the EU risk not only entrenching present development differentials, but also establishing new dividing lines in Europe. The current hesitation and procrastination concerning CEECs' eventual membership is having a particularly detrimental effect, to the extent that the present situation has been described 'abysmal' (Lorentzen, 1998: 17). First, discrimination between fast-track accession and backmarker countries inevitably widens the gaps between them. Second, the very demanding procedures candidates must undergo before achieving membership – that is, to comply with the 'acquis', requires enormous deployment of resources – both financial and other. The fact that the acquis is a moving target (since the body of legislation is in a state of constant expansion), and that it is not accompanied by a fixed term for actual formal accession has the effect of substantially increasing uncertainties without working towards con-vergence. The problem is that in the meantime, EU economies are moving forward. As a result, the longer CEEC candidates are kept in the waiting room, the greater the risk of widening gaps. What is more, the process itself contains intrinsic elements of division. Since it is both cumbersome and expensive, only those firms which are best prepared and most informed will be able to first identify the body of legislation relevant to their activity, and then engage the necessary transformations. In short, foreign-owned firms or joint ventures which can benefit from some form of imported knowledge will be favoured as opposed to local firms less used to mastering EU procedures.

Thus, far from being an instrument to promote growth and development, the process of complying with the acquis may actually widen a series of gaps between CEECs' first and second tiers, between locally-owned and foreign-owned firms within CEEC economies, and, finally, between the EU and the accession countries as a whole. In this context, some argue that CEECs would be well advised to employ the resources they are currently devoting to compliance with the acquis to reach other more compelling priorities in terms of development. Thus, on the face of it, the more optimistic commentators consider the acquis as a formidable incentive to engage rapid and profound transformation in CEECs which would speed up the processes of change that will be necessary in any event.

The enlargement paradox: EU policies and the temptation of entrenched differentials

Accession procedures are not the only measures that can be incriminated as doing little to reduce development differentials between the EU and CEECs. The fact is that EU policies and approaches to neighbouring Eastern countries have long been based on the deepest of possible divides; the Berlin Wall. With such historical antecedents, it has proved difficult and sometimes vain to try and depart from a line which has taken differentials for granted. Past relations and approaches still weigh heavily in the structuring of present ones.

Although the political frontier crumbled very suddenly on 3 October 1989, dismantling the economic one was a far more progressive process. Though limited, exchanges were allowed to take place before the 1989 events (with German firms being the almost exclusive beneficiaries of these windows of opportunity), and the opening up of CEECs which followed has been, in fact, a protracted and uneven process. Free trade was not established at once, and time has been used as a factor to determine the benefits and the beneficiaries of trade liberalisation. Hence, the 'Europe Agreements' which provide for the establishment of free trade over a period of ten years have been one potentially powerful instrument to influence patterns of trade and production specialisation. In certain cases, the process of trade liberalisation has further entrenched asymmetries between CEECs and EU countries but not necessarily in the expected direction.[11] There is an extensive literature criticising the EU approach to CEECs on this topic. For example, the bilateral stance adopted by the EC/EU when negotiating with CEECs has been held responsible for fostering a 'hub-and-spoke' structure of economic relations (Baldwin, 1994).[12] In addition, the Europe Agreements have been accused of overt and hidden protectionism. While making access to EU markets for the so-called 'sensitive goods' particularly difficult (Rollo and Smith, 1993), a fine tuning approach to liberalisation was adopted, and numerous discrete actions taken such as the multiplication of safeguard clauses and other anti-dumping measures (Messerlin, 1992, 1993).

The OPT arrangement must be analysed in this context of policy measures entrenching old differentials and giving rise to new dividing lines in an enlarged Europe. It is a remarkable example while illustrates the mentality and the approach adopted by EU/EC politicians and policy makers when devising policies dealing with CEECs. This specific custom regime grants preferential trade access (under the form of a reduction and sometimes a suspension[13] of tariff and/or access to additional quantitative restrictions – specific OPT quota) to CEEC exports to the EU which are actually *re*-exports, that is, which were preceded by imports of material sent by EU producers to CEECs in order to be processed there.

This measure was devised on the model of a US measure, and at a time when the international crisis triggered – or accelerated – the decline of traditional sectors in developed countries, eroding their competitiveness and putting employment at risk. In this context, the OPT measure was expected to enable the relocation of EU firms' production activities abroad, while keeping the process under close political monitoring so as to minimise adverse consequences for domestic employment levels. Indeed, the preferential treatment extended to re-imports into the Single European Market is granted to EU producers only if these producers respect the many stringent conditions concerning the level of production maintained at home. At the same time, the OPT mechanisms help protect against imports from competing CEEC firms.

Thus, it is in a very literal sense that the OPT regime influences the distribution of gains resulting from trade liberalisation. Since it is foreign partners who source the input and market the output, local CEEC producers are deprived of their market power at both ends of the production chain. This implies that CEECs' comparative and local firms' competitive advantages are exploited, not directly by local firms, but indirectly by their EU partners. The OPT mechanisms are thus a clever way of transforming potentially rival patterns of specialisation into complementary ones (Zysman and Schwartz, 1998) in such a way that the interests of EU producers are preserved (Ellison, 1999: 268).

Overall, there is a strong tension between the tradition of EU policies towards CEECs based both on exploitation of heterogeneity between the two areas and on the principles of convergence and cohesion which have been driving the European integration process until now. It is not in the least paradoxical that the whole process of enlargement actually posits that CEECs catch up rapidly with EU levels and standards, while the enlargement policies of the EU do very little to offer CEECs effective means of development – if they are not actually contributing to the entrenchment of development differentials between the two areas.

Corporate strategies: espousing or blurring the divides?

If decisions taken in the political sphere are important elements influencing the terms under which divergences across Europe are made compatible, in the end, it is corporate strategies which are the ultimate determining factor. The opening up of CEECs offers many opportunities to both Western and Eastern firms to boost their competitiveness. The question is thus how, or whether at all, these potentials are being seized, and for whom exactly the benefits – if any – of liberalisation are *in fact* accruing. Does corporate integration contribute to further entrenchment of the differentials now characterising an enlarged Europe? Is it helping reduce these gaps? Or, is it creating new dividing lines? Lastly, to what extent does the policy framework set up by the EU determine corporate strategies?

One major drawback regarding the literature on East–West integration is that trade and foreign direct investment (FDI) tend to be analysed separately, while OPT itself is little analysed – if at all. This is rather unfortunate. First, this is because OPT is an important – if neglected – aspect of East–West corporate integration; in addition, the three are different facets of economic/corporate integration, not fully-fledged separate sorts of integration vehicles. In fact, OPT is in-between arm's length trade and FDI: it takes place between firms that are legally independent, but it involves a close partnership between two firms, so that it is appropriate to talk about vertical 'quasi-integration' and 'quasi-intra-firm trade'. These three vehicles of integration will be briefly reviewed in the following sections to try and ascertain whether corporate integration contributes to the imperative of 'convergence' posited by the enlargement process.

Trade

The *quantitative* contribution of foreign trade with the EU to CEECs' economic performances is without contest. Indeed, CEECs have been very successful in reorienting their trade relations towards Western Europe. In 1994, the EU had already become the most important market for CEECs' exports, accounting for over half the total. However, different asymmetries characterise this general statement. First, four CEECs account for over three-quarters of total imports and exports with the EU while the other CEECs trailed well behind. In decreasing order of magnitude they are: Poland (30 per cent of total trade with the EU), the Czech Republic (20 per cent), Hungary (16 per cent), and Slovenia (10 per cent). Table 1.2 shows how the degree of trade dependence on the EU can vary across CEECs.

Second, for nine out of the ten CEECs listed in Table 1.2, Germany is the single most important trading partner in the EU. In trading terms, Germany is in fact often many times more dominant than the second most important EU partner. Overall, Germany accounts for about half of total EU exports to and imports from CEECs.

Finally, there are persistent trade surpluses in favour of the EU even though the latter appear to be quite manageable for most CEECs (the average amounted to 5.7 per cent of GDP in 1996).[14]

There is much debate and uncertainty concerning the question of whether the structure of CEECs' foreign trade is moving as a whole towards more elaborate products, as well as to considerable methodological difficulties. A number of studies testify to the fact that CEECs are not locked into traditional specialisation patterns and that they are also developing new capacities.[15] In particular, there are encouraging signs

Table 1.2   EU share of CEECs' world imports in 1995 (%)

	1995
Slovenia	79
Poland	69
Hungary	67
Czech Republic	66
Estonia	65
Bulgaria	56
Romania	54
Latvia	45
Slovakia	44
Lithuania	37

Source: Grabbe, Hughes (1997).

regarding the strengthening of the technological content of CEECs' trade (Hotopp and Radosevic, 1999). Of specific concern, however, is the fact that all these studies note to some extent increasing disparities throughout the region with respect to the ability of CEECs' export structures to shift in favour of more capital- and skill-intensive products.

Foreign direct investments

There is much expectation placed on foreign direct investment (FDI) as an instrument to spur restructuring processes in CEECs, but its actual contribution is rather controversial. An assessment of the role of FDI in CEECs transformation process is possibly even more difficult since strong variations take place almost on a firm-by-firm basis. However, a few aggregate features appear. First, levels of FDI are generally considered to be low compared to expectations and to other regional experiences.[16]

Table 1.3 shows the marked country differences characterising FDI in the region. Roughly, two 'tiers' can be identified, with the first four countries taking around 80 per cent of FDI to the region. Germany and the US share first position as far as the source of FDI is concerned. It is interesting to note that in this instance there is less of a polarisation (dependence) on Germany than is the case with trade. However, German firms hold the first position for FDI in Hungary and a German presence is strongest in the Czech Republic (30 per cent of the stocks of FDI in 1995). In Poland, German firms occupy first position in terms of the number of local firms with German participation, but they rank third for the total amount of invested capital. Overall, German FDI in the region is characterised by certain specific features such as variations in Germany's share of FDI across countries and the low amount of capital engaged, a feature which probably reflects the involvement of German small and medium-sized enterprises ('Mittelstand') in CEECs.

Table 1.3   FDI inward stock in 1997 (M $), and cumulative FDI inflow per capita in 1998 ($)

	1998	
	Stock	*Flow*
Czech Republic	6 763	1 010
Hungary	15 882	1 720
Poland	16 463	385
Slovakia	1 293	267
Romania	2 467	180
Bulgaria	943	131

Sources: World Investment Report (1998) and UNECE (1999).

In terms of inflows of capital,[17] local firms count on FDI in a manner beyond expectations in order to gain access to market and technology. However, FDI to CEECs have been generally documented as taking place for market access reasons (Meyer, 1998; Widmaier and Potratz, 1999: 19). MNCs engage relatively large FDI with the main aim of securing market shares of what is expected to be a fast growing regional market. Although at the beginning of the transition process, FDI mostly consisted of joint ventures, since 1993, the establishment of 'greenfield plants' (i.e. enterprises that are newly established and 100 per cent owned by the foreign investor) has become the preferred form of involvement. Implications for the possibility of spillover are problematic. The traditional view has it that greenfields create more value (i.e. activities with higher knowledge and R&D content) and can involve new suppliers. On the other hand, greenfields can be held to be more likely to operate either in isolation, or in 'enclaves' consisting of domestic suppliers who followed their customers (Benacek *et al.*, 1999). Overall, besides the involvement of German *Mittelstand*, FDI in CEECs appears to be a game played by big multinationals more concerned by first mover advantage than by the effective spillover of knowledge and techniques to their local partners. Considering how high were the expectations placed on FDI as an 'engine of growth',[18] it is perhaps no surprise that disillusionment quickly followed. Foreign direct investment has been the object of several waves of criticism which accused foreign investors of buying the family silver (Sinn and Weichenrieder, 1997), and of rendering local economies excessively vulnerable to cyclical downturns in the home economies of the firms which have invested in CEECs.

Most of the analyses of East–West integration stop here, after they have considered trade and/or – more often 'or', in fact – direct investments. They thus miss the fact that an important part of the (re)organisation of international production in CEECs actually takes the form of OPT.[19] If they are not compared with, or complemented by data on OPT, the above figures might 'hide more than they reveal' (Stopford and Strange with Henley, 1991: 18). This is a drawback this study intends to address.

Outward processing traffic

Evidence on OPT presents a sudden rectification to the previous analysis of trade and FDI. The fact that a significant part of East–West economic transaction is actually undertaken under this very peculiar arrangement devised at EU level presents the most serious contention that EU policies play(ed) a role in the process of CEECs' trade and production specialisation.

The OPT measure has been an important factor contributing to past and present trade performances of CEECs. This 'temporary' trade still accounts for a non-negligible proportion of CEECs foreign trade, and, in certain sectors and countries, it keeps growing. There are many technical difficulties, however, in keeping track of this specific type of trade. In particular, there is a strong mismatch between EU sources (EUROSTAT) and local ones. For example, in 1997, the arrangement was estimated by local sources to account for 26 per cent of both Hungarian and Czech exports to the EU,[20] a figure roughly confirmed by UN sources (which apply to Poland as well)[21] (UNECE, 1997). However, the corresponding figures produced by EUROSTAT for 1997 amount to approximately 10 per cent for the three countries. For the sake of consistency (and the longer time span covered), the EUROSTAT data are highlighted below. These data are lower, yet they still display relatively high proportions. For example, in 1993/94 (a peak), around 20 per cent of Polish and Hungarian exports to the EU, and 12 per cent of Czech exports to the EU were in fact *re*-exported after processing of material 'temporarily' imported from the EU.

As to the source of OPT activities, here again there is no surprise. In fact, the role of German actors, which characterises East–West patterns of interdependence in general, is even more markedly important in the case of OPT. As a matter of fact, Germany makes far more use of the arrangement than do counterparts from other EU countries. Not only does Germany undertake 2.5 times more OPT in CEECs than other EU firms, but they are also characterised by a preference for OPT as opposed to FDI. In Hungary for example, the German share in EU OPT is 80 per cent, whereas the German share in FDI ranges between 40 per cent and 45 per cent. All this suggests that a distinctive feature of Germany's involvement in CEECs is its greater engagement with sub-contracting activities. Whether development of German OPT results from activity of the 'Mittelstand' or whether it takes place at the instigation of larger firms is of specific relevance to understand whether and how the opening up of CEECs can engineer a deep restructuring of the German industrial basis (Hughes, 1996).

The fact that an important part of CEECs' foreign trade is due to the internationalisation of EU (German) production activities in the form of OPT poses a number of questions concerning the terms of economic interdependence developing between the EU and CEECs. As a matter of fact, the mechanisms described above promote the vertical division of labour on a regional scale, and tie CEEC firms into vertical production chains controlled by EU firms. In the face of the very low entry and exit costs that the arrangement offers to foreign firms, local partners are being cut off for some time from both upstream and downstream linkages. Deprived as they are from their market power at both ends of the production chain, local firms are therefore placed in a quite vulnerable position if foreign partners decide to withdraw from their engagement. If EU – effectively German – partners take advantage of the flexibility that the arrangement offers to withdraw from their commitment, is this to say that between 10 per cent and 20 per cent of CEECs' foreign trade is at risk? Conversely, but equally detrimentally, foreign partners may actually stay committed to their local partners and lock the latter into the low end of their production chain.[22] In one word, OPT would promote the 'maquiladorisation' of CEECs (Ellingstad, 1997) and contribute to a pattern of specialisation based on low wages of the least dynamic sort.

A more favourable prospect would be that local firms take advantage of their partnerships to learn new techniques and know-how so as to be ready when – end if – their partners leave – and engage in production on their own. Finally, local firms might well remained tied to the production chain of their partners but they can develop the capacity necessary to upgrade their position in their partner's value-added chain.

As a very preliminary conclusion drawn from the above broad picture, it is important to emphasise the fact that in the different aspects of integration described, and in OPT in particular, German firms figure as pre-eminent economic partners, responsible on some occasions for overwhelming proportions of CEECs' foreign economic relations. A second striking characteristic of EU–CEECs economic relations is their degree of unevenness, nurtured to varying degrees by corporate strategies under the influence of EU policies. Corporate integration does not seem to be helping to reduce gaps between the EU and CEECs. Rather, it reproduces and even introduces dividing lines among CEECs. These very much reflect the political position of candidate countries in the accession process. As Grabbe and Hughes (1998) put it, 'investors show the same preferences as the EU and NATO in terms of (CEECs') relative progress'.

It is in this difficult context that CEECs are expected to catch up and converge towards EU levels of development. In the face of relative uncertainty regarding the ability of the EU not only to provide CEECs with effective means to achieve this objective, but even simply to refrain from making the process more difficult than it already is (and because corporate integration does not show signs that it can be the only motor fostering growth and development in CEECs), it is imperative that CEECs engage their own strategies of development. In Ellison's words:

The deepening of relations between CEECs and the EU should depend less upon the ability of the CEECs to conform to EU standards, and much more on the ability of the EU to offer significant benefits to the CEECs, and on the ability of the CEECs *to develop long-term economic growth potential.* (Ellison, 1999: 283)[23]

For this, CEECs need to take into account a completely different set of difficulties which is no less compelling, but which at the same time offers many new opportunities: what is loosely termed 'globalisation'.

The globalisation imperative: learning to catch up

Coping with the contradictions of the enlargement process is a quite challenging task. To this must be added another source of constraints as well as opportunities resulting from the drastic changes that have been place in the world economy in the last 20 years. CEECs' opening up has indeed come at a specific time in the history of international competition, characterised by fast moving changes. 'Globalisation', that is, the multiplication of risks and opportunities in the world economy, is bearing upon the way firms compete. This cannot but have direct repercussions on the development paths and strategies of individual countries. The very notion of globalisation blurred as it is, is highly controversial, although this is not the place to resolve the issue. What is of interest here, is to briefly outline some of the main features characterising present 'competitive conditions' and then assess the implications for countries entering the 'development race', at this peculiar point in time in general, and for CEECs in particular.

The new terms of international competition

The opening up of CEEC markets happens at a quite peculiar moment in the history of international competition. It is vain to try and characterise the latter in an exhaustive and synthetic manner. The reason has precisely to do with a fundamental feature characterising competitive conditions in a 'global era': the increasing *volatility* with which firms and states are confronted (Stopford and Strange with Henley, 1991: 4). In other words:

> this era lacks a dominant style. It is distinctively diverse and uncertain. It is not just that the terms of corporate competition have been altered. Rather, a multiplicity of corporate and national strategies compete to capture advantage in volatile markets. (Borrus and Zysman, 1998)

Increased economic uncertainty materialises at different levels on the production as well as on the demand side. Ultimately, however, it is connected to a 'changing relationship of knowledge to production' in the context of the overhaul of the old Fordist model of mass production and consumption (Mytelka, 1991). This has several implications in terms of what CEECs need to master if they are to catch up in a context of heightened world-wide competition.

Cost versus knowledge

At the core of these developments lies a change in the components of competitiveness. The 1980s were marked by 'the diminishing significance of low labour costs and access to raw material as a source of competitive advantage, and the increasing importance of quality production methods and proximity to markets' (Porter, 1986).[24] Competitiveness thus increasingly includes 'soft' elements such as the ability to compete on delivery, to differentiate products – and to do this rapidly. The fact that technological competitiveness develops at the expense of cost competitiveness implies that more emphasis in the production process is placed on innovation and knowledge. 'Innovation' should be understood here in a broad sense. It certainly refers to technological *breakthrough*, the accelerated pace of which has, as a main consequence, drastic cuts in product cycles. The notion also extends its reach below the technology frontier. It is

> a process by which firms master and implement the design and the production of goods and services that are new to them irrespective of whether or not they are new to their competitors – domestic or foreign. (Ernst *et al.*, 1998: 13)

However, if competition is more knowledge-based, it does not mean that costs are no longer relevant. On the contrary, minimum costs are taken for granted so that simply competing on this basis is not enough. What is more, the ways to actually reduce costs are in essence more innovative. In short, quality and costs are still necessary conditions to compete successfully. However, 'knowledge' now makes the critical difference.

Regional corporate integration and international production networks

To comply with the requirements of the increasing knowledge content of production and in order to face uncertainty, firms need to be as flexible as possible. In order to achieve this, they increasingly resort to non-equity forms of inter-firm agreements. An 'organisational response' to globalisation, international production networks (IPNs) is woven throughout the world economy by multinational corporations (MNCs)[25] and generally retain a strong regional structure (Borrus and Zysman, 1998; Ernst, 1999). They can have many different forms,[26] but they are characterised by a common trend towards the de-integration of the production chain. This applies at all levels, from outsourcing at an upstream stage to mergers and acquisitions (M&As) and other forms of strategic partnering further downstream of the production chain. This corresponds to the development of what can be defined as 'knowledge-based networked oligopolies' (UNCTAD, 1999; Delapierre and Mytelka, 1998). In 'true' global industries, like the automotive sector, suppliers are organised into different tiers, the first of which is responsible for the modularised production of whole sub-assemblies. Hence, and new and more flexible production methods such as Just-In-Time (JIT) can be implemented the cost burden passed on to local suppliers.

Implications for development strategies: what is specific about CEECs?

What are the implications of all this for CEEC firms and governments those presently engaging strategies so as to catch up? First, and importantly, low wage specialisation of the least dynamic sort is less than ever tenable. This is not to say that CEECs should try and specialise in high tech sectors at all costs. Many alternatives exist, including strategies such as specialisation into market 'niches,' those where demand is particularly dynamic.[27]

More fundamentally, strategies of development need to be devised on the one hand according to the specific 'moment' characterising competition conditions, and on the other hand on the level (and *nature*) of development of a country as well as other features proper to the particular history, practices, and institutions of the considered country. In short, 'one-size-fits-all' policies are simply untenable. Depending on whether firms and countries are to 'catch up', to 'keep up', or to 'get ahead', different objectives will need to be pursued (Ernst *et al.*, 1998).[28] In a catch up phase, what matters is the ability to change and adapt, that is, to *learn*. In fact, to be more precise, Ernst *et al.* (1998), borrowing the notion from Stiglitz, insist that what is central is 'learning to learn'.[29] The objective of making possible the conditions for innovation should thus not be taken in too technicist a sense, and its successful achievement should not be measured (only) in terms of R&D intensity. Rather, the emphasis should be placed on the ability of local firms to *learn* processes and practices which are new to them. How?

The literature on national innovation systems (NIS)[30] helps determine the general conditions under which innovation activities develop. Innovation is an interactive process socially, and institutionally embedded. It involves a large range of actors linked through networks. Interactions and linkages between 'users' and 'producers' of technology enable exchange and diffusion of the decisive tacit component of knowledge on which competitiveness is based (Lundvall, 1988)[31].

The main drawback of this stream of literature is that it – deliberately[32] – fails to take into consideration the international dimension of the learning process. In fact, the pervasive and highly influential activities of MNCs in the world economy, and, in particular, the trend towards the de-integration of their production chain, cannot but have important implications for the way in which NIS develop and function. By offering local firms in developing or emerging countries multiple opportunities to link with their production networks (Stopford and Strange with Henley, 1991: 39, 86), MNCs' influence the conditions under which innovation as defined above can develop. Thus, besides traditional 'network organisers' which are national,[33] it would be worth considering international firms as increasingly important potential candidates capable of playing this role. What, then, is the contribution of the production networks established by foreign firms to an interactive process leading to learning and capability formation (Martin, 1998; Lorentzen, 1998)? In particular, are the interactions between MNCs and (smaller) local firms included into their subdelivery network (Herrigel, 2000) conducive to the strengthening of local capabilities?[34]

The role that the production networks established by international firms play in the formation of NIS is a topic that requires further research (Ernst, 1999; Mytelka, 1999a), something which has a specific relevance in the case of CEECs (Radosevic, 2000). In fact, in common with other countries embarking particularly late on a catch-up process, CEECs show a greater reliance on foreign sources of knowledge as they have had 'few[er] opportunities to build their innovation system on localized clusters' (Ernst, 1999). International linkages are decisive for CEECs since these linkages have to substitute for domestic ones severely disrupted through the demise of the command economy and the subsequent vacuum of innovation system (Radosevic, 2000; Inzelt, 1999). Furhtermore, CEECs must move quickly as the enlargement process gains momentum, something that in turn leaves them very little time to build innovation capabilities by themselves. Finally, the fact that CEECs are latecomers among latecomers means that they face particular constraints through the internationalisation imperative since competition to be included into IPN is harsher than ever.

In short, to catch up, CEECs must both conform to the new requirements of 'global competition' and consolidate the knowledge basis of their competitive edge. For CEECs one crucial component of this process of building up new systems of innovation is the inclusion of local firms into IPN. The causality between NIS formation and the inclusion of local firms into IPN works both ways since the two are mutually reinforcing processes. If 'learning to learn' through partnership with foreign firms can be expected to make a crucial contribution to the formation of NIS, an appropriate institutional framework is an essential factor to facilitate the learning process at company level.

Considering the potentially crucial contribution of international linkages to the process of building up knowledge-based economies in latecomer CEECs, the role which is currently assigned to them is rather disappointing. Among countries that have recently engaged in the development race, and in CEECs in particular, there is a strong focus on attracting FDI. Emulating the example of developed countries – which trigger incentives 'tournaments' to maximise inward investment – countries with a lower degree of attractiveness have indeed been particularly concerned by the possibility of being left out of this global game. However, on the basis of the extreme variability of corporate strategies and of their respective impact on host economies, the viability of strategies aimed exclusively at attracting FDI is highly questionable (Myant, 1999; Mytelka, 1999b). A cause for concern is that the objective of attracting FDI goes unquestioned and thus risks becoming an objective *per se*: FDI tends to be credited (a little too quickly and automatically) with generic benefits such as access to 'capital', 'market' and, especially, 'technology'. Policy makers need to be clear both about tasks assigned to foreign investors and the expectations placed on them. For a start, host states have to engage partnership-style relations with foreign firms so that the 'two parties can co-operate to promote their mutual interests' (Stopford and Strange with Henley, 1991: 95). In addition, the attention should shift away from narrowly defined FDI towards IPN in general, that is, in their non-equity dimension as well. As a matter of fact, if the objective is to 'learn', then non-equity forms of co-operation might prove particularly favourable. Indeed, the interactions identified in NIS literature as being especially conducive to innovation processes are not necessarily internalised within firms; indeed, the contrary is more likely to be the case.[35]

To sum up, development strategies in CEECs should aim at knowledge-creation taking into account various specific criteria. First among these should be the development levels pertaining in the considered national economy and the 'moment' characterising competitive conditions in the world economy. For CEECs, having to catch up at this particular point in time, together with the establishment of international linkages and policies helping local firms link up to international production networks, are going to be critical.

The content of the book: why outward processing traffic (OPT)?

CEECs have entered the 'development race' in a particularly difficult context, where (a) they must fulfil the requirements of the enlargement process; and (b) meet the challenge arising from drastic changes in the world economy. The present moment is thus characterised by a formidable indeterminacy: that is, whether EU and CEEC policies, the enlargement process itself and the whole European edifice are suited to weather the challenge of globalisation.

It is proposed to offer some insight into these important and rather challenging questions on the basis of evidence inferred from outward processing traffic (OPT). The question of the development of OPT between the EU and CEECs is a largely neglected one. As argued above, however, OPT has been, and still is, one important dimension of corporate integration between the EU and CEECs. This reason alone would justify an in-depth analysis of East–West OPT patterns. But the definitive argument for choosing OPT as a source of evidence, as argued above, is that it is at the core of the major issues at stake in the process of enlargement.

The OPT arrangement was devised in the 1970s to regulate the relocation of EU production activities abroad. This was before anyone could have dreamt that a unified European economy would be possible one day, and when the above transformations of the terms of competitiveness were yet to materialise. Its raison d'être was initially very clear: to exploit low wages in developing countries in general and in the then COMECON countries in particular, and to jettison the threats of cheap labour imports from these very countries, and of developing unemployment in EC/EU countries.

Ten years later, CEECs have become 'emerging markets', struggling to become part of the EU sooner rather than later. Yet OPT is still an important feature of East–West economic relations. How could the arrangement go through this fundamental redefinition of the context in which it developed? This in turn raises a fundamental question: does OPT now help CEECs reach what is now their top priority – to catch up with

Western levels of development? Beyond this, does it acquire a wider relevance, as far as the future development of CEECs are concerned, in this respect?

In fact, the OPT story is full of unexpected developments. The most notable one is probably the fact that, in the light of new conditions of competitiveness in the world economy, the arrangement offers the improbable potential of being a vehicle for implementing new production methods in line with the requirements of international ('global') competition. Symmetrical to the very 'dependency' bias of the OPT mechanisms, the arrangement presents outstanding potential to fulfil many of the requirements associated with the changing terms of international competition as depicted above. For example, what may be presented as a threat, that is, the facility with which foreign partners can withdraw from their commitment, becomes, in the new context of international competition, a decisive asset. If seized by partner firms, the potential of the arrangement in terms of flexibility combined with proximity enables the former to apply new production methods such as 'Just-In-Time', particularly apt at competing on world markets.

More fundamentally, OPT data are a source of evidence to trace the formation of international production networks (IPN) in CEECs. As shown above, these are expected to be of crucial importance in the process of building local capabilities. By offering a rare chance to explore empirically the under-researched question of the impact IPN have on the formation of innovation systems, this analysis of OPT is expected to give insight into whether and under what conditions – and at the instigation of whom – 'knowledge-based economies' are emerging in CEECs.

Overall, this book tells the story of a policy instrument transformation. Based on the exploitation of development differentials between Eastern and Western Europe, this measure has the potential to become an instrument to help CEECs catch up with Western levels and standards. By determining whether and how this is happening, this book ultimately aims to characterise the potential that the process of enlargement has to transform CEECs into viable members of the European Union.

Chapter 2 begins by illustrating the quantitative importance of OPT in the development of East–West interdependence since the fall of the Berlin Wall. Contrary to what the neglect of OPT data in the literature might one lead to think, CEECs' trade performances owe much to the arrangement. This means that a significant proportion of East–West trade is in fact of a 'quasi-intra-firm' nature, and that the development is – apparently – monitored by EU regulations.

Chapter 3 explores the exact nature of OPT partnerships at firm level. On the basis of extensive fieldwork carried out at local firms in the Czech Republic and Hungary, mainly in the textile and clothing and the electrical machinery sectors, it will identify different ways in which firms 'up-grade' their capabilities and strengthen their competitive position within an OPT partnership. It takes the OPT case as a useful test to see whether and under what conditions IPN develop at the instigation of EU firms operating in CEECs. It will also consider whether, and under what conditions, the latter promote learning and innovation in CEECs' economies.

Chapter 4 sets out to identify the determinants of OPT and its outcome so as to make sense of the large array of differentiated types of partnerships found in Chapter 3. It contrasts the institutional factors of OPT with firm-level variables, and assesses their respective weight in the structuration of OPT relations. It will become clear that much depends on the use firms of different sizes from different countries and in different sectors make of the arrangement. The chapter thus illustrates the transformations undergone by the OPT policy instrument. In particular, it will stress that some German firms carrying out OPT in CEECs might, in certain circumstances, avail themselves of the role of 'network organisers'.

Chapter 5 looks back at the decision-making procedures that led to the adoption of the OPT arrangement by the EC/EU to recognise and understand the motive that incited EU policy-makers to set up the measure. The chapter will show that, contrary to expectations, the OPT developments did not give rise to any real centralisation of competence at the Community level. The latter are more the result of the overheating of the functioning of EU mechanisms than the product of a conscious strategy of industrial policy possessing precise contours.

Chapter 6 draws some lessons from the OPT story that are relevant for economic theories of regional integration. It argues that the drastic changes in the world economy which underlie the OPT developments – in particular, the increasing knowledge-content of competition – call for a profound reconsideration of theories both of international trade and international production.

The concluding chapter will attempt to pull together different findings made throughout the study. In particular, it draws conclusions from the high firm-level variability found in Chapter 3 and the missed centralisation over OPT matters at the EU level identified in Chapter 4. It will, on this basis, assess the efficacy of policy measures adopted at EU level and offer insight into how the governance of an enlarged European economy can be carried out at a time of 'global competition'. It argues that the OPT developments testify to some important shifts in the locus and exercise of structural power in today's world economy.

2
The Neglected Importance of OPT in CEECs' Foreign Trade

Outward processing traffic (OPT) is an important feature characterising patterns of East–West economic interdependence. Indeed, OPT may prove relevant, if not decisive, in influencing the terms under which such interdependence develops. Notwithstanding this, the now vast literature on CEECs' trade (and production) specialisation is characterised by a sustained neglect of OPT developments. A succinct literature on OPT does exist, but its findings are rarely taken into account in 'mainstream' trade analyses. Nor does the literature actually bother to refer to the latter. As a result, very little connection is established between the development of OPT and CEECs' trade performance. In addition, OPT studies are often biased by the negative approach adopted so that when the impact OPT may have on the development of East–West economic interdependence is explored, it is almost always concluded that the measure brings with it only adverse consequences.

This chapter adopts a trade perspective and looks at OPT in aggregate terms. The objective is to take a first step towards a thorough assessment of OPT's contribution to the regional dynamics of integration by providing as fair a picture of OPT patterns as possible. This will hopefully correct some of the inaccuracy that characterises OPT literature and identify some surprising correlations between the conclusions reached by classic trade studies and the OPT developments themselves. A brief review of the trade and OPT literatures, followed by a 'map' of the OPT relations which have been developing between the EU and CEECs, should clarify this point.

Trade and production specialisation of CEECs in the literature: findings and shortcomings

There is an extensive literature that analyses CEECs' trade and production specialisation since the beginning of the CEECs' transition process. A number of different approaches have been used and different questions addressed concerning the development of EU–CEEC trade patterns.[36] Despite the great variety of indicators used, and the sometimes discordant results obtained, there are nevertheless some converging findings reached by studies on CEECs' trade specialisation.

A first group of (early) studies tried to determine the comparative advantages characterising CEECs' economies in the aftermath of the demise of COMECON by using revealed comparative advantage indicators.[37] Of particular interest are synthetic indicators. Graziani (1994a), for example, groups the different categories of products according to the characteristics of their production process. He successively weights resource-based versus non-resource-based products, mature versus new products, standardised versus unstandardised,[38] and labour versus capital-intensive products. In his findings, the stylised good exported to the EC is no longer resource-based; rather it is a mature, standardised and labour-intensive product. Moreover, low technology products dominate CEEC exports.

Klodt (1994), provides a similar synthesis. He computed the revealed comparative advantage (RCA) of the goods that CEECs traded with Germany in 1980 and 1992, grouping them into four categories according to the relative factor intensity of their production processes. Klodt concluded that there are (1) resource-intensive; (2) physical capital-intensive; (3) labour-intensive; and (4) technology-intensive products. This latter category is itself divided into 'mobile-Schumpeter goods', and 'immobile Schumpeter goods'. Interestingly enough, these results show that the highest RCA is still recorded by Czechoslovakia in resource-intensive goods. However, as compared to the other CEECs, Czechoslovakia and Hungary present the highest RCA in capital-intensive goods, and one of the lowest RCA in labour-intensive goods. Technology-intensive products are clearly characterised by negative values of RCA, even though the relative disadvantage is comparatively inferior to that of other CEECs. Neven (1995) distinguishes five types of industries according to their factor content,[39] and computes their respective RCA for the five CEECs and the former USSR. In general, he finds a consistent pattern of CEECs comparative advantage in low-skilled sectors, and sectors intensive in physical capital. In conclusion, he notes that long-term comparative advantage lies rather 'where a comparative advantage has recently emerged (...), namely in the labour intensive industries'.

Overall, studies of the early CEECs trade specialisation patterns all point to labour-intensive as well as resource- and energy-intensive products as the goods for which CEECs' economies have a comparative advantage (Landesmann, 1994 and 1998; Dobrinsky and Landesmann, 1995). Interestingly enough, some first evidence of differentiated patterns of specialisation shows that Hungary and the former Czechoslovakia/Czech Republic stand apart. The Czech Republic is remarkable for the number of industries with a comparative advantage and Hungary for having comparative advantages where other CEECs have comparative disadvantages.

Although the early studies mentioned above converge in identifying labour as a source for comparative advantage, they stress that this is probably only a temporary feature of CEECs' economies. As a veiled recognition of the limitations of insights gained from RCA indexes, the very intuitive notion of 'potential' comparative advantage based on what is generally thought to be the high level of education of CEECs' populations is often referred to. This is the case for the Centre for Economic Policy Research (CEPR) (1990: 9), Hamilton and Winters (1992: 95), Graziani (1994: 226) and Halpern (1994: 21). Deemed to be equally important are the good R&D capabilities of these countries. On the basis of a more or less explicit correlation between scientific skills and comparative advantage in mid-tech goods in Western countries, these studies conclude by pointing to the likelihood for certain CEECs to become exporters of sophisticated products. The comparative edge in human capital and the R&D capabilities of CEECs in general should, in the long run, be reflected in their trade specialisation.

Interestingly enough, it is often mentioned that these developments are more likely to materialise with the impetus given by foreign capital: foreign investment is deemed necessary to spur the exports of upgraded value added goods. Klodt (1994) refines the argument and distinguishes between high tech goods, the research stage of which can be geographically separated from the production process (mobile Schumpeter goods[40]), and those high tech goods whose research and production phases can hardly be disentangled from each other (immobile Schumpeter goods[41]). As NICs managed to attract foreign investment in the former sectors, they also specialised their trade in the corresponding products. Successful CEECs might be expected to do the same, with the difference that rather than micro-electronic goods, CEECs would be more prone to specialise in chemicals or software. As an empirical confirmation of such a view, Klodt provides some estimation of RCA for both mobile and immobile Schumpeter goods. Although he considers both to be negative, the RCAs of the former are slightly higher than those of technology-intensive and immobile Schumpeter goods.

More recent studies have obtained contrasting results concerning the question as to whether CEECs are 'moving up-market' and specialising in more technologically demanding goods. Rather worrying, however, are the findings made by Neven (1995) that CEECs' patterns of comparative advantage have scarcely changed over five years, even though trade volumes have been increasing at quite a remarkable rate. Likewise, Guerrieri (1997) examined country-specific patterns and found an increase in the export of labour intensive products for which CEECs doubled their share of world exports. Landesmann (1998), too, found consistent evidence of changes toward labour-intensive branches and away from capital, R&D and skill-intensive branches. Worse, Myant (1999) evoked CEECs' 'structural regression', arguing that contrary to Asian tigers, the latter are undergoing a process of structural change where low skill and labour-intensive products are promoted in CEECs' trade structures.

Other studies, however, demonstrate that to some extent the product structures of CEEC exports are moving towards higher value-added products such as engineering goods (UN: ECE, 1997; Lemoine, 1998). Evidence presented by Freudenberg and Lemoine (1999), for example, shows that even though CEECs have maintained a comparative advantage in 'traditional' sectors, these countries are 'despecialising', that is, their comparative advantage is decreasing, especially in textile and clothing (T&C) and footwear. What is more, the most dynamic sectors are 'new' ones, in which CEECs *used* to have a comparative disadvantage.[42] Sectors such as engineering, motor vehicles, and electrical machinery are now emerging, in particular in the Czech Republic and Hungary.[43] This fact testifies to the fact that CEECs are not locked into traditional specialisation, but that they are also developing new capacities. Of particular relevance is the fact that all the studies mentioned above note, to some extent, a growing differentiation among CEECs. For example, Landesmann (1998) finds increasing differences in CEECs' specialisation patterns.

Interesting new developments characterising CEECs' patterns of specialisation, such as their growing share of intra-industry trade, have been detected. This suggests that determinants other than comparative advantages are increasingly important in influencing EU–CEECs' trade; these include economies of scale or product differentiation (Landesmann, 1998; Lemoine, 1995, 1996). Freudenberg and Lemoine (1999) show that the kind of intra industry trade (IIT) developing in CEECs' trade is vertical. It results from the exchange of similar goods differentiated on the basis of quality and price.[44] Most of this IIT is taking place in down market segments, leading the authors to evoke a 'qualitative division of labour' (Freudenberg and Lemoine, 1999: 8).

However, here, too, the authors found evidence of an upgrading process. What is more, the development of IIT concerns only a small set of countries and sectors. Again, many divergences were found among CEECs. Freudenberg and Lemoine (1999), for example, found that IIT develops mostly in fact in the Czech Republic, Hungary and Slovenia.

The link between trade and international production in CEECs has recently been emphasised. A second important finding made by Freudenberg and Lemoine (1999) is indeed that CEECs are taking part in the international segmentation of the production process. This is indicated through an increase in the proportion of intermediate goods in CEECs' import and export structures. Indeed,

> The structure of CEECs trade by stage of production reveals that intermediate products form the largest and the most dynamic part of trade flows, suggesting an increased participation of the region in the international division of the production process. (Freudenberg and Lemoine, 1999: 69)

In static terms, CEECs are often more specialised in the whole production process. In dynamic terms, however, one can pinpoint important exceptions where CEECs hold comparative advantages in certain stages of the production process and comparative disadvantages in others. In the latter case, CEECs generally specialise in downstream stages of the production process. However, there are situations where they also position themselves in upstream stages. Once more, country differences are important. Whereas a great many exchanges in intermediate goods takes place in the engineering sector in Central Europe, in more Eastern countries, trade in intermediate goods develops in natural resource-intensive industries. Overall,

> the international division of production process may have a role in the evolution of Central European countries and influence the change in their specialisation patterns. (Freudenberg and Lemoine, 1999: 32)

Of particular note are findings within a number of 'unconventional' trade studies interested in the changing technological basis of CEECs' trade.[45] Hotopp and Radosevic (1999), for example, offer insight into the potential for CEECs' catching up by analysing changing product composition of trade, explaining the latter by different 'learning' patterns. Following Grossman and Helpman (1991), they suggest that

> Trade is an essential aspect of the catching up process through the several learning mechanisms it entails. (Hotopp and Radosevic, 1999)[46]

Labour intensive products are generally shown to have a continuing importance, but encouraging signs indicating the strengthening of the technological content of CEECs' trade are also detected.

Very few of the above studies offering comprehensive analysis of CEECs' foreign economic relations do in fact mention OPT, let alone carry out an analysis of it. This is regrettable as many of the developments these studies address are related to OPT developments in one way or another. The upgrading process of CEECs' product specialisation, the growth of IIT, the role of intermediate goods in CEECs' exports, increased differentiated trade performances across CEECs, and last but not least, 'trade-related learning processes', are all developments that OPT trends confirm, and perhaps even contribute to determining. Thus, even though Freudenberg and Lemoine (1999) address such questions as the place of CEECs in the international segmentation of the production process, and even if their study recognises that

> Studies on outward processing have underlined that subcontracting activities have played a decisive role in the export performance of CEECs in individual sectors (. . .) (Freudenberg and Lemoine, 1999: 10),

they do not further elaborate on the issue.[47]

Against this background, studies which devote major attention to OPT are the exception (Eichengreen and Kohl, 1998a, 1998b; Graziani, 1998; Lemoine 1998; UNECE, 1995, 1997; Naujoks and Schmidt, 1994; Baldone and Sdogati, 1997). The problem is that it is often taken for granted that OPT is a marginal and transient phenomenon, developing in 'traditional' labour-intensive, low value-added sectors. This idea is possibly nurtured by OPT studies which look at OPT developments, but only in the textile and clothing sector (UNECE, 1995). An example is given by Freudenberg and Lemoine who recognise that OPT underlies the development of a vertical specialisation in intermediate products in the T&C sector. However, even taking into account the fact that they did find that the same process takes place in 'new' sectors like electrical machinery, transport equipment and telecommunication equipment, they omit OPT as a factor accounting for this trend (Freudenberg and Lemoine, 1999: 38).

What is more, because it is regularly postulated that OPT develops mainly, if not exclusively, on the basis of wage differentials, there is an expectation that OPT business in CEECs will be wiped away as soon as the latter become unfavourable. Indeed, several studies detect a decrease of OPT. Apart from gross generalisations about OPT for example, 'dropping there since 1992' (Zysman *et al.*, 1998: 12), some studies argue – perhaps a little too quickly – that the arrangement has no future (Hamar, 1999; Lemoine, 1998). As a corollary, it is also sometimes considered that OPT follows waves of relocation in countries further East. For instance, the process of 'despecialisation' that Freudenberg and Lemoine detect in T&C and footwear is, in fact, attributed to a relocation of OPT eastwards which confirms that OPT is 'losing momentum' (Freudenberg and Lemoine, 1999: 16).

It is also interesting to note that OPT is often considered only in terms of its *trade* dimension. Even when the *production* dimension of OPT is acknowledged, it is again considered to be a minor vehicle of international production. In Kurz and Wittke (1998), OPT is assimilated with 'extended workbenches' carried out by German small and medium-sized enterprises in neighbouring CEECs in order to loosen the constraints represented by high wages in their home economies.[48] The best that can be expected is if OPT gives rise to FDI and/or if it is a first step that leads towards complex capital-intensive IPN Borrus and (Zysman, 1998: 42).

Yet another drawback underlying virtually all the literature on OPT is that its specificity as an EU policy instrument is hardly acknowledged. OPT data are taken as such with little understanding of the mechanisms involved, with a straight correspondence being established between OPT and sub-contracting. Again, exceptions are to be found in Eichengreen and Kohl (1998a, b), as well as in Graziani who insists that OPT provides only an 'indirect indicator of subcontracting trends' (Graziani, 1998: 242).

Overall, the general view has it that:

> although subcontracting had a crucial role in the first phase of the transition, it seems to have rapidly exhausted its potential effect on export growth. (Lemoine, 1998: 159)

With respect to the many issues above, the findings made by Eichengreen and Kohl (1998a, 1998b) stand apart. They characterise OPT as a development worth considering on its own and across all sectors concerned. OPT is regarded on a par with FDI as an important motor of growth in CEECs' development strategies. In particular, they acknowledge the fact that OPT, like FDI, can bring about positive spillover:

> High tech FDI and OPT, once started, have worked to disseminate technological and organizational knowledge and to attract additional FDI and OPT. (Eichengreen and Kohl, 1998b: 3)

Also, the fact that OPT develops:

> into newer, more technologically sophisticated, skilled-labour-intensive products (Eichengreen and Kohl, 1998: 37),

and that it does so in some countries (the Czech Republic, Hungary) but not in others (Romania), leads Eichengreen and Kohl to hold OPT as one factor responsible for the performance differential noted across CEECs.

Interestingly enough, however, after having noted its potential, Eichengreen and Kohl revert to a view in which OTP is regarded as a second best in comparison to FDI. Indeed,

> the technological and organizational implications of OPT are less obviously favourable [than FDI] (Eichengreen and Kohl, 1998b: 51)

and

> In the region's less advanced economies where FDI is largely absent, integration into the world economy takes the form of OPT and assembly which affords less opportunity for investment in human capital, employment, of skilled labor, and local R&D. It is found in low-wage, labor-intensive, technologically unsophisticated sectors like textiles, apparels, and footwear, thought to afford few domestic spillovers. (Eichengreen and Kohl, 1998b: 51)

These contrasting assessments, together with the relative paucity of evidence to support them, extend a persuasive invitation to carry out an in-depth analysis of OPT between the EU and CEECs, first in quantitative and aggregate terms.

A map of OPT relations between the EU and CEECs

The neglect of OPT is rather unfortunate given the potentially wide-ranging and complex implications the measure entails on patterns of trade and production specialisation in CEECs. In order to gain as comprehensive an understanding of the latter as possible, it is first necessary to have a clear idea of where, and at the instigation of whom, OPT develops.

At this preliminary methodological juncture, it is necessary to stress that what follows is not a neutral description of a phenomenon which exists independently from the statistical instrument describing it. In fact, 'Outward Processing Traffic' would not exist if there were no trade barriers as, indeed, OPT transactions owe their statistical existence to the specific custom regime easing the restrictions faced by EU firms relocating part of their activities abroad. Hence, OPT is – directly – the product of the legislation providing for it, and – indirectly – the consequence of trade barriers remaining in place during the process of trade liberalisation engaged between the EU and CEECs.

An important implication of this concerns the integrity of OPT data. As they owe their statistical raison d'être to trade barriers in place between the EU and CEECs during the transition towards free trade, OPT data lose their relevance as these protection measures are being dismantled. In other words, as time goes on, OPT statistics increasingly underplay OPT transactions. OPT decreases are thus *partially* due to a 'statistical effect'.[49]

The origin of the legislation has to do with a dilemma posed by the internationalisation of production activity. Firms willing to relocate either the totality or part of their production activities abroad on the grounds of exceedingly high domestic labour costs might be dissuaded from doing so by the presence of trade barriers. In fact, 'reimporting' products which have been processed abroad might be constrained by trade measures enforced to protect against *any* exports from low labour cost countries. The solution proposed by the OPT arrangement is to discriminate between the imports of local producers and 're-imports' resulting from the relocation strategies of Community producers, that is, between 'direct' and 'temporary' trade flows. If a product exported by a Community firm in order to be processed abroad faces 'normal' trade restrictions when it is re-imported into the Community, then OPT makes it possible to lift such trade protection measures either partially, or, in certain cases, completely. This requires a specific custom regime, and a resulting statistical monitoring of the transactions taking place under this regime.

Comparative static picture[50]

A first main characteristic of OPT[51] is the important share it has been occupying in CEECs' foreign trade. In 1998, proportions of OPT in total CEECs' exports to the EU were reduced because of the above statistical effect. They amounted to 9 per cent in Poland; 6 per cent in both the Czech Republic and Slovakia; 7 per cent in Hungary; 24 per cent in Romania; 14 per cent in Bulgaria; 17 per cent in Lithuania, and 7–8 per cent in Estonia and Latvia. In 1993, however, around 20 per cent of the total trade of Hungary and Poland was dependent on OPT, and slightly less than 13 per cent of that of the former Czechoslovakia. In 1995, the proportions were 15 per cent for Poland 13 per cent in Hungary and 11 per cent in the former Czechoslovakia (Table 2.1).

Countries

A major country-specific feature characterising OPT in CEECs is that the bulk of this is undertaken by German firms: 74 per cent and 60 per cent of EU OPT to the CEEC6 and CEEC10, respectively, was of German origin in 1997.[52] Indeed, German OPT in the CEEC10 amounts to ECU 3.8 bn. Italy is second, having 780 M engaged in OPT transactions, whereas Austria, which used to be the second biggest source of OPT, now commits no more than ECU 325 M. France, the Netherlands and Denmark follow (ECU 350 M, 240 M and 200 M, respectively). A final category consists of countries marginally and anecdotally involved in OPT operations (Belgium, and the UK, for example, were countries registering barely more than ECU 50 M of OPT in CEECs in 1995) (Table 2.2).

The major recipient of OPT is, in absolute terms, Poland (around 30 per cent of EU15 OPT). Romania, Hungary and the Czech Republic each accounted for approximately 20 per cent of EU15 OPT to the CEEC4 exactly. In last position, Slovakia and Bulgaria attracted less than 10 per cent of EU OPT. The rest went to the Baltic States.

German OPT in CEECs is highest in Poland and the Czech Republic. Romania is in third place, before Hungary. Italian firms are comparatively more prone than Germans to undertake OPT with Hungarian partners but they are mostly active in Romania. Austrian firms, not surprisingly, conduct OPT with neighbouring Hungarian partners while Danish as well as Dutch firms are engaged almost exclusively in Poland. To a lesser extent, French firms also have privileged partnerships with Romanian, Polish and Hungarian firms. Finally, with much lower absolute levels, Swedish firms are engaged in Poland and Estonia, and Finnish ones in Estonia.

For the host countries, the strong German engagement in OPT activities assumes a slightly different aspect. There is sometimes a pronounced, if not exclusive, orientation of CEECs' OPT activities towards Germany, combined with a high proportion of OPT in total trade to the EU. However this 'dependence' on OPT with German partners is characterised by important differences of magnitude. Czech firms, in particular, are

Table 2.1   OPT re-exports (M ECU) and proportion in total exports (%) to EU countries

	1991		1992		1993		1994		1995		1996		1997		1998	
	opt	*%*	*opt*	*%*	*opt*	*%*	*opt*	*%*	*opt*	*%*	*opt*	*%*	*opt*	*%*	*opt*	*%*
Poland	838.9	13.5	1 122.7	15.9	1 407.2	18.6	1 684.7	18.5	1 881.9	15.4	1 934.0	15.8	1 672.6	11.8	1 400.8	8.7
Czech Republic	na	na	na	na	601.1	12.4	796.8	12.5	968.4	10.8	1 034.6	10.6	996.5	8.5	829.4	5.7
Slovakia	na	na	na	na	156.3	13.5	225.4	12.0	286.6	9.3	346.9	10.1	372.4	9.4	300.4	5.6
Hungary	669.3	18.5	805.1	20.2	800.6	20.3	862.3	17.5	982.1	12.9	1 160.9	13.2	1 182.3	10.2	1 024.4	7.1
Romania	287.7	19.6	385.3	27.4	502.6	29.7	702.4	28.0	862.8	25.5	1 052.4	29.3	1 202.4	27.2	1 247.6	24.4
Bulgaria	53.7	7.1	89.5	9.9	129.4	13.6	153.5	11.4	206.6	11.3	250.0	14.6	276.2	13.2	319.4	14.3
Estonia	na	na	0.7	0.8	8.4	4.6	10.2	3.9	56.8	6.4	75.2	6.9	93.7	6.2	144.5	8.2
Latvia	na	na	2.3	0.5	17.5	2.8	36.7	5.0	55.3	4.9	66.9	5.9	85.5	6.7	95.4	6.9
Lithuania	na	na	9.5	2.1	42.2	6.6	77.6	10.3	125.6	12.9	164.2	15.1	217.3	16.6	235.5	16.7
Slovenia	na	na	191.4	12.1	340.5	11.9	307.1	9.0	273.8	6.4	244.0	5.7	241.0	5.2	222.5	4.3

Table 2.2   OPT re-exports (M ECU) and proportion in total OPT re-exports (%) in 1997

	Poland		Czech Republic		Slovakia		Hungary		Romania		Bulgaria		Estonia		Latvia		Lithuania		Slovenia		CEFCs10
		%		*%*		*%*		*%*		*%*		*%*		*%*		*%*		*%*		*%*	
Germany	1 112.9	66.2	854.0	85.8	217.8	58.7	565.6	48.9	633.6	52.9	95.7	34.7	6.8	7.3	56.9	66.6	122.6	57.1	180.2	75.2	3846.2
Italy	45.6	2.7	19.4	2.0	65.2	17.6	176.8	15.3	368.1	30.7	68.6	24.8		3.1	3.6	2.4	1.1	30.4	12.7		779.4
Austria			55.3	5.6	28.9	7.8	225.5	19.5			8.8	3.2							6.4	2.7	324.8
Sweden	31.5	1.9											43.4	46.4	3.9	4.6	6.8	3.2			85.6
Netherlands	128.2	7.6	11.4	1.1	24.7	6.6	61.1	5.3	14.5	1.2											239.9
Finland													32.5	34.8							32.5
Denmark	198.4	11.8																	198.4		
France	88.4	5.3	24.4	2.5	18.4	5.0	77.6	6.7	100.5	8.4	31.6	11.5					2.8	1.3	10.3	4.3	354.1
EU	1681.8	100	995.8	100	371.3	100	1156.1	100	1198.7	100	276.1	100	93.5	100	85.4	100	214.8	100	239.7	100	6313.2

remarkable in that they have the strongest CEECs dependence on a German presence: the German share of total OPT carried out in the country is highest, at 86 per cent in 1997. Polish firms are also very dependent on OPT of German origin (accounting for more than 60 per cent of total Polish OPT exports to the EU). However, they manage a slightly higher degree of diversification and a number of these are also in relation with Danish and Dutch companies.

The remaining CEECs are dependent on German companies for more than half of their OPT activities. This is the case in Slovakia (60 per cent), Latvia and Lithuania (66 per cent and 57 per cent, respectively), and finally Romania (53 per cent). Notably, Bulgarian firms (and to a lesser extent Romanian ones) regard OPT partnerships with Italian companies in equally favourable terms. Italians companies also offer an alternative to German partnership for Hungarian and Slovak firms. Hungarian partners are the most diversified, comprising – beside German and Italian companies – Austrian firms as well. Finally, German firms are privileged OPT partners for firms in Latvia, and more specifically in Lithuania. In contrast, Estonian companies are engaged in OPT partnerships with Swedish firms.

The most important bilateral relations which do not involve partners of German origin are those between Danish and Polish firms (ECU 200 M), between Italian and Hungarian firms (slightly less than ECU 180 M), and between Dutch and Polish firms (130 M).

Sectors

Among recipient sectors, the textile and clothing sector (unsurprisingly) comes first, with an overwhelming share of total OPT relations between the EU and CEECs (ECU 4.3 bn, i.e. 68 per cent in 1997). Quite a way below this, the next sector to be most concerned by OPT transactions is the electrical machinery industry (830 M).[53] Other sectors important for OPT include furniture, footwear and mechanical machinery (100 to 300 M). With lower absolute levels, the automotive industry, plastic, leather and the edible preparations sector all register OPT activities. With a frankly insignificant share of output, the iron and steel sector is a source of some OPT of non- negligible absolute value. Even more marginal but almost systematically characterising the product structure of member states are the optical, toy and clock sectors, as well as the printing sector and glassware industry (Table 2.3).

Countries and sectors: synthesis

The quantitative disparity already mentioned between Germany and the other EU countries as a source of OPT is reflected in the product structure

Table 2.3   OPT product structure: OPT re-exports (M ECU) and proportion in OPT re-exports (%) of the CEEC 10 to the EU15, in 1997

Sector	OPT	%
Total trade	6,313.2	100.0
T&C	4,303.5	68.2
Electrical machinery	829.6	13.1
Footwear	265.3	4.2
Mechanical machinery	197.3	3.1
Furniture	117.7	1.9
Cars	97.0	1.5
Plastic	83.4	1.3
Edible preparations	62.8	1.0

of OPT in CEECs. First, there is no sector where a degree of OPT is registered and from which German firms are absent. The range covered thus goes from T&C (as expected), to electrical and mechanical machinery, footwear and furniture. Second, in these sectors, OPT of German origin does often occupy a largely pre-eminent share. In T&C, for example, German firms undertake about 10 times more OPT than firms from the other EU members (ECU 1.9 bn as against to a maximum of 270 engaged by Dutch firms in 1996). This unmitigated German domination is equally affirmed in the sectors of both electrical and mechanical machinery: 70 per cent of OPT in electrical machinery and slightly less than 90 per cent of EU OPT in CEEC4 for mechanical machinery (ECU 420 M, and 140 M, respectively) is in fact of German origin. In furniture, Germany is virtually the only country to carry out OPT in the sector (ECU 150 M). The same goes for much lower absolute levels, for the sector of edible preparations (37 M) (Tables 2.4a and 2.4b).

Austrian firms represent the second most important source of OPT in CEECs after those of Germany (11 per cent of EU OPT in CEEC4 in 1996). These have very predictable patterns of OPT activity in the sense that, as previously noted, they are mostly engaged in neighbouring countries (especially Hungary), undertaking OPT almost exclusively in T&C and in the electrical machinery sector. These two account for more than 80 per cent of total Austrian OPT in CEECs. In this latter sector, Austrians are the unique second source of OPT after Germans (17 per cent of EU OPT in CEEC4 in 1996).

Italy also has a very concentrated distribution of OPT. This occurs, however, in other sectors and Italy's OPT activities are more widely spread across countries. Most of the Italian OPT is carried out in T&C (70 per cent

Table 2.4a Proportion of OPT in total exports (%) and OPT re-exports (M ECU) between EU countries and CEECs

1996	Germany	Austria	Italy	Netherlands	Denmark	France	Sweden	EU15
All products								
Poland	21.1	1.0	4.1	22.2	33.2	5.9	7.8	1.9 bn
Czech Republic	15.2	5.9	3.8	4.6	1.1	3.0	0.3	1 bn
Slovakia	10.4	7.5	13.5	22.1	2.4	2.9	2.9	330 M
Hungary	13.6	15.5	16.7	16.9	7.8	8.3	6.2	1.1 bn
CEEC4	*2.9 bn*	*320 M*	*290 M*	*280 M*	*190 M*	*223 M*	*47 M*	*4.3 bn*
T&C								
Poland	86.1	40.4	58.0	89.4	93.5	70.0	60.0	1.5 bn
Czech Republic	63.3	49.1	17.1					430 M
Slovakia	67.2	60.3	54.3	80.7		47.0		250 M
Hungary	79.4	83.8	75.6	84.0		77.0		710 M
CEEC4	*1.9 bn*	*170 M*	*200 M*	*242 M*	*170 M*	*172 M*	*36 M*	*2.9 bn*
Electrical Machinery								
Poland	18.8					14.0		100 M
Czech Republic	26.9	23.4		29.2				240 M
Slovakia	11.8	21.6						30 M
Hungary	14.4	21.0		13.0				220 M
CEEC4	*420 M*	*100 M*		*16 M*		*28 M*		*590 M*
Mechanical machinary								
Poland	4.6							20 M
Czech Republic	11.2							80 M
Slovakia	11.3							10 M
Hungary	3.9		8.9					40 M
CEEC4	*140 M*		*10 M*					*160 M*
Furniture								
Poland	14.3							
CEEC4	*150 M*							*160 M*
Footwear								
Poland	9.9		18.9		89.1			20 M
Czech Republic	30.0		27.8					20 M
Slovakia	1.1		17.7					10 M
Hungary	27.1		31.1					60 M
CEEC4	*60 M*		*40 M*		*10 M*			*110 M*

of total Italian OPT in the CEEC10 in 1997), and in the footwear industry (20 per cent). In this latter sector, Italians are a very significant source of OPT, just after the Germans who are – in relative terms – less involved (Italy represented 58 per cent of EU OPT to CEEC10 in the sector in 1997). Interestingly, Italians are also responsible for a non-negligible share of EU OPT in mechanical machinery, behind the Germans. In addition, despite

Table 2.4b Proportion of OPT in total exports (%) and OPT re-exports (M ECU) between EU countries and CEECs

1997	Germany	Austria	Italy	Netherlands	Denmark	France	Sweden	Finland	EU15
All products									
Romania	47.0	5.0	24.5						1.2 bn
Bulgaria	21.4	12.4	12.8						276 M
Estonia			3.0				12.3		94 M
Latvia	17.1								85 M
Lithuania	27.4								215 M
Slovenia	8.8		3.0						240 M
CEEC6	*1.1 bn*	*26 M*	*473 M*	*64 M*	*81 M*	*145 M*	*58 M*	*33 M*	*2.1 bn*
Textile and Clothing									
Romania	87.9	30.8	56.3	63.5		64.2			1 bn
Bulgaria	56.4	72.5	38.7	58.8		41.7			225 M
Estonia	25.6						24.0		27 M
Latvia	64.6				71.7				69 M
Lithuania				78.0	91.0				210 M
Slovenia	39.5		15.3	50.5		56.4			201 M
CEEC6	*990 M*	*23 M*	*321 M*	*54 M*	*79 M*	*129 M*	*28 M*		*1.8 bn*
Electrical machinery									
Romania	14.7								16 M
Bulgaria									
Estonia							28.7	63.0	50 M
Latvia	72.3								14 M
Lithuania									
Slovenia									
CEEC6	*33 M*						*26 M*	*25 M*	*88 M*

Table 2.4b (*continued*)

1997	Germany	Austria	Italy	Netherlands	Denmark	France	Sweden	Finland	EU15
Footwear									
Romania			23.0			93.8			95 M
Bulgaria			31.4			93.8			34 M
Lithuania									
Latvia									
Estonia									
Slovenia									
CEEC6			*111 M*			*10 M*			*138 M*

very low absolute levels, Italian firms engage some OPT in the sectors of plastics, and pharmaceuticals[54] and in organic chemicals. For their OPT activities, Italians mainly go to Hungary and Poland, but also – and this is a distinctive trait of Italian OPT patterns – to Romania (for T&C, and to a lesser extent footwear), to Bulgaria (for footwear, and to a lesser extent T&C), and to Slovakia.

Firms from other EU countries involved in OPT operations in CEECs have even more concentrated product and country structures which are generally very focused on T&C. Dutch firms, for example – and to a lesser extent, French firms – are massively engaged with Polish partners in the T&C sector. The same goes for Danish firms. However, whereas the former undertake some OPT in the sector of electrical machinery as well, the latter have some residual OPT in the footwear industry.[55]

From the viewpoint of host countries, the OPT picture is slightly different. Even though T&C systematically comes first in the product structure of all the CEECs, it is Poland which is the most specialised in this area. The OPT business in the Polish sector was worth ECU 1.9 bn in 1996 (around 80 per cent of total OPT carried out in Poland, and 30 per cent of EU OPT in CEEC10 in the sector). Another interesting feature concerning the Polish OPT product structure has to do with the furniture sector, this being almost the only destination for EU OPT (more than 90 per cent of all EU OPT to CEECs in furniture).[56]

The Czech structure is far more diversified with a lot of sectors concerned; OPT in T&C represents a lower share compared to the other CEECs (only 43 per cent of the OPT activities of Czech firms). It is not particularly attractive to EU firms (less than 10 per cent of EU OPT in CEECs goes to the Czech Republic). On the face of it, the electrical machinery sector occupies quite an important second position with rather high absolute levels (around ECU 250 M – i.e. 25 per cent of total Czech OPT). The Czech Republic is also a preferred destination for OPT activities of EU firms in the mechanical machinery sector (ECU 80 M in 1996). In addition, it is worth noting that a large range of Czech sectors register some OPT, even if in marginal proportions. These are: the automotive industry, iron and steel, photography, printing, base metals and glassware.

Hungary occupies an intermediate position, at least as far as T&C is concerned. This sector is more important than in the Czech Republic, but less so than in Poland (ECU 710 M in 1996, – i.e. 65 per cent of the total Czech OPT). Electrical machinery is in second position and, as in the case of the Czech Republic, it attracts very significant amounts of OPT from the EU (slightly more than ECU 200 M). Some OPT also exists in the mechanical machinery sector (of both German and Italian origin), but less than in the Czech Republic. Footwear is an additional pole of relative specialisation.

Romania is a privileged destination of EU OPT in the T&C sector (around 25 per cent of all EU OPT resided in this sector in 1997), as well as in the footwear industry (36 per cent of total EU OPT). The same goes for Bulgaria which attracts a particularly significant share of EU OPT in the footwear sector (13 per cent – i.e. 34 M, and 200 M in the T&C industry).

In sum, Germany is the country largely responsible for the levels of OPT carried out across CEECs. The most important partnerships Germans conduct are in T&C and furniture with Polish firms, and in the electrical machinery sector with Czech and Hungarian companies. Other firms are responsible for far lower absolute levels of OPT transactions, and they are far more specialised. Italian firms have privileged OPT relations with Hungarian partners. These have developed mainly in T&C and in the footwear sector as well as in the plastics industry. Austrian firms undertake OPT in the Hungarian T&C and electrical machinery sectors, whereas Dutch firms predominate in the Polish T&C and in the Czech (and Hungarian) electrical machinery sector. The OPT relations of Danish firms take place overwhelmingly, if not exclusively, with Polish partners in T&C. Finally, French firms are engaged in Romania, Poland and Hungary for T&C, and in the electrical machinery sector in Poland, the Czech Republic and Hungary. Swedish firms have privileged partnerships with Polish and Estonian firms, mainly in the T&C sector. Overall, Poland is a preferred destination for OPT in T&C, and it is almost the only location for EU OPT in furniture. The Czech Republic and Hungary, in contrast, attract comparatively more OPT in the electrical and mechanical machinery industries. OPT in Romania and Bulgaria is concentrated in the T&C and footwear industries.

'OPT dependence'

OPT often accounts for a significant per centage of exports in the above sectors. The Polish T&C sector, for example, distinguishes itself by outstanding rates of dependence on OPT. More than 80 per cent of total Polish exports of T&C to the EU was undertaken under the OPT arrangement in 1996, compared to around 76 per cent of total Hungarian exports to the EU and only 50 per cent of Czech EU exports. Other sectors characterised by high rates of dependence on OPT are the Czech and to a lesser extent the Hungarian electrical machinery sectors (respectively 23 per cent and 14 per cent and to a much lesser extent, Poland). In 1996, the Czech and Hungarian footwear sectors were also still significantly dependent on OPT (20 per cent to 25 per cent of total exports) and the Polish furniture sector previously had very high rates of dependence on OPT.

Most of these OPT proportions are in fact ascribable to partnerships engaged with German firms: 86 per cent and 80 per cent respectively of Polish and Hungarian exports to Germany in T&C were, in fact, OPT re-exports. In the electrical machinery sector, it is remarkable to note that Germans were actually responsible for more than 80 per cent of the amount of OPT undertaken in the Czech sector. Thus, OPT re-exports account for no less than 27 per cent of Czech exports to Germany, and 20 per cent of total Czech exports of electrical machinery to the EU as a whole in 1996. This compares with 14 per cent of Hungarian exports to Germany, and 7 per cent of Hungarian exports to the EU. Finally, export performances registered in the Hungarian footwear industry and in the Polish furniture sector are characterised by the same feature. The same proportion of 15 per cent of Hungarian exports of footwear to the EU and 15 per cent of Polish exports of furniture were OPT re-exports to Germany in 1996 (20 per cent in 1995 for the Hungarian footwear sector).

A second category of sectors which are less important for the general trade performance of CEECs attracts nevertheless, relevant OPT activity in relative terms. These sectors are particularly numerous and diversified in the former Czechoslovakia: optical instruments, leather,[57] toys, printing, miscellaneous manufactures, clocks and optical instruments are all sectors that are dependent on OPT for up to 15 per cent – 40 per cent of total exports. In Poland, electrical machinery and edible preparations, while in Hungary (with lower absolute levels), furniture and leather are sectors in a similar position.

The dynamics of OPT relations

OPT is not a new phenomenon connected to the opening up of the CEECs' markets since the fall of the Berlin Wall. In fact, starting levels of OPT in the then Centrally Planned Economies were already non-negligible in 1991. At that time, more than 18 per cent of Hungarian exports to the EU12 were actually ascribable to OPT (the highest proportion registered in the region), and Poland was the privileged OPT partner of the EU12 in absolute terms (ECU 0.8 bn in 1991 – i.e. 13.5 per cent of total Polish exports to the EU12). The former Czechoslovakia was characterised by the lowest starting point with a total amount of OPT exports to the EU 2.5 times lower than that of Poland (ECU 0.3 bn – i.e. 8 per cent of its total exports to the EU12).

OPT contribution to CEECs' trade performance

Between 1991–95, total OPT transactions increased by 161 per cent between the EU and the CEEC10 (from ECU 2.1 bn to ECU approximately ECU 6 bn in 1995 – i.e. between 11 per cent and 14 per cent of total trade between the two areas over the considered period) (Table 2.5). As a result, OPT exports inflate the growth rate of total exports by around 5 per cent in the former Czechoslovakia, and by around 10 per cent in Poland between 1991 and 1995 (+158 per cent increase of total trade, but 'only' +150 per cent without OPT for the Czech trade. For Poland: +79 per cent with OPT, and +72 per cent without). Overall, according to the contribution ratio,[58] OPT re-exports 'explain'[59] 14 per cent of CEECs' exports growth to the EU12 between 1991 and 1996. This breaks down in the following manner: OPT growth explains 20 per cent of total export growth from Poland to the EU12, and 13 per cent and 7 per cent of total exports growth from the former Czechoslovakia and Hungary, respectively.

OPT growth was extremely dynamic at the beginning of the transition process, and slower afterwards. Until 1993/94, CEECs' OPT clearly followed an increasing trend in all the CEECs and until 1993, OPT growth was in general stronger than that of direct trade.

Table 2.5 Evolution of direct exports, OPT re-exports, and OPT proportion in total exports to the EU 15, base 100 previous year

		1992	*1993*	*1994*	*1995*	*1996*	*1997*	*1998*	*1993–98*	*1991–98*
	Czech Republic	–	–	131.2	144.2	108.6	123.3	128.6	326.2	–
	Hungary	107.7	99.0	128.8	163.2	115.7	136.3	128.7	426.7	455.1
Direct	Poland	110.9	103.7	120.2	139.8	99.5	121.5	117.4	198.3	273.9
trade	Slovakia	–	–	164.0	170.0	109.7	117.4	140.2	503.5	–
	Romania	86.4	116.6	152.1	139.9	100.7	126.7	120.2	214.5	328.6
	Bulgaria	116.9	100.7	144.8	137.0	89.6	124.1	105.7	233.0	274.0
	Czech Republic	–	–	132.6	121.5	106.8	96.3	83.2	157.0	–
	Hungary	120.3	99.4	107.7	113.9	118.2	101.8	86.6	128.0	153.0
OPT	Poland	133.8	125.3	119.7	111.7	102.8	86.5	83.8	83.1	167.0
	Slovakia	–	–	144.3	127.1	121.0	107.4	80.7	192.3	–
	Romania	133.9	130.5	139.8	122.8	122.0	114.3	103.8	177.6	433.7
	Bulgaria	166.6	144.6	118.6	134.6	121.0	110.5	115.6	246.8	594.3
	Czech Republic	–	–	100.9	86.0	98.5	79.9	66.7	35.6	–
	Hungary	109.3	100.3	86.5	73.7	101.9	77.3	69.6	34.9	38.3
OPT%	Poland	117.4	117.0	99.7	83.0	102.8	74.6	73.8	46.8	64.4
	Slovakia	–	–	89.4	77.1	109.3	92.2	59.9	41.6	–
	Romania	140.0	108.4	94.2	90.9	114.9	92.8	89.7	87.0	124.2
	Bulgaria	138.3	137.7	84.0	98.4	130.0	90.5	108.1	105.1	200.2

It was not until 1994 that direct trade growth overtook OPT in dynamic terms, while OPT increases began to decelerate across the region. OPT rates of growth decelerated in 1994 in the Czech Republic, Poland, Slovakia and Bulgaria, whereas it continued to increase in Hungary until 1996. OPT started to decrease in absolute terms in 1997 in the Czech Republic and Poland, and one year later in Hungary and Slovakia.

In general, OPT trends in Hungary are more regular and sustained than in the former Czechoslovakia and in Poland where OPT growth was vigorous at the beginning and weaker later. It is worth drawing attention to a peculiarity characterising OPT in Hungary: OPT actually recorded a positive increase in absolute terms in recent years, even though the figure is marginal (+4 per cent between 1995 and 1998). Over the same period, OPT clearly decreased by 14 per cent in the Czech Republic and by 26 per cent in Poland. This is all the more remarkable given that the dismantling of trade protection measures provides an incentive not to resort to this arrangement.[60] Thus, these figures actually underplay real – and increasing – trends.

In Romania and Bulgaria, OPT increases are very substantial. In Romania, OPT followed a slightly decelerating trend in 1997, while continuing to increase in Bulgaria. In no case is an absolute decrease recorded as in the first fringe of CEECs. The development of OPT in the Baltic States is much more recent, and more uneven. Lithuania attracts much of the OPT to the region, and is comparatively more dependent on the arrangement. However, Estonia has been undergoing a remarkable catch up even though it is still Lithuania which attracts the largest amount of OPT in absolute terms (approx imately 200 M as against less than 100 M for Estonia).

The different trajectories of OPT took place in quite different contexts throughout CEECs, particularly with regard to the evolution of direct trade. It is interesting to note that the relatively strong increases of OPT recorded in Hungary were concomitant with a very strong dynamism of direct flows (+53 per cent and +355 per cent respectively between 1991 and 1998). This is also true of the Czech Republic, but with lower performance of direct trade (+57 per cent, and +226 per cent respectively over the 1993–98 period). In contrast, Poland is relatively more dependent on OPT (+67 per cent), while the performance of direct trade is slightly 'poorer' (+174 per cent). Slovakia is characterised by higher figures in both cases (+400 per cent and +92 per cent for direct and OPT respectively between 1993 and 1998).

Trends characterising Romania and Bulgaria depart from those recorded in the 'first fringe' of CEECs (the Czech Republic, Poland,

Hungary and Slovakia). In these latter countries, OPT increases are generally lower than direct trade dynamism, this is not the case in the two countries which record much higher OPT growth rates, especially at the end of the period (overall +330 per cent and +400 per cent for OPT and +230 and +170 per cent for direct exports respectively).

Thus, whereas in Hungary (and to a slightly lesser extent in Slovakia), direct trade is clearly more dynamic than OPT, in Poland and even more so in Romania and Bulgaria, OPT remains an important source of total trade dynamism. Direct trade in this latter group of countries is characterised by weaker increases than in the case of Hungary and Slovakia. In the Czech Republic, the performance of direct trade is intermediate.

The differentiated developments of direct and OPT trade result in distinct patterns of evolution of OPT dependence. Whereas absolute levels continue to increase, OPT dependence started to decrease in these three countries in 1993/94. However, the Czech Republic, and especially Hungary, are clearly more successful in reducing the share of OPT in their total trade than Poland. In Hungary, OPT proportions decrease by 26 per cent between 1991 and 1995, and by a further 45 per cent between 1995 and 1998 (respectively by 65 per cent between 1993 and 1998). In the Czech Republic, OPT proportions decrease by 47 per cent between 1995 and 1998 (respectively by 64 per cent between 1993 and 1998). Conversely, in Poland, OPT dependence increased between 1991 and 1995 (+22 per cent), whereas it decreased by 43 per cent between 1995 and 1998.

Overall, OPT proportions decreased by 36 per cent in Poland and by 62 per cent in Hungary between 1991 and 1998. Thus, while Hungary had the highest proportion of OPT in total trade in 1991, OPT increases were kept under control, so that the subsequent and particularly strong dynamism of direct trade resulted in a steady decrease in the proportion of OPT. On the face of it, with a lower starting level of OPT dependence, Poland experienced early and very sudden growth of OPT which was not accompanied by strong direct trade increases. As a result, the evolution of OPT proportions in total exports proved to be more resilient.

From the perspective of home countries, German OPT activities in CEECs increased at the very respectable rate of 130 per cent between 1991 and 1997. Two other countries registered similar growth of OPT: France and the Netherlands (+122 per cent and +126 per cent). Denmark is characterised by slightly more dynamic evolution (+300 per cent). However, the most remarkable feature concerns Italy, an extremely dynamic newcomer to the business. Italian OPT in CEECs grew by more than 1600 per cent between 1991 and 1997.

By measuring the proportion of total trade growth which is in fact due to OPT evolution, 'contribution' indicators synthesise the fundamental role that OPT played in trade reorientation towards EU markets of certain sectors of the CEECs. The contribution of OPT in one sector to the growth of the aggregate figure of total trade[61] displays low figures, which nevertheless identify those sectors responsible for the dynamism of OPT and total trade, respectively. In particular, they stress how pronounced country differences are. T&C comes, unsurprisingly, at the top of the ranking of the strongest contributions, but in quite a different manner over the three countries under scrutiny. In Poland, OPT in the sector explains 10 per cent of the growth of Polish total exports to the EU12 (17 per cent between 1991 and 1996) whereas the corresponding figures are 4 per cent and 5 per cent in the Czech Republic and Hungary, respectively.

The second most significant contribution that OPT made to the evolution of CEECs' foreign trade is in the electrical machinery sector. Here, the measure was more significant in the Czech Republic than in Hungary and Poland (2.6 per cent, 2 per cent and 1.5 per cent respectively).[62] It is also worth noting the contributions of OPT in the sectors of Polish furniture (1.1 per cent between 1991 and 1996), Czech mechanical machinery (less in Hungary: 0.7 and 0.5 per cent, respectively), as well the negative contribution registered by OPT in the footwear sector across the three countries. Overall, apart from footwear, therefore, it appears that the sectors identified in the static analysis as being major recipients of EU OPT activity are also the most important in driving CEEC export performances.

OPT contribution, by sector

However, a slightly different computation of the contribution indicator makes possible a deeper analysis of the role that OPT played in explaining the trade performance of individual sectors of CEECs.

Table 2.6, column 1, ranks sectors according to their contribution to the growth of CEECs' exports to the EU: mechanical and electrical machinery in the three Central European countries, but more markedly in Hungary; T&C, especially in Poland, and even more so in Romania and Bulgaria; the automotive industry, especially in Slovakia, the Czech Republic and to a lesser extent Poland; and finally, the furniture industry in Poland, are all sectors of particular importance for the overall trade performances of the

Table 2.6 Sector's contribution to total exports, and OPT contribution to sector's total exports (%)

Czech Republic	1993–98 sect. cont.	1993–96 opt cont.	1996 opt %	Hungary	1991–98 sect. cont.	1991–96 opt cont.	1996 opt %	Poland	1991–98 sect. cont.	1991–96 opt cont.	1996 opt %
Cars	21.2	3.7	4.3	Mechanical machinery	36.0	0.6	2.6	Electrical machinery	16.3	11.5	11.1
Mechanical machinery	15.5	4.7	7.7	Electrical machinery	26.3	7.9	13.7	T&C	14.5	88.1	81.5
Electrical machinery	15.4	17.6	22.2	Cars	8.7	–1.7	1.5	cars	14.4	0.8	1.7
Plastic	5.7	9.3	7.3	T&C	6.1	79.6	75.8	Furniture	11.6	9.3	12.1
T&C	5.1	60.7	50.0	Plastic	3.1	18.9	7.4	Mechanical machinery	6.3	–1.3	3.0
Furniture	4.4	–2.6	3.0	Furniture	2.1	–2.0	7.9	Plastic	3.7	0.5	1.3
Glassware	2.7	–4.1	0.9	Optical instruments	1.3	1.4	4.1	Glassware	1.6	–1.0	0.3
Optical instruments	1.8	18.5	17.6	Footwear	1.3	–61.8	24.4				

Slovakia	1993–98 sect. cont.	1993–96 opt cont.	1996 opt %	Romania	1991–98 sect. cont.	1991–97 opt cont.	1997 opt %	Bulgaria	1991–98 sect. cont.	1991–97 opt cont.	1997 opt %
Cars	37.0	–1.9	1.5	T&C	43.4	68.0	65.0	T&C	32.2	48.4	47.0
Electrical machinery	12.5	10.9	13.7	Footwear	13.9	14.3	19.2	Footwear	6.1	36.0	31.1
Mechanical machinery	8.1	7.6	2.6	Electrical machinery	5.8	11.2	9.2	Mechanical machinery	5.6	1.4	
T&C	8.0	63.7	75.8	Mechanical machinery	5.4	2.4	1.8	Plastic	3.3	0.1	0.1
Plastic	3.7	4.7	7.4	Furniture	3.4	–39.3	0.6	Glassware	2.1	0.5	0.4
Footwear	2.7	–0.6	24.4	Plastic	2.2	3.2	2.5	Electrical machinery	1.8	6.3	2.5
Furniture	1.9	1.9	7.9	Glassware	1.6	–2.2	0.2	Furniture	1.4	0.0	0.0
Transport equipment	1.8	–0.1	0.6	Cars	1.2	67.3	48.9				
Glassware	0.9	–0.4	0.8	Leather	1.0	5.3	4.9				

concerned CEECs. In fact, most of these sectors are themselves quite dependent on OPT for their dynamism. Thus, OPT explains 88 per cent, 86 per cent and 80 per cent of the growth of exports in the T&C industry of Poland, Romania and Hungary, respectively, between 1991 and 1996. This is especially important for Poland and Romania, where the sector is particularly dynamic and drives the country's trade performance.

In the Czech Republic, OPT plays an important role in the electrical machinery sector which is crucial to the country's foreign trade structure. Not only does OPT contribution to the sector's performance rank high (18 per cent), it also represents a significant proportion of the sector's total trade (more than 20 per cent). OPT is also relatively important in the electrical machinery sector of Poland (even though it accounted for only 11 per cent of Polish exports in 1996). What is more, OPT in furniture played a significant role in the trade performances of the Polish sector (10 per cent OPT contribution in a sector which ranks fourth among the biggest exporters).

In Hungary, the contribution of OPT is substantial in the electrical machinery sector (as well as in the T&C, although this latter sector is less important in the Hungarian overall trade structure). Otherwise, it is remarkable to note in other sectors the many contributions which are 'negative' or close to zero and which sometimes play a crucial role in Hungarian trade performance. This is the case, particularly in the mechanical and automotive industries. Finally, OPT in the footwear industry appears to follow quite peculiar patterns of evolution. OPT made a strongly 'negative' contribution to Hungarian exports, while representing quite high proportions of the sector's exports in 1996 (24 per cent). In Romania and even more so in Bulgaria, OPT has been making a strongly positive contribution in similarly high proportions (around 30 per cent of the sector's exports for Bulgaria, and 20 per cent for Romania in 1997/98).

CEECs' sectoral distribution sometimes displays significant changes particularly with respect to OPT proportions in total trade (Table 2.7). The trend of OPT dependence is characterised by a sectoral distinction between T&C on the one hand, and on the other hand most other sectors. Indeed, OPT in T&C increased in the CEEC3 until 1996. It was also in this very same year that OPT proportions started decreasing. The same went for Romania and Bulgaria, although the two countries distinguished themselves by maintaining extremely high growth rates, alongside a minor ability to reduce the proportion of OPT in total exports. Notably, Bulgaria's performance is characterised by an increase of OPT dependence over the 1991–98 period.

Table 2.7   Evolution of OPT re-exports and OPT proportion in total exports to the EU 15, base 100 previous year

		1992	1993	1994	1995	1996	1997	1998	1991–96*	1991–98	1993–98	1995–98
Textiles and clothing												
	Czech Republic			140.6	117.0	105.3	78.2	64.2	173.2		97.3	52.9
	Hungary	113.2	110.5	110.5	123.2	110.2	93.0	74.4	187.8	129.8	103.8	76.2
OPT	Poland	130.1	130.7	120.7	115.6	102.4	83.0	78.2	242.9	157.8	92.8	66.5
	Romania	151.8	132.2	141.8	129.7	121.2	110.0	96.1	447.4	473.2	235.8	128.2
	Bulgaria	174.3	122.7	121.1	143.9	118.5	106.0	119.0	441.9	557.4	260.7	149.5
	Czech Republic			112.0	97.3	103.6	70.5	57.8	77.2		36.6	42.2
	Hungary	95.4	103.8	103.3	102.4	102.0	84.2	65.9	107.0	59.4	59.9	56.6
OPT%	Poland	101.1	104.4	103.0	100.1	101.7	78.8	68.0	110.7	59.4	56.2	54.6
	Romania	115.3	101.3	108.7	104.8	103.8	84.9	77.1	138.2	90.4	77.4	67.9
	Bulgaria	99.2	113.8	103.4	113.5	103.9	80.2	96.7	137.5	106.7	94.5	80.5
Footwear												
	Czech Republic			114.9	65.5	64.6	89.5	101.8	48.6		51.4	58.8
	Hungary	120.1	90.6	95.3	58.3	94.9	122.7	93.0	57.3	65.4	60.1	108.3
OPT	Poland	141.4	118.5	83.4	95.4	56.8	81.3	107.3	75.8	66.2	39.5	49.6
	Romania	86.1	138.5	164.1	90.7	112.8	148.4	196.4	200.1	583.5	489.5	328.8
	Bulgaria	320.7	1896.9	140.3	96.5	130.8	159.4	91.8	10774.2	15768.7	259.2	191.5
	Czech Republic			99.4	60.3	78.6	84.3	93.7	112.9		26.7	62.1
	Hungary	93.2	92.3	89.9	48.7	84.1	104.3	94.7	31.7	31.3	36.4	83.1
OPT %	Poland	133.2	132.4	83.9	74.6	53.0	84.5	106.1	58.5	52.4	29.7	47.5
	Romania	65.5	71.8	101.1	65.8	93.0	111.8	173.6	29.1	56.5	120.0	180.5
	Bulgaria	112.4	1605.1	125.7	92.6	99.4	116.3	95.3	2087.7	2312.7	128.2	110.1
Mechanical machinery												
	Czech Republic			107.8	161.8	95.1	103.7	127.2	165.8		227.5	125.4
OPT	Hungary	102.4	47.7	120.8	147.6	151.7	113.8	114.5	132.0	172.1	352.5	197.7
	Poland	93.0	46.1	98.4	149.6	134.4	137.9	90.5	84.9	106.0	247.3	167.9

Table 2.7 (continued)

		1992	1993	1994	1995	1996	1997	1998	1991–96*	1991–98	1993–98	1995–98
	Czech Republic			76.8	98.5	77.9	84.7	89.8	24.9		34.5	59.2
OPT%	Hungary	94.1	42.8	74.9	72.4	118.8	63.6	76.8	25.9	12.7	31.4	58.0
	Poland	90.3	47.3	76.1	97.6	110.1	121.3	74.6	34.9	31.6	74.0	99.6
Electrical machinery												
	Czech Republic			106.2	161.5	123.1	111.7	92.3	211.2		254.2	127.0
OPT	Hungary	171.2	114.4	97.2	117.1	158.0	127.1	104.2	352.3	466.6	238.2	209.3
	Poland	176.0	101.7	183.9	135.8	131.1	145.4	84.9	586.3	723.8	404.2	161.8
	Czech Republic			67.9	102.3	102.5	87.2	68.0	58.9		36.2	60.8
OPT%	Hungary	125.3	84.8	65.8	67.5	108.0	82.2	83.9	51.0	35.1	33.0	74.4
	Poland	140.0	67.3	130.0	81.9	106.1	98.5	64.8	106.4	67.9	72.0	67.7
Transport equipment												
OPT	Hungary	137.7	40.3	123.8	56.8	135.4	122.4	78.5	52.8	50.8	91.4	130.1
OPT%	Hungary	70.0	43.6	73.7	24.6	106.0	92.5	52.8	5.9	2.9	9.4	51.8
Edible preparations												
OPT	Poland	175.1	89.3	103.8	72.9	141.7	93.1	112.3	167.8	175.3	112.1	148.0
OPT%	Poland	162.1	98.4	104.9	52.6	139.4	82.5	121.8	122.8	123.3	77.3	140.0
Furniture												
OPT	Poland	119.7	140.9	123.6	95.9	101.2	63.6	105.5	202.2	135.7	80.5	67.9
OPT%	Poland	92.8	105.5	97.3	66.7	90.6	54.3	90.0	57.6	28.1	28.7	44.2

[a]: 1993–96 for the Czech Republic.

On the face of it, in the other sectors, and notwithstanding the country concerned, OPT is characterised by its decreasing proportions. This trend generally started much earlier. That said, there are numerous country-specific features and trends in the non-T&C sectors are generally far more differentiated. The fact that Poland was less successful in reducing the proportion of OPT in its total trade is reflected at sectoral level. Virtually all the Polish sectors registering OPT have slower rates of decrease of OPT proportions, not least those of the food processing sector, one of the few across CEEC3 to be characterised by increase of OPT proportions between 1991–98 which therefore take place at the expense of direct trade, and which occurred in the context of a rather depressed overall trade performance. However, in furniture, an important sector in the Polish trade structure, a significant reduction of OPT proportion was registered: –31 per cent between 1991–95, and –72 per cent between 1991–98. OPT represented around 20 per cent of total Polish exports between 1991–94 (in absolute terms this meant an increase from around ECU 60 M to more than ECU 130 M). The rate suddenly fell to 13 per cent in 1994 and then 6 per cent in 1998 (ECU 86 M). This decrease of OPT proportions was actually accompanied by absolute decreases of OPT in the sector between 1994–95 and since 1996. As opposed to the sector of edible preparations, this evolution of OPT took place in the context of very dynamic trends of overall export performance (slightly less than 400 per cent growth between 1991–98).

It has previously been noted that electrical machinery is important in the OPT product structure of the Czech Republic and Hungary. If, overall, OPT dependence decreased by similar proportions (–67 per cent in Hungary and –64 per cent in the Czech Republic between 1993–98), this is a result of distinct patterns. In both countries, the sector used to be characterised by high and similar proportions of OPT (with a peak in 1992 of 34 per cent in Hungary, and 36 per cent in Czechoslovakia). In the Czech Republic, OPT still represented 22 per cent of exports in the sector in 1996 (from around 30 per cent in 1993), and OPT in the sector increased by 150 per cent between 1993 and 1998. This is particularly significant when considering that the sector is one of the most important generators of exports from the Czech Republic.[63]

In Hungary, OPT proportions in the sector are even more relevant given the sector's extreme dynamism and its very privileged position in the Hungarian export product structure.[64] What is especially interesting is the yearly evolution of OPT in the Hungarian case. OPT did in fact increase steadily, even experiencing an acceleration towards the end of the period. Unlike OPT to the Czech Republic, *absolute* levels constantly grew until

1998. Overall, OPT levels increased by no less than 366 per cent between 1991 and 1998. However, with direct exports developing even faster in Hungary, Hungarian firms managed to reduce their dependence on OPT, doing so to a larger extent than Czech firms. In the final analysis, absolute levels of OPT were slightly higher in Hungary than in the Czech Republic in 1998 (ECU 300 M as against ECU 250 M) but OPT proportions of total exports are lower (9 per cent as against 13 per cent).[65]

OPT patterns in the mechanical machinery sector are also very distinct in the Czech Republic and in Hungary. Here again, even though decreases of OPT proportions are very similar (–66 per cent in the Czech Republic between 1993–98, and –69 per cent in Hungary), OPT proportions have been more important in the Czech Republic in the context of weaker general performance of the sector (as measured by total exports). The rate of dependence in the Czechoslovak sector in 1991 was quite significant (17 per cent, compared to 10 per cent in Hungary). It was then reduced to slightly less than 6 per cent, but due to the lower importance of the sector's direct exports, the absolute value of OPT was actually not negligible (more than ECU 100 M). Conversely, in Hungary, trade performance in the sector is clearly stronger (mechanical machinery is the single most important sector driving general trade performance), while OPT played a much minor role.

One sector marked by important country-specific features is the footwear industry. While OPT dependence decreased markedly in the first fringe of CEECs, OPT absolute levels and proportions have undergone steady increases in second fringe countries, especially in Bulgaria, where OPT grew dramatically. With virtually no OPT in the sector in 1991, Bulgaria later experienced an outburst of OPT, mostly concentrated in 1993. It is the only country in the region where growth of OPT constantly outpaced growth rates of direct trade, resulting in OPT proportions steadily increasing in the country's exports.

The trends undergone in the first fringe of CEECs stand in sharp contrast to this. The decrease of OPT proportions were sharp in both Hungary and the Czech Republic (–64 per cent and –73 per cent respectively between 1993–98). Starting levels were quite different, however. In 1991, no less than 77 per cent of total Hungarian exports of footwear were actually OPT re-exports (i.e. ECU 100 M), compared with approximately 20–30 M (i.e. slightly less than 30 per cent of the total trade in the then Czechoslovakia). In 1998, proportions were still non-negligible: 24 per cent for Hungary and 16 per cent for the Czech Republic (respectively ECU 66 and 22 M). Interestingly enough, these OPT trends took place in the context of a rather poor performance of total trade. Between 1993 and 1997, exports in the sector grew only by 68 per cent, 31 per cent and 9 per cent in Hungary, Poland and the Czech Republic, respectively.

OPT product structure

Comparing the ranking of sectors attracting the most important values of OPT in 1991 and 1997 clarifies that the product structure of OPT in CEECs has been undergoing a general process of upgrading, but that this is uneven throughout the region (Table 2.8).

In a first 'fringe' of countries comprising the Czech Republic, Poland, Hungary and Slovakia, the share of EU OPT undertaken in T&C clearly decreases, together with its proportion in CEECs exports to the EU. The same goes, to an even greater extent, for the footwear industry (from 8 per cent of EU OPT in CEECs in 1991 to not more than 3 per cent in 1997),

Table 2.8 OPT re-exports (M ECU) and proportion in OPT re-exports to the EU15 (%)

CEEC4

	1991				1997		
	OPT	*%*	*struct (%)*		*OPT*	*%*	*struct (%)*
TT	1 840.7	13.2	100.0	TT	4 223.8	10.2	100.0
T&C	1 182.0	62.1	64.2	T&C	2 558.3	56.6	60.6
Footwear	153.1	48.1	8.3	Electrical machinery	752.8	13.3	17.8
Electrical machinery	114.3	20.7	6.2	Mechanical machinery	180.8	3.5	4.3
Mechanical machinery	106.0	12.0	5.8	Footwear	127.0	18.9	3.0
Furniture	87.4	16.1	4.8	Furniture	112.3	5.2	2.7
Cars	43.0	9.0	2.3	Plastic	92.2	5.0	2.2
Leather	35.7	18.2	1.9	Cars	70.5	1.7	1.7
Edible	24.0	6.3	1.3	Edible	50.2	10.5	1.2

Romania and Bulgaria

	1991				1997		
	OPT	*%*	*struct (%)*		*OPT*	*%*	*struct (%)*
TT	341.4	15.4	100.0	TT	1 478.6	22.7	100.0
T&C	255.9	52.4	74.9	T&C	1 247.9	60.8	84.4
Furniture	42.8	17.2	12.5	Footwear	129.3	21.3	8.7
Footwear	32.3	46.2	9.5	Cars	25.7	42.0	1.7
				Electrical machinery	16.9	7.7	1.1

Baltic States

	1995				1997		
	OPT	*%*	*struct (%)*		*OPT*	*%*	*struct (%)*
TT	237.6	8.0	100.0	TT	396.6	9.7	100.0
T&C	198.7	40.8	83.6	T&C	309.1	38.6	78.0
Electrical machinery	25.7	24.6	10.8	Electrical machinery	64.2	25.6	16.2
Mechanical machinery	3.0	3.0	1.3	Mechanical machinery	5.7	4.0	1.4
Furniture	2.3	2.8	1.0				

except that OPT in the sector also registered decreases in absolute terms. Furniture, another low value-added sector, also decreased its importance in total EU OPT carried out in CEECs (below 5 per cent of EU OPT).

Compensating for these decreasing positions, the electrical machinery sector became the object of a remarkable promotion. It represented slightly more than 6 per cent of total OPT in CEECs in 1991 and around 20 per cent in 1997. At the same time, its share in CEECs' foreign trade fell from 20 per cent to 13 per cent. The plastics industry became another very dynamic sector, even though absolute levels remained marginal. Interestingly enough, the Baltic States also managed to reduce the share of OPT taking place in T&C. While the latter occupied 84 per cent of EU OPT to the three countries in 1995, this proportion was reduced to 78 per cent in 1997. Parallel to this, the electrical machinery sector grew from 10 per cent to 16 per cent of total EU OPT. Romania and Bulgaria both entrenched their OPT specialisation in T&C: indeed, the sector attracted a greater proportion of OPT in 1997 compared to that of 1991 (from 75 per cent to 84 per cent of total EU OPT in CEECs). As a result, the share dedicated to OPT in the footwear industry remained stable at 9 per cent even though absolute levels of OPT grew very strongly (from 30 to 130 M ECU between 1991 and 1997). Thus, contrary to the first fringe of CEECs and the Baltic States, these trends in T&C and in footwear took place to the detriment of the development of OPT in other – higher value-added – sectors.

There are, however, interesting country variations *within* these broad groupings. For example, as the electrical machinery sector was promoted in both the Czech and the Hungarian OPT product structure by four points, both countries conduct comparatively more OPT in this area than other CEECs (23 per cent and 20 per cent of total OPT in 1996, respectively). This promotion took place, especially in Hungary, at the expense of sectors such as footwear (from 14 per cent to 5 per cent of total Hungarian OPT between 1993–96, and from 8 per cent to 2 per cent in the Czech Republic) or furniture.[66]

The evolution of the OPT product structure of Poland was slightly different. The already high share of T&C in total OPT carried out in Poland increased between 1993–96 from 77 per cent to 80 per cent, whereas in both the Czech Republic and Hungary, the share remained stable (at around 40 per cent and 60 per cent of total OPT in the two countries, respectively). Otherwise, the furniture sector remained in second position and represented 7 per cent to 8 per cent of total OPT carried out in the country. If Poland is also doing more OPT in the electrical machinery sector this is not very significant, given the marginal position of the sector in the overall Polish OPT product structure.

In the other CEECs, it is T&C which is gaining over the other sectors in terms of OPT attractiveness. Very impressive in this respect is the case of Slovakia; it was initially characterised by virtually no OPT in the sector and subsequently saw a drastic increase (from 6 per cent in the Slovak OPT structure in 1993 to 73 per cent in 1996). Besides this promotion of OPT in T&C, exactly the same happens in electrical machinery (from no OPT in 1993 to slightly more than 10 per cent of all OPT carried out in the country). Among the Baltic States, Estonia, despite quite low absolute values, is remarkable for a drastic reorientation of OPT away from T&C to the electrical machinery sector.

Conclusion

Overall, OPT has been occupying an important share of CEECs' foreign trade. In fact, decreasing trade measures notwithstanding, OPT remains a major feature characterising the development of East–West economic interdependence. Furthermore, OPT has played an important role in the reorientation process of CEECs' trade towards EU markets. Indeed, those sectors which have been driving the process of reorientation in single CEECs are also sectors that have received significant shares of OPT. What is more, there is a peculiar parallelism between CEECs' strength ('comparative advantage') as identified in the review of trade studies in the first section and sectors where OPT has been particularly important.

As can be seen from the discussion so far, a major characteristic of OPT developments in CEECs is that it is a peculiarly German story. This is thoroughly reiterated by the above different indicators. However, two in particular deserve specific attention: the fact that around 70 per cent of EU OPT in CEECs is of German origin, and the fact that around 15 per cent of German trade with the CEEC10 is actually undertaken under the specific OPT regime (compared to an average of 10 per cent for the other member states concerned in 1997).

The other important features characterising OPT in CEECs are more specific. To be precise, one striking peculiarity pertains to distinct patterns of OPT distribution and evolution, depending on the sectors and the host country concerned. There is, first, a strong sectoral division between T&C on the one hand (dominant position in the OPT product structure; increasing OPT shares at the expense of direct trade), and the other sectors (more 'marginal' in the overall OPT product structure; generally characterised by decreasing OPT proportions in the context of strong direct trade dynamism).

Finally, there are many country-specific features. A broad distinction may be made between three areas or 'tiers': the Czech Republic, Hungary and Poland, first; followed by Romania and Bulgaria; and finally, the three Baltic States. Roughly speaking, OPT in the first group is more diversified across sectors; with a characteristic tendency to develop in more value-added sectors; this tread is accompanied by a generally decreasing share occupied in total trade. OPT in Romania and Bulgaria, instead, is mainly concentrated in T&C and in footwear, while remaining a very (nominal) source of trade dynamism. As to the Baltic States, OPT developments are more both recent and more occasional. OPT in the footwear industry in particular seems to espouse these dividing lines. Whereas this decreases in absolute and relative terms in the first 'tier' of CEECs, it follows an extremely dynamic trend in Romania and Bulgaria.

That said, there are a number of country differences within these groups of countries, in particular, between Poland, the Czech Republic and Hungary. First, in static terms, OPT in these countries develops in different sectors. Poland attracts OPT in the T&C and furniture sectors, whereas the Czech Republic and Hungary experience a far higher share of OPT in the sector of electrical machinery (around 20 per cent of Czech and Hungarian exports to the EU in this sector have been, in fact, OPT re-exports in recent years). Second, in dynamic terms, Poland appears to be relatively less successful in reducing its OPT share in the context of trade performances, which are extremely positive in the absolute, but slightly less dynamic than trends observed in the Czech Republic and Hungary. In this latter country, in particular, a remarkable evolution is underway: the simultaneous very strong growth of direct trade and OPT. Most notably, OPT in the Hungarian sector of electrical machinery continues to increase in absolute terms; it is due to even stronger growth rates of direct trade that OPT proportions actually decrease.

Generally speaking, the dynamism of OPT goes together with that of *total trade*. This happens in two ways. In T&C, OPT evolutions account for overall trade performance of the sector, that is, that the growth of OPT re-exports more than compensates for stagnating direct exports. In other sectors such as electrical machinery, particularly in Hungary (and in the Czech Republic), the dynamism of OPT goes together with that of *direct trade*, that is, that OPT growth adds to direct trade dynamism.

Beyond the straight quantitative importance of OPT in CEECs' foreign trade in both static and dynamic terms (something that is underplayed by the figures quoted above), what is of specific relevance for the purpose of this book is that a sizeable proportion of CEECs' foreign trade *has been*, at one time or another, channelled through the arrangement. The question to be tackled at length in the following is: even if OPT is decreasing (and notwithstanding this being a statistical effect), what exactly will the consequences be for local firms and economies of the high dependence on OPT?

Concerning *interpretation* of these features, and their relevance for the terms under which East–West economic interdependence develops, no hasty conclusions should be formed on the basis of statistics alone. It will first be necessary to explore the possible consequences that OPT entails at the level of the firm, and then to acquire a deeper understanding of the general context in which OPT develops.

3
OPT Partnerships at Firm-Level: a 'Learning Approach'

The picture of OPT relations is very different at firm-level and in aggregate statistical terms. Thus it is necessary to go beyond a statistical analysis and conduct a more qualitative assessment of the very nature of OPT partnerships that are concluded between EU and CEECs firms. The 'aggregate' dependence of CEECs' trade on OPT, highlighted in Chapter 2's statistical section, corresponds to a 'microeconomic' dependence of local firms on their foreign OPT partners which can take many different forms. It is important to understand the nature of these OPT inter-firm relations as they coincide with different opportunities for CEECs' firms to take advantage of the measure. In fact, they trigger different 'learning mechanisms' which are important factors determining the chances that CEECs transition economies have to catch up. This chapter thus identifies different possible types of OPT partnerships mainly on the basis of fieldwork analysis carried out with local firms in the T&C and electrical machinery sectors in the Czech Republic and in Hungary.

An approach to OPT at firm-level

The above statistical evidence suggests that OPT has had a beneficial effects on CEECs' trade performance. The measure was indeed instrumental in helping the process of CEECs' trade reorientation towards EU markets. However, going beyond a mere trade approach and examining the corporate networks which give rise to OPT trade flows yields a rather more mitigated assessment. In fact, regarding the question of the terms under which OPT integrates CEECs' production facilities, no simple and definitive answer is to be proposed. If the measure has been so successful, it is no doubt because this provides firms with appropriate solutions to their respective problems. However, the OPT mechanisms also raise much concern about the way in which this measure integrates local firms into the Western corporate sphere.

Pros and cons at firm-level

At first, OPT appears to have been a providential solution to many of the problems that faced CEECs at the dawn of their economic transformation process in 1991. In particular, OPT has been decisive in helping to fill often huge production capacities left with no raison d'être by the sudden demise of the CMEA (COMECON) in 1991. In addition, OPT has offered a solution to the shortage of good quality input necessary for successfully weathering international competition. The measure has also facilitated CEECs' access to EU markets. Indeed, OPT eases trade restrictions set up by the EU which would otherwise dissuade exports to the Community. Besides, OPT offers a means for exporting abroad without having to fulfil often very demanding conditions in order to penetrate local distribution channels. Furthermore, OPT is an ideal solution to the problem of 'adverse selection' that forces producers with no popular trademark to fix their prices lower than if their brand were renowned. Last but not least, OPT is a straightforward solution to solving the difficulties pertaining to lack of managerial experience in the field of international relations.

The price to pay for the above advantages, however, is costly in terms of independence. A local firm engaging in OPT activities has to sacrifice its market power to the benefit of its foreign partner as it becomes dependent on the latter, first, for inputs, and second, to market the output. Additionally, a series of mechanisms exists which actually deepens the state of dependence of local firms, making it difficult for them to recover autonomy. For example, the fact that goods produced under an OPT agreement are traded under the trademark of the EU partner prevents a local brand from gaining the recognition necessary for potential subsequent autonomous penetration of foreign markets. This is particularly pernicious as the ability of a local partner to take over production on his own in the case of withdrawal of an EU firm is seriously jeopardised.

Another drawback is that OPT concerns often very simple and labour-intensive transformation tasks. These may potentially neglect or even erode the potential technological capabilities of local partners, forcing the latter to specialise in labour-intensive goods. What is more, it can be argued that the profitability conditions attached to OPT are likely to be unfavourable. For example, if the depreciation of machines used in the production process is not taken into account in the computation underlying an OPT contract, margins of profit decrease with time. The life span of the machinery then determines the end of the co-operation between the two partners – and perhaps ultimately the closing down of a local firm.[67] Equally unfavourable can be the outcome in terms of development activities of a local OPT firm. Involving only primary tasks, an OPT co-operation agreement necessarily makes a limited contribution to promoting the spill-over of technology and know-how that may be expected from close contacts between partner firms. Finally, at the macroeconomic level, the major criticism to be addressed to OPT is the consequence of local partners' dependence for input. If undertaken on a significant scale, OPT might sever linkages between industries concerned by OPT and upstream sectors.

The state of dependence in which local partners are placed is particularly worrying in the face of the extreme ease with which foreign partners may withdraw from their commitment. Were dissuading factors to materialise, foreign partners would find almost no 'exit' costs pertaining to their withdrawal. One such factor is wage increases in CEECs. As soon as advantage of CEECs in terms of labour costs becomes less advantageous, foreign partners could find it more convenient to terminate their OPT engagement as OPT contracts do not demand long-lasting commitment. They can indeed last only the time of one order (for example, three months), and be renewed subject to further demand.

Overall, the negative aspects of OPT are mitigated when taking into account the question as to whether an alternative to OPT was within reach of firms concerned at the time of CEECs' opening up. The distinction between *dependent* and *independent* exports (Stopford and Strange with Healey, 1991: 25) helps us to understand why. If compared to independent exports, OPT is clearly characterised by more negative aspects; however, OPT becomes a 'second-best' if independent exports are difficult or impossible to achieve. Undoubtedly, in this respect, OPT represented for a majority of CEECs' firms an almost providential solution to the demise of the CMEA in 1991.

That said, however, OPT seems to unite all the elements to place the 'family silver' in foreign – i.e. German – hands (Martin 1998: 9; Sinn and Weichenrieder, 1997). If the arrangement proves to be a good second-best, making possible trade reorientation to Western markets, it is not clear what its benefits for local firms are in the long term. Two sorts of risks are associated with the OPT type of co-operation.

The OPT measure is the European version of an American provision which gave way to the development of *maquiladora* in the Mexican US border region.[68] Records are mixed, but, overall, *maquiladora* have been accused of locking local firms into low value-added activities, without offering them real chances for upgrading along the production chains of their partners. *Maquiladora* were also charged with keeping wage increases below productivity rises and of bringing about small backward linkages with other local Mexican firms (Ellingstad, 1997).

Symmetrically, another possible drawback of OPT is if wages are allowed to increase. Foreign partners who possibly engaged in OPT business with the objective of exploiting low labour costs in the short term would then withdraw massively from their commitments, severely damaging local firms' access to inputs and markets.

Primary evidence from statistics

The patterns of OPT evolution identified in Chapter 2 reveal something about whether and which of the scenarios above actually materialise. By comparing OPT to direct and total trade, it was shown that OPT follows different evolutions. These, in fact, correspond to different possible types of OPT partnerships at firm-level. In a first approach, it is therefore worth trying to infer what type of inter-firm relations the different patterns of OPT evolution identified in Chapter 2 correspond to.

In Chapter 2, it was demonstrated that total trade is in general very dynamic in sectors where OPT develops. This belies, as a rule of thumb, a scenario in which the trade performances of local firms are harmed by the sudden withdrawal of foreign partners. There is a notable exception, however. In the footwear sectors of Poland, the Czech Republic, Hungary and even more markedly in the Polish food processing industry, OPT follows absolute decreases and these decreases are not systematically compensated by direct exports. At the same time, OPT follows an extremely dynamic trend in Romania and Bulgaria. There are also variations depending on the home country concerned. German OPT relations with Hungarian partners in footwear radically contrast with Italian OPT in Hungary (and, with lower absolute levels involved, in Poland), and with German OPT in the former Czechoslovakia where OPT increased strongly and much faster than direct trade. The facility with which the geographical distribution of EU OPT in footwear shifts illustrates, at firm-level, the relative 'short-termism' of strategies adopted in the sector. The simultaneous decrease in the first fringe and increase in the second fringe of CEECs suggests waves of re-relocation eastwards at the expense of export performance where OPT partners withdraw from their commitment.

That said, in other sectors, there is, generally speaking, no evidence of destruction of local export capabilities resulting from the cessation of OPT activities due to wage increases. Indeed, the opposite trend may be observed: OPT activities go hand-in-hand with the strengthening of trade performances. However, this can correspond to distinct situations. It was shown that OPT continues to increase in the context of two possibilities: either OPT increases faster than direct trade (increasing proportions of OPT), or OPT increases are slower than the growth of direct trade (decreasing proportions of OPT). OPT in textile and clothing falls into the first category. OPT is characterised by exponential OPT growth rates, irrelevant increases (if not decreasing trends) of direct trade, and resulting high and rising proportions of OPT in total trade (ranging between 60 per cent and 80 per cent). Interestingly enough, the strong growth of OPT that later occurred in Romania, Bulgaria and possibly the Ukraine, does not actually take place at the expense of OPT in the first fringe of countries, as in the footwear case. Thus, these trends testify to a first type of prolonged OPT partnerships. Foreign partners prolong their presence in the OPT business in the first fringe of CEECs, engaging new partnerships in the second fringe. This takes place at the expense of the development of direct – untied – exports. However, since OPT relations continue, this does not harm overall trade performances.

In the other cases, OPT tends to be characterised by a decreasing share of OPT in total trade. In particular, it was stressed that OPT proportions have been very significantly reduced in the electrical machinery sector of Hungary and the Czech Republic, in the context of very dynamic absolute growth of OPT and particularly strong increases of direct exports. As already noted, these trends are particularly striking as, contrary to rising OPT quota in T&C, decreasing tariffs offer lessening incentives to resort to the OPT arrangement. In fact, for OPT to continue to display increasing trends, 'real' upward trends more than offset any statistical effect due to the trade dismantling process.[69] These patterns also reflect the permanence of foreign partners, but in a different context. The fact that OPT transactions remain high while direct trade follows extremely dynamic trends is encouraging: foreign OPT partners are still present and these prolonged partnerships are not detrimental to the development of 'independent' exports. One might even be tempted to infer a sense of causality from this positive correlation between OPT and direct exports performances. OPT continuing growth in the context of strong dynamism in direct trade suggests that OPT partnerships are paving the way for the development of direct exports. Again, this can take place in two ways. The strong dynamism of direct trade can reflect the fact that local firms are taking over OPT production and that they are becoming able to export on their own. However, the strong dynamism of direct trade is not accompanied by symmetrical decreases of OPT. This implies the permanence of foreign partners' involvement and the fact that, to a certain extent, local firms still rely upon OPT to access Western markets and to acquire input. Alternatively, the increase of direct trade can also mean that OPT partners prolong their co- operation with local firms, but under altered forms so that their trade-related activities are no longer recorded as 'OPT'.[70] Hence, part of the dynamism of direct trade could be attributed to the activities of former OPT partners who transformed the terms of their co-operation. This is the case, for example, if an increasing recourse to local sourcing occurs, or if the output is no longer geared back to EU markets.

This second hypothesis fits better with the fact that OPT continues to grow, albeit at a slower pace, especially in Hungary. Rather than testifying to the takeover of OPT exports by local firms recovering their autonomy, the surge in direct trade can be interpreted as resulting from a transformation of OPT partnerships, not a termination of them. Symmetrically, the dynamism of direct trade mitigates a negative interpretation of high levels of OPT taken as indicating that the circular – captive – scheme is reproduced with negative impact on the development of local backward linkages in CEECs.

In this respect, it is worth insisting on the difference of magnitude noted between OPT in the electrical machinery sectors in Hungary and the Czech Republic. In the former case, OPT is mostly characterised by sustained increases of OPT absolute levels, which are accompanied by particularly dynamic trends of direct trade. In other words, Hungarian firms are to some extent better at taking over OPT production or at transforming the terms of their co-operation with their partners, depending on which hypothesis is validated.

Overall, after having significantly contributed to CEECs' trade reorientation, OPT does not seem to subsequently erode the export capability of CEECs' firms. On the contrary, OPT actually contributes to the further strengthening of these. In the T&C sector, the evolution of OPT drives the performance of total exports in the context of very weak direct exports. In the electrical machinery sector, conversely, OPT dynamism goes together with that of direct trade. It is only in the footwear industry that the arrangement seems to give rise to quite volatile (Literally, footloose perhaps!) inter-firm relations. Thus, generally speaking, OPT is not a transient phenomenon embraced by Western firms to take advantage of low wage levels on a very short-term basis. On this point, OPT in CEECs differs from off-shore activities carried out in developing countries.

In fact, OPT statistical evidence supports the hypothesis that local firms are integrated into the production chains of their foreign partners on a long-term basis, even if this takes place in different ways depending on the sector and the country concerned. The question remains open as to the terms under which this prolonged co-operation takes place. Can local firms count on an upgrading of their OPT relations, for example if their foreign partners ask them to make increasing recourse to local sourcing? Do foreign firms even perhaps engage capital and thus transform OPT into FDI? In short, more firm-level analysis is needed to lift the fundamental indeterminacy of trade statistics, in particular to determine whether OPT partnerships give way to the development of autonomous export capabilities, or to altered forms of co-operation.

Evidence from fieldwork

The objective of the present section is to complement the above statistical analysis with case studies of local firms engaged in OPT partnerships (see the Appendix). For this purpose, fieldwork was carried out in the Czech Republic and Hungary, in both the T&C and electrical machinery sectors. These case studies make clear that there is a wide range of possible outcomes associated with OPT which entail quite differentiated local consequences at the level of the firm. In the following section, an exploration of the different profiles of the firms visited is proposed. The objective is to identify the possible ways in which local firms can take advantage of their co-operation with EU partners so as to 'upgrade' their capabilities.

OP and Styl

OP (Prostejov, Moravia), and Styl (Szombathely, Hungary) are two large firms in the T&C sector (5000 and 2100 employees, respectively, in 1994), privatised in the immediate aftermath of the 'revolution'. They produce mainly men's suits and women's ready-to-wear dresses. OPT proportion was high in 1995: 90 per cent for Styl, 50 per cent for OP (three-quarters of its exports). Both firms had a privileged relation with one of their OPT partners: Hugo Boss for OP, and Baumler for Styl. The latter has invested in Styl and holds the majority of its shares. Confidence in the future was the main feature characterising the position of both management staffs at the time. In none of the two firms the necessity of reducing the share of OPT in production was stressed. OP, however, was at least in principle, more inclined to develop its own exports. Styl was very positive about OPT and intended to keep up with this situation as it did not fear competition, be this from Asia, Romania, or the former Soviet States. Interestingly enough, in both firms the average salary was slightly higher than average for the sector. Moreover, the average salary on the respective production lines of Hugo Boss and Baumler was higher than the average at the level of the firm taken as a whole. It worth noting that Styl, as opposed to OP, was engaged in OPT with Baumler before the demise of the COMECON (in approximately the same proportion: 85 per cent versus 15 per cent). Instead, OP was entirely geared to Russia, and started OPT in 1989.

Four years later, the Moravian firm was still working under the OPT arrangement in co-operation with its long-time partner Hugo Boss. However, the proportion of exports accounted for by the partnership with the German firm was 9 per cent (while exports were representing 70 per cent of OP's production capacities).

There was general satisfaction concerning the evolution of relationship between the two firms and the benefits OP could draw from this. In particular, transfer of know-how was stressed to have been taking place on a large scale. Not only could OP learn new designs either 'by-doing' or through the documentation Hugo Boss provided for the Moravian firm, the latter also benefited from more concrete advantages such as training for the workforce. Overall, OP's managers reported being able to dramatically improve discipline and product quality, attributing the increase of OP's sale to these factors.

OP also successfully concluded co-operation agreements with British partners willing to buy ready-made clothes from them (i.e. outside the strict definition of the OPT regime). What is more, these new partners were reported to pay higher prices for OP's output than Hugo Boss was doing. Thus, OP was able to increase the proportion of its output produced under its own brand. Furthermore, it was actually able to sell these goods at higher prices than those agreed with Hugo Boss (which used to be the reverse). However, some features are worth noting like, for example, the fact that wages used to be higher at OP than in the rest of the local industry, which was no longer the case. As a general objective, OP was aiming at increasing the proportion of branded clothing in its total output.

CKD-Elektrotechnika

CKD-Elektrotechnika (1000 employees) was in 1995 mainly oriented to the local Czech market (90 per cent of local sales, and 10 per cent of exports).[71] However, 40 per cent of CKD-Elektrotechnika's exports were ascribable to one OPT agreement with a German partner (SFM, a producer of medical equipment). Here, OPT activities are undertaken in a special workshop that makes needles. It was physically isolated from other divisions and employed 100 workers. Of the input, 100 per cent comes from their German partner, and 100 per cent of the output is exported back to them. Although it would be incorrect to consider that CKD-Elektrotechnika as a whole was dependent on OPT, SFM was nevertheless in the position of fully controlling activities undertaken within the workshop. An important premise for understanding the nature of the relationship between the two partners is that CKD-Elektrotechnika had to make a significant investment in a climatisation system so as to sterilise the air. This was a condition, a *sine-qua-non*, for undertaking the kind of tasks required by the OPT agreement concluded with SFM. Another interesting feature of the agreement has to do with the apparently very long-term horizon of the co-operation. Besides the fact that the Czech managing staff referred to a minimum period of ten years, SFM had invested in a greenfield company established in the Czech Republic (SeFeMed) which was dealing exclusively with OPT relations between CKD and SFM. In addition, the OPT contract contains certain guarantees for the Czech partner, including the obligation for SFM to give six months' notice of any intention to decrease orders, and to inform its Czech partner five years before taking the decision to cease the co-operation completely. Reciprocally, the contract contained a clause stipulating that wages should increase according to inflation (i.e. around 10 per cent a year). Finally, it is worth noting that there was no chance for CKD to assume production on its own as distribution of the concerned products in Western Europe is completely controlled by a Belgian firm in a monopoly position. The managers added that they are very satisfied with profit conditions (something which was also stipulated in the contract).

When visited for a second time, CKD-Elektrotechnika was approximately in the same position as four years previously. Even though changed, the ownership structure was not much clearer and still depends on the gigantic and ailing CKD concern.[72] Various indicators were rather worrying. Production, for example, dropped in 1995, before recovering its 1994 levels in 1999. In fact, the product concerned is very susceptible to cyclical downturns on world markets. Also, the number of employees, 100, was approximately the same as earlier. Despite contact with another firm which eventually came to nothing, the workshop was still devoting its entire production of OPT to its unique partner, the German SFM. The activity, and the nature of the very labour-intensive work carried out in the workshop, did not evolve at all. New machinery had been brought to the Prague facility by CKD's partner, but no technical improvement was introduced. The only real difference compared to what was noted during the previous visit, was the realisation that were SFM to increase its demand for production as a result of an upsurge on world markets, CKD could not satisfy it due to its exiguous facility, and the lack of capital to acquire a new climatisation system necessary to sterilise the air. Moreover, there were strong complaints concerning the very high cost pressures that CKD's partner was placing on the firm. Wages were set to the minimum (the workshop employs mainly women incidentally), and it was hinted that contrary to what had been agreed, payments made by SFM to CKD (for one hour of production) were actually not even indexed to inflation.

ABB Elektro-Praga

A case of long-lasting OPT relations in the electrical machinery sector is offered through the example of ABB Elektro-Praga. OPT with one partner which is also the main investor (ABB) forms a large part of ABB Elektro-Praga's exports; the products in question are electric wall switches. What is particularly interesting in this case is that avoiding tariff duties was openly an important element in the decision to undertake OPT. Whereas it was agreed that wage rises can represent a real danger, it is to be stressed that ABB Elektro-Praga was investing in order to increase productivity faster than wages could be expected to rise. The future of the co-operation was considered to be dependent on prospects on the market for the concerned product.

Timo

Timo, a Czech producer of underwear, with 800 employees, is an example of a firm which managed to successfully take over some production on its own. Split from Triola in 1992, and one of the biggest T&C firms under communist times (20 000 employees), it maintained the OPT relation Triola had with the German company Felina. The decision was taken to rely on OPT for no more than 30 per cent of total production. The proportion decreased to 10 per cent to 12 per cent while the firm diversified its partners. In particular, some OPT contracts had been concluded with Italian firms whose approach was said to differ totally from the traditional relations the Czech firm had been having with its German partner, for example, items were more fashionable, more technically demanding; contracts were short term, depending on market demands; time delivery was more constraining, and the operations apparently had a higher profitability – for the Italians).

The staff stressed how important OPT proved to be for getting to know about the latest developments in fashion and for becoming acquainted with the most sophisticated techniques. It was considered to be extremely valuable for short-term advantages such as not having to pay for material;

being able to obtain the proceeds immediately was also deemed very helpful. However, the profitability associated with independent exports was higher than with OPT.

Vilati

In the electrical sector, the Hungarian firm Vilati used to be in an initial difficult situation. The firm was state-owned with 480 employees producing process control systems, printed circuit boards, and electrical and electronic equipment. Up to 90 per cent of the total production was made for around ten OPT partners; however, one of these (Brunswick from Germany) accounted for 50 per cent of total OPT contracts. The manager used to distinguish between three types of partners:

1. long term-ones, necessary to give a long-term horizon to the firm's strategy (in order to invest), account for 80 per cent of the total number of partners;
2. occasional partners represent around 20 per cent of the total number;
3. potential partners which are very important in order to maintain contact with demand, and to publicise and promote Vilati's capabilities.

None of these, however, would acquire a share when the firm became privatised. The main reason advanced for Vilati's reliance on OPT was the price of inputs. In fact, inputs had to be imported, meaning that foreign firms were almost always in a more favourable position in this respect. Moreover, to the price of imported input had be added transport costs and tariff duties. Finally, to undertake independent exports the firm would have had to pay other tariff duties on the way to European markets (in conformity with the rules of origin legislation). Vilati definitely did not have sufficient capital to advance in order to cover such expenses. As a result, the choice between independent exports and OPT did not really exist. Regarding the foreseeable future, a realistic position prevailed: it would have been advantageous to increase the proportion of independent exports – however, it was safer to focus on keeping up with the technological pace in order to continue to present an attractive profile for OPT partners.

Four years after the first visit, Vilati was in a remarkably stronger position. First, the firm had successfully undertaken the sensitive process of its privatisation.[73] Moreover, many indicators had improved such as its number of employees (100 in Budapest, and 500 in Eger), as well as the level of investment and the turnover (2 bn Ft in 1998, between 2 and 4 in 1999). Net profit was 400 M Ft in 1998.

Most notably, Vilati succeeded in diversifying its activities. These are now grouped into four main categories:

1. Mechanical engineering represents around 70 per cent of Vilati's total activities, and is undertaken mainly with German partners. In particular, Vilati is pursuing its 15-year-old partnership with the German company Brunswick. Interestingly, whereas Vilati used to deliver processed goods back to Germany, it now supplies the greenfield plant that Brunswick established in Hungary recently. It is worth noting that Vilati is not the only supplier of Brunswick. The second most important contract Vilati has is with Liebher, a large supplier of Deutsche Bahn. This partnership does not properly fall within the OPT category since, Vilati simply obtains the blueprint from Liebher. Vilati is otherwise responsible for the purchase of inputs it needs, and does so where it is cheapest: in Hungary or in Austria.

   In general, partnerships in this area of activity are stable and characterised by long-term horizons.

2. Electronical engineering is the second most important activity carried out by the Hungarian firm (around 10 per cent). Partners are particularly diversified. In general, they are established first tier suppliers of firms in the automotive industry or in electrical machinery. For example, Vilati has concluded a partnership with the Swiss firm APAG, which in turn supplies companies like Mercedes[74] Audi,[75] but also Bosch and other companies in the Czech Republic. The partnership with APAG is a strict OPT relationship in the sense that the Swiss company actually supplies Vilati with inputs. The partnership between Vilati and APAG is quite 'close' in that the later 'depends' on Vilati for around 75 per cent of its input. Another example of Vilati's partnership is with an Austro-German firm, Avb-Zöllner, a very competitive company producing parts for motorcycles. In this case, Vilati itself sources the material. Activity in this sector is cyclical, subject to highs and lows.

3. The third sector of Vilati's activity is cables and harnesses (12 per cent of Vilati's activity). Here, Vilati has concluded a contract with the German Leoni Hungaria. The two have established for the purpose of their co-operation a 'custom free area' as, this is encouraged by Hungarian provisions. The partnership is an OPT contract in a strict sense: Leoni Hungaria provides the blueprint, the material, and even production equipment and machinery. In return, Vilati supplies only labour. This co-operation was expected to terminate at the end of 1999.

4. Finally, electrical equipment occupies the last position in Vilati's speciality. Some of this co-operation falls into the occasional category and are conducted usually over a short-term period, sometimes without even a contract signed. At any rate, Vilati had no privileged partnership underway in this branch of its activity at the time it was surveyed for this study.

Overall, the general impression was very positive. Vilati had clearly played the card of a second tier sub-contractor and had done so successfully. It was in fact an early decision, which the manager had cearly stuck to, all the uncertainties – notably due to the privatisation process – notwithstanding. The other main feature of this strategy is the diversification of Vilati's activity and partners, together with a strengthening of the quality of these relations. In particular, Vilati management made clear that the long-term commitment of its partners gave Vilati enough time to plan investment – a crucial necessary condition to the development of the firm – and its ability to keep up with the pace of technological innovation. Another choice paid off, such as the early priority to comply with ISO 9000 and other EU standards. This strategy proved to be particularly realistic given the relatively small size of the firm. It enabled Vilati to avoid the risks which would have resulted from both the temptation of purporting to operate under its own brand, and the illusion that it could act as the principal supplier of a big MNC like General Electrics, Philips, or Siemens.[76] Its 'realistic' character and deep understanding of the rules of the 'global' competition game are two general striking features of Vilati's strategy. For example, Vilati's manager insisted that Vilati had little competitive edge other than that of costs,[77] even though the firm had a long-established tradition of technical excellence. However, at the same time, he insisted that the solidity of the firm's relationship with its partners very much relies on Vilati's capacity to learn and swiftly apply the requirements of the latter. He also had no expectations that one of his partners would take over a majority share in Vilati's capital. Overall, the firm is resolutely geared towards the future – the next project at the time of this interview was to supply the winner of the bid for the mobile licence. This was due to take place shortly afterwards.

Fekon

Fekon was a Hungarian state-owned clothing firm which used to be based in Budapest and specialised in shirts (1200 employees). It depended on OPT for 90 per cent of its production with 12 different partners. Although the managing staff said they were determined to take over production on their own (they mentioned a time-horizon for OPT in the sector limited to five years), they admitted that Fekon was not in a position to do so. What the firm longed for was an injection of capital in order to make the necessary investments and change product lines. Interestingly, none of their actual OPT partners indicated any intention of acquiring a stake in Fekon when privatisation would come. The firm went into bankruptcy in 1993.

Tos Hostivar

The state-owned enterprise Tos Hostivar, a manufacturer of grinding machines with 550 employees,[78] stressed how valuable OPT is. OPT co-operation accounted for 30 per cent of their total production in 1994 (the other 70 per cent was exported under their own brand). Tos had five or six partners. One of these, a German firm, established a separate workshop in Tos's hall where German supervisors worked hand-in-hand with Czech (sometimes Ukrainian) workers to produce post office printing machines. The Germans were settled for '10 years' according to Tos's manager; moreover, they would start to source locally. Tos was willing to increase OPT, even though it was acknowledged that such a form of co-operation had a lifetime in general of only five years. OPT was considered valuable in that it occupies production capacities, introduced more updated techniques, and rendered market mechanisms familiar. The firm was, however, closed down shortly afterwards.

Tesla Karlin and CKD Tatra

Tesla Karlin (electrical equipment; 1000 employees) and CKD Tatra (heavy transport equipment; 1100 employees) are two firms based in Prague that used to export massively to the Soviet markets. Both clearly had negative experiences with OPT. The main matter for grievance concerned the end of the OPT co-operation that both firms had had with a foreign partner (Siemens and AEG Westinghouse, respectively). Siemens' engagement in an OPT co-operation with Tesla Karlin took place in a wider context: co-operation between the two partners commenced with Tesla Karlin producing under Siemens' license. Subsequently, Siemens provided Tesla Karlin with a new machine in exchange for an OPT contract (for a value amounting to 15 per cent of the total turnover of Tesla Karlin). This probably constituted a means by which Siemens could test Tesla for potential future co-operation. However, Siemens was not satisfied and decided to reduce the initial repayment schedule of four years to two years, thus bringing considerable pressure to bear upon their partner. No other co-operation was on the agenda. Tesla Karlin has been looking for other partners. It had already had some sporadic OPT co-operations on a much lower scale (less than one per cent of the turnover), but these were just temporary contacts. It might be speculated that these foreign partners were more concerned to explore the Czech market than to conduct 'serious' OPT. Similarly, it was the premature withdrawal of AEG Westinghouse that led CKD Tatra's disillusionment with OPT. In principle, CKD Tatra would not undertake OPT as it used to source locally. However, it concluded such a contract as a first step towards a more thorough co-operation with AEG Westinghouse; the formation of a joint venture was contemplated. The contract amounted to 100 millions Kcs, but the value of OPT actually performed was only 70 to 80 per cent of that sum. In mid 1995 it was decided that the agreement would not be renewed. Contracts were then transferred to another firm of the same holding (CKD-Lokomotivka). Tatra maintained that it benefited from this co-operation in terms of training and technological upgrading – they would 'desperately' seek for other OPT partners, but they remained very disappointed that there were so few of these.

Pal and Ateso

Pal (4000 employees), and Ateso (3100 employees) are two Czech firms in the automobile industry which were carrying out some OPT on a marginal basis in the early 1990s. The less involved was Ateso, its main activity was to supply Škoda. Ateso purchased 90 per cent of its input locally. However, Ateso conducted some OPT in one of its plant with its joint venture partner (Lucas). The products concerned were brake wheel cylinders. Pal was doing more OPT, but this was still a marginal activity (3 per cent of total output, and 15 per cent of exports). Its main activity also consisted in supplying Škoda (85 per cent of total production, with the rest being exported). Pal would have liked to increase its level of OPT, and was considering that the time-horizon of such activities was about ten years. Indeed, what was consider to matter was not only convenient wage levels, but also low transport costs. Apparently, both firms were satisfied with the profit margins associated with OPT.

Different types of OPT partnerships

A number of features can be inferred from the above firms' stories to help distinguish between different types of OPT partnerships at firm level. A first impression is that OP and Styl were, at the beginning, in a similar position inasmuch as they were both large concerns dependent on OPT to a high extent (for up to 90 per cent of their total production), carried out on behalf of one main partner. This accounted for the vast majority of the two firms' OPT contracts. In both cases, the foreign partner was committed on a long-term basis as well as in qualitative terms. Indeed Hugo Boss and Baumler 'invested' time effort, and even machinery so as to increase the level of their partner's quality up to their own standards.

However, the similarity stops there. First, Styl was already engaged in OPT partnership with Baumler before the fall of the Berlin Wall, whereas OP had just started its co-operation with Hugo Boss in 1991. Subsequent developments further entrenched differences which are particularly telling of the two distinct routes available to local firms. Whereas OP opted for the development of its own brand while diversifying its OPT partners, Styl consolidated its privileged partnership with Baumler by forming a joint venture with the German firm. In this, Styl is a good example of how OPT partnerships can give rise to FDI, and how the two forms of co-operation can take place simultaneously. The question as to whether OP will be successful in imposing its own image remains open.

Another example of an exclusive OPT partnership which evolved in yet another direction is offered by the case of CKD. Like Hugo Boss and Baumler, SFM was unlikely to suddenly withdraw from its commitment on the basis of wage increases. If anything, this is because pressure has been very strong to keep wages in the workshop as low as possible. The local firm may hope that its partner will augment its stake or transform partnership into FDI. However, why would SFM invest capital if, thanks to OPT mechanisms, it already has near-complete control over its local partner? SFM is unlikely to do so and CKD appears to be caught in a trap of low value added specialisation, with a remarkably unfavourable bargaining position. The way out, consisting in recovering independence, was completely out of reach. The only solution would have been to try and diversify, but attempts were unsuccessful.

It is worth noting the important role played by impediments to market access in all three cases of strongly privileged OPT relations with one partner. A common point between OP and Styl is, indeed, that trade restrictions (quotas) rendered access to EU markets impossible without OPT. The same goes for CKD-Elektrotechnika but for different reasons, related to the difficult penetration of distribution schemes in the sector, which enables SFM to extend a considerable degree of control over its partner without having to commit capital. There is almost 'quasi-integration' between the two firms. Thus, in certain cases, difficulties pertaining to market access made a recourse to OPT imperative.

At the other extreme, there is the case of local firms that are engaged in OPT co-operation contracts, with not one main partner, but with several.

This case corresponds to two different situations, however. Again, contrasting the cases of two firms – Timo and ONA, for example – is useful to understand why similar firms can choose very different strategies. The example of Timo illustrates how successful the choice of having recourse to different partners can be in the context of a strategy aiming at re-gaining market shares for its own branded products. Its strategy is to some extent comparable to that of OP as far as the diversification of partners and the development of an own brand is concerned. However, differences in the size of the two firms certainly played an important role in determining their eventual respective success. With larger production capacities, OP is more dependent on OPT than its smaller counterpart because as more likely to encounter trade protection by filling quotas more rapidly. For this very same reason, OP is also more attractive to big MNCs in the sector. Conversely, Timo can be more flexible and, provided it takes advantage of its partnerships to learn new techniques and keep apace with latest fashion developments, it can specialise in certain niche markets. This gives Timo a chance to get in contact with more dynamic and innovative medium-sized firms in the sector.

Vilati is also very concerned about diversifying its partners. In contrast with the two T&C firms, however, it does not aim to develop its own products. In fact, the case of Vilati is extremely interesting in exemplifying a thriving strategy designed to consolidate local firms' position as good quality suppliers among as wide as possible a spectrum of partners. There are other examples of success stories like that of Vilati in Hungary. Raba, for example, is a large producer of truck components which is able to strengthen its R&D as a result of – and in order to keep – contracts to supply MNCs in the country.[79] In the T&C sector, another positive example is offered by Duma, which is supplying Nike and Adidas. Duma has favoured OPT partnerships for a long time and it is now developing its own brand thanks to significant levels of investment. It has its own designers and sources the material it needs by itself.

However, diversifying partners – and activities – is not a sufficient condition for success. An unsuccessful version of this option is illustrated by the cases of firms like ONA or Fekon which are (were) in the difficult position of being highly dependent on numerous and quite volatile partners. Needless to say, having to rely on such partners was not their preferred option.

Several firms in the machinery sector were reported to be in a similarly difficult position. In need of a deep restructuring process, such firms are not in a position to achieve the quality standard that would allow them to compete in the world markets. Tos is a good example of the huge effort that needs to be undertaken in this respect. Here, OPT offered just a transient solution which simply postponed closure of the firm which would have taken place anyway sooner or later. The step from a situation in which local firms rely for their survival upon numerous and uncommitted partners to one in which local firms find it increasingly difficult to have OPT partners at all, is only a small one. For local firms in such difficult situation (for example, when productivity levels are so low that they offset the advantage of low labour costs), the problem is not so much that they have too many volatile OPT partners, but rather they *lack* them. They can be either small (ONA, Fekon, TOS) or larger, as illustrated by the cases of CKD Tatra, and Tesla Karlin.

Whether local firms choose to diversify their OPT partners and activities or, on the contrary, whether they decide to concentrate on one privileged partnership are good criteria from which to discriminate between various OPT strategies. Diversifying the number of partners is a way of reducing risks incurred in case one of these retracts. It offers, however, no solution in the case of the collective withdrawal that would happen if foreign partners have short-term views and are wage-sensititive.

Thus, in principle, the motives underlying strategies adopted by foreign partners are also important in determining the faith of an OPT partnership. For example, medium-sized enterprises whose main objective is to take advantage of low labour costs for the time being, without becoming enmeshed in a more demanding co-operation, would re-relocate their production elsewhere – possibly further east – once wages reached unfavourable levels. Local firms would be forced to close down in the event of lacking time to upgrade their capabilities, and/or if their asset had been exploited or eroded as a result of an OPT partnership.[80] OPT would, in this case constitute an advantageous substitute for foreign direct investment for foreign partners.

Another possibility is if foreign partners are in fact larger firms, possibly MNCs, which engage in OPT activity in the context of a complex rationalisation of their strategy on a regional scale. The cases of CKD Tatra and Tesla are interesting in this respect. First, they demonstrate that MNCs are indeed a potential source of OPT. Second, they make clear how extremely demanding the expectations that the latter have with respect to would-be local partners are. The two Czech firms formally fulfilled the conditions to become Siemens' and AEG's suppliers in terms of size (production capacity) and labour costs. However, their levels of productivity and qualitative requirements such as the ability to deliver on time and to comply with quality and technical standards, were not up to Siemens' and AEG's levels.

In fact, ultimately, these case studies suggest that if the strategies adopted by foreign partners play an important role in determining the nature of an OPT partnership, the eventual outcome – that is, whether local firms benefit from OPT relationship – is very much dependent on the initial situation and profile of the latter. In other words, the type of strategy adopted by foreign partners is not decisive. In particular, local firms in difficult would have had to close down *anyway* with or without OPT. Symmetrically, if OPT performs no miracles for firms in difficult positions, it can make a very valuable contribution to those with healthier records which are able to take advantage of the measure. Overall, the causality relationship between foreign and local firms' strategies is not one way and local firms can, to some extent, influence the decisions of their partners. The key in this respect is to *learn* from the partnership, whatever the type of (initial) agreements concluded. This does not mean achieving fundamental technological breakthroughs; rather, it involves a daily improvement of organisational practices.

Different upgrading mechanisms

These case studies demonstrate that the outcome of OPT partnerships can be astonishingly varied and that there are different ways for local firms to take advantage of the OPT measure to upgrade their capabilities.

A first possible option open to local firms is to try and reduce their reliance on OPT.

Firms in T&C in particular may try to impose a brand while simultaneously diversifying OPT partners and reducing their share of total output (OP, Timo). The objective is, in this case, the development of autonomous production and export capacities paving the way for a complete take over. Local firms thus take advantage of OPT to learn new techniques, fashion trends and soon and eventually develop their own brand.

Alternatively, local firms can chose to deepen an OPT relationship with one privileged partner. Large firms in the T&C sector are apparently able to secure the relative long-term and exclusive commitment of their foreign partners, and this can give rise to FDI (Styl). There are some examples in the electrical machinery sector as well (ABB). However, in the event of a foreign partner not engaging capital, such exclusive partnerships might well turn out to be vehicles for placing local firms in positions of real structural dependency (CKD). An opposite strategy is to specialise in OPT business and use the arrangement to become suppliers. In the electrical machinery sector, medium/larger-sized local enterprises, far from regaining independence, can acquire a fully-fledged status of supplier. Rather than aiming at becoming first tier suppliers of big MNCs (Tesla, CKD), a more realistic approach is to specialise in the second tier (Vilati). Here, local firms 'upgrade' their capability in the sense that they undertake more complex tasks, develop the capacity to source their input, and possibly progress from a third or second tier of suppliers to the first tier.

Finally, there is the possibility of carrying out a mixed strategy: while supplying MNCs, local firms produce goods under their brand. This is not, however, tantamount to carrying out OPT as a provisional activity so as to prepare for recovery of full autonomy. The two can run together in parallel for some time, which is rendered possible by specialisation on different quality segments of a considered market.

Clearly, local firms may not have this choice and the strategy of their foreign partners might represent an important constraint. However, it is worth insisting that profile of local firms (in particular, their size), and their behaviour *does* appear to be of primary importance in determining how OPT partnerships develop. Even if the search for better production costs is (has been) an obvious primary determinant of OPT strategies adopted by EU firms, local firms have room for manoeuvre in taking advantage of their partnerships. In fact, the key is to *learn* new practices and techniques, as well as the new rules of the competition game. This learning process prepares local firms either to carry out production on their own (and take over OPT production), or to specialise in the supplier business, and invite foreign partners to upgrade their commitment and enter into more equal partnerships.

A tentative conclusion could be formulated in the form of what might, in a first approach, resemble a paradox: dependence on OPT may constitute, under certain circumstances, the best way for securing the positive aspects of OPT. In the face of the seriously challenging task of succeeding in imposing a brand on domestic and/or world markets, a strategy which consists of getting the most out of an inclusion into a system of international division increasingly based on sub-assembly operations is surely in line with the new conditions of world competition. Indeed, from the panel of firms interviewed, the one which seemed to be better off was Vilati: depending on several serious partners had proved to pay off. However, staying on the edge is not easy, and the risks are high for local firms become hopelessly dependent on a single or on several volatile foreign firms.

Synthesis

In the following section, it is proposed to relate the evolution of aggregate trends of OPT at country and sector level analysed in Chapter 2, and the

Table 3.1   OPT firms and the evolution of OPT and direct trade

	Dynamic OPT increases	*Slowing down of OPT increase*	*OPT decreases*
Dynamic direct trade increases	Vilati (OP)	Styl	–
Stagnant direct trade/or decrease	OP	CKD-Elektrotechnika	footwear?

different types[81] of OPT partnerships at firm-level that were identified through fieldwork. Drawing together evidence from statistics and from the case studies thus enables to 'quantify' which type of learning mechanism is most likely to materialise and where – that is, in which sector and between which countries (Table 3.1).

In column two, top, a slowing down of OPT increases is apparently taken over by direct trade. This could coincide with the case of Styl, in the T&C sector, which has transformed its OPT partnership into proper FDI. Rather than corresponding to truly independent exports carried out by 'local' firms, this case illustrates how OPT can be a first step before full vertical integration through FDI takes place. According to statistical evidence, however, this case is not the most frequent as few cases of symmetrical rises of direct trade and decrease of OPT were detected. There are exceptions in the T&C sector, however, especially in the Czech Republic and in Hungary. It is also possible that this outcome develops in the electrical machinery industry, although this is more likely in the Czech Republic than in Hungary (as in this latter country OPT continues to increase).

In contrast, in column one, bottom, the case of OP corresponds to continuing OPT re-exports. Whether the firm manages to reduce its share of OPT and impose its own brand will determine its position in either column one, top or column one, bottom (see Table 3.1, above).[82] This is typically the situation in T&C in virtually all countries. For the moment no evidence of direct trade dynamism has been noted (far from it), which suggests that strategies aiming at recovering independence are not entirely successful. However, this could very well be because items produced outside the OPT arrangement are geared to local markets. Thus, firms in the T&C sector trying to produce under their own brand, might do so if they content themselves with the domestic markets, but not if they want access to the international markets.

In column one, top, the case of Vilati fits with the *simultaneous* growth of OPT and direct trade. This is when local firms 'specialise' in the OPT job:

they do not purport to recover independence, so aggregate levels of OPT continue to increase. However, these firms successfully manage to diversify and upgrade their partnerships so that as a result, direct trade increases as well. The strategy of these firms is indeed to establish their reputations as reliable and technologically updated suppliers of larger firms. It has been shown that this is characteristic of the case of electrical machinery in Hungary – to a lesser extent in the Czech Republic.

The worrying case of CKD-Elektrotechnika is shown in column two, the bottom. The firm continues to conduct OPT for its only partner so that OPT flows are still statistically recorded. However, it is not successful in imposing a brand nor at transforming its partnership, so direct trade registers no increase. For how long could this last? This case would be representative of local firms locked into the production chains of their foreign OPT partners, with little chance to access international markets independently or to transform their OPT partnership. In short, they would be integrated 'on the cheap'. In this case, prolonged OPT relationships can only be possible on the basis of wages that are kept low. In a word, it corresponds to a *maquiladora* scenario. OPT statistics tend to dismiss a scenario of this sort developing on a large scale.

Finally, column three, bottom, presents the most damaging scenario for local firms and economies. Here, foreign firms are engaged in the OPT business only to take advantage of comparative advantages based on low labour costs. When wage differentials are no longer advantageous, such firms withdraw from their commitment, helped by the very low exit costs associated with this form of international production. Fieldwork did not reveal many such cases, but statistical evidence suggests that this is happening in the footwear sector, especially in the first fringe of CEECs.

Conclusion

The OPT measure appears to promote the development of very different inter-firm relations which have different consequences for local firms and economies. By using the quantitative evidence presented in Chapter 2, and combining this with the above case studies, it was possible to assess the respective weight of different types of learning mechanisms associated with OPT partnerships. The range of possibilities open to local firms is wide and continuous, and if there are cases where OPT partnerships operate to the detriment of local firms, there is also room for manoeuvre for the latter to take advantage of a measure which was at first designed to exploit them.

The most favourable cases were found in two opposite situations, but with different chances for success. These occurred when local firms diversified their partners and increased their activities (especially in electrical machinery), and when they were able to secure the steadier commitment of an exclusive partner so that OPT was transformed into FDI (with lower probabilities, though). The two cases then gave rise to increased direct trade.

However, some evidence was also found which supported the hypothesis of a *maquiladora* type of OPT development, with the withdrawal of foreign partners causing damage to local export capabilities (in the footwear sector), and/or the worrying position of strong dependence of local firms upon one foreign partner with no prospect of improvement.

Finally, the combined fieldwork and statistical analysis is also interesting for what it did *not* find, that is, the complete take-over of OPT activity by local firms.

These results pave the way for a more thorough assessment of the contribution that OPT makes to the dynamics of regional integration. To arrive at the right interpretation, however, it is first necessary to be clear about the framework of constraint and opportunities in which firms decide on their OPT strategies.

4
The Transformation of a Policy Instrument

An analysis of OPT relations between the EU and CEECs makes clear two fundamental features characterising the development of economic interdependence between the EU and the transition economies. These include the fact that economic interdependence develops at the same time in the very politicised framework of opportunities and constraints shaped by EU policies, and in the context of profound changes at work in the world economy, broadly referred to as 'globalisation'.

The present chapter proposes to pull together the findings of the above statistical analysis and case studies so as to understand the nature of the 'market linkages' the OPT measure contributes to establishing between Western and Eastern Europe. In order to rightly interpret of the trends observed in Chapters 2 and 3, the chapter will therefore proceed by assessing the two broad ranges of factors determining OPT developments: EU policies and 'globalisation'.

Institutional determinants: the process of trade liberalisation

OPT owes its raison d'être to the permanence of trade barriers before full trade liberalisation took place as of January 2000. In this respect, the 'politicisation' of OPT determinants appears to be double-faceted: first, directly, the development of OPT owes much to the mode (the speed and the form) of trade liberalisation; and second, indirectly, the process of trade liberalisation on which OPT depends is itself ascribable to more general considerations which assume their full significance in the context of political relations between the EU and CEECs.

Trade liberalisation: historical perspective, political function and controversies

Economic transactions between west and east traditionally developed in a very politicised environment. Two contending principles governed these: the belief in economic interdependence to spur political convergence, and the reliance on economic containment as a political instrument to isolate CEECs (Bertsch, Vogel and Zielonka, 1991). Relations between the European Community and Central and Eastern European countries took place in this context. Until 1988, they were characterised by unilateral measures taken by the Community in the framework of a trade regime designed to deal specifically with 'state trading economies'.[83] Apart from unilateralism, a second feature of the EC-CEECs' relations was that 'agreements' were adopted by the EC, with each CEEC taken separately.[84] Such agreements were most often confined to particular and restricted issues; they were actually used to endorse measures taken at the national level by member states.

On 25 June 1988 a joint declaration between the EC and the COMECON was signed, establishing mutual recognition. However, the regime governing trade relations was not upgraded in the hierarchy of trade treatment granted by the EC to third countries. Moreover, due to the rapid decay[85] of the organisation, no measures were implemented to develop closer co-operation. Instead, a series of truly bilateral agreements were signed, starting with Hungary in 1988. Part of the so-called 'first generation agreements' (Daviddi, 1992: 272), they dealt with economic issues and paved the way for the removal of quantitative restrictions. However, most of the measures contained in this first wave of agreements were in turn rendered obsolete by the conclusion of the more ambitious PHARE programme in July 1989. Dealing initially with Poland and Hungary, this was subsequently extended to all former COMECON countries.[86]

To keep up with the pace of change in CEECs, and for the sake of a more consistent and systematic scheme of co-operation, the Commission decided in August 1990 to conclude 'Europe Agreements' with the CEECs, adopting once more a bilateral formula. They were signed on 16 December 1991 with the CSFR,[87] Hungary and Poland, then in March and February 1993 with Bulgaria and Romania, respectively. Each agreement contains eight main sections.[88] It is, however, the establishment of a free trade area by the year 2000 which is their central objective. 'Interim Agreements' were adopted in March 1992[89] in order to speed up the coming into force of trade and trade-related measures contained in the Europe Agreements (EAs).[90] The process of implementation rests on the principle of asymmetry, whereby the EU is committed to fully liberalise

CEECs' exports by 1997, that is, five years before the complete liberalisation of EU exports to CEECs. It is worth stressing that what is at stake in the economic chapters of the Europe Agreements is the establishment of a free trade area (with the liberalisation of goods, services, persons and capital), and *not* the implementation of a Custom Union that would require a common external tariff and, possibly, harmonised trade policies. In this sense, the Europe Agreements differ substantially from 'Association Agreements' the EU has concluded with other countries.

A salient feature of the EAs is that they consider full membership of CEECs as their ultimate objective. Although of a highly indeterminate form, and despite repeated attempts to procrastinate on the issue of any clear-cut timetable, integration was considered by the Community to be an eventual outcome of the EAs, co-operation scheme. The objective was more clearly restated at the European Council in Copenhagen (June 1993), and a White Paper was issued in June 1995 to provide guidelines on policy reforms to be adopted. The EAs were thus an important pillar of the pre-accesssion strategy engaged by the EC/EU.[91] A second phase of the enlargement process started with the Intergovernmental Conference launched in 1996, and Agenda 2000, presented in July 1997 by the Commission as a single framework tackling together the many issues at stake in the enlargement process.[92]

In the approach adopted by the EC/EU, establishment of a free trade area was therefore the first step in a process intended to culminate in the all-encompassing political integration of CEECs into the EU.

The influence that EU policies have had on the development and terms of East–West economic interdependence has been widely debated. Past relations have been accused of weighing heavily in the definition of present ones. This is clear in the 'hub-and-spoke' criticism made by Baldwin concerning EU-CEECs' relations (1994), due to the fact that CEECs have never been considered together by the EU/EC. Several related developments, such as the difficulty of agreeing on a pan-European cumulation of rules of origin, have been considered to be detrimental to the development of intra-CEECs' relations. However, it has been shown that these rules of origin have not had much influence on the way MNCs organised their activity throughout the region (Lorentzen, 1998).

Concerning the Europe Agreements, there have been many protests related to the suitability of trade protection measures imposed by the EU precisely on products where CEECs seemed to have a comparative advantage, the so-called 'sensitive goods'.[93] However, Brenton and Di Mauro (1998) argue that the incriminated protection measures on 'sensitive' products actually had no restrictive effect and that trade in sensitive goods would not increase as a result of further trade liberalisation, in contrast to the sceptical conclusions reached by Vittas and Mauro (Black, 1997). Also criticised were measures of protection developing at quite refined levels. Messerlin (1992, 1993), for example, demonstrated that depending upon the speed and modality of distribution of quantitative restrictions, certain products and producers in various countries were advantaged at the expense of carefully chosen others. Parallel to this fine-tuning of protection is the implementation of measures that are more visible yet relatively uncommon and, thus, more difficult to monitor. This is the case with measures such as anti-dumping, countervailing duties and safeguard clauses, certain of these, for example, antidumping, are used quite extensively.

The OPT measure

The OPT measure is to be considered in this context of this tradition of controversial protectionist attitudes of the EU towards its Eastern neighbours. As noted above, the raison d'être of OPT is the – residual – presence of trade barriers during the process of trade liberalisation which it helps circumvent. An immediate consequence flows as far as the incentive to resort to the arrangement is concerned: the more binding the latter, the more compelling the recourse to the arrangement. If, on the contrary, trade protection measures are marginal, or if they are not binding, there is no point in having them lifted. There is therefore little incentive to undertake and/or to declare OPT. To understand how effective the incentives to resort to OPT are, it is therefore necessary to assess the bindingness of trade restrictions imposed on East–West trade.

General schedule of trade liberalisation

Far from establishing free trade all at once, the process of trade liberalisation between the EU and CEECs has taken place in an uneven and protracted manner. As a result, numerous trade protection measures have continued to constrain trade flows before being eventually lifted. Such a transition period lasted, at best, six years for CEECs' exports to the EU and ten years for EU exports to CEECs. During this transition period, the major CEECs' exports have faced 'substantial' tariffs and non-tariffs barriers (Messerlin, 1993: 12). In the following, the identification of trade protection measures still in place during the transition process will make possible the assessment of their bindingness.

The entry into force of the Interim Agreements marked the liberalisation of a significant number of barriers constraining trade between the EU and Associated countries. The remaining trade obstacles were expected to undergo progressive elimination according to a precise schedule. The Europe Agreements provided for the abolition of around half of enforced tariffs upon the entry into force of the Interim Agreement on 1 March 1992. At the Copenhagen European Council held in June 1993, it was decided that the majority of the remaining half would be eliminated by no later than 1 January 1995, instead of 1997 as previously agreed. As to quantitative restrictions, in principle these were lifted in 1992. However, textile and clothing MFA products, together with CSCE products, were subject to quotas (at least until 1997). As far as OPT is concerned, textile and clothing MFA products that were eligible for the arrangement benefited from a complete exemption of tariff from the entry into force of the Interim Agreements.[94] Moreover, quantitative restrictions specific to OPT in the T&C sector were completely eliminated on 1 January 1998. It goes without saying that no duties were any longer associated with OPT when tariffs were themselves completely eliminated (on 1 January 1995). It means that *in principle*[95] OPT figures are no longer available as of 1 January 1995 for products subject to tariffs, and as of 1 January 1998 for T&C products still subject to quantitative restrictions. Table 4.1 outlines the detailed schedule of liberalisation as provided for by the Europe Agreements, and the Copenhagen Declaration.

Since there are two types of protection measures – quotas and tariffs – there are two OPT regimes which differ according to the type of preferential treatment they grant. The so-called 'economic' regime – economic OPT – consists in granting additional specific quota applying to OPT transactions. In the 'tariff OPT' regime, instead, tariffs on re-imports are suspended either partially or – in the case of CEECs – entirely.[96] This has significant relevance as far as the incentives to resort to OPT are concerned. Indeed, since quotas and tariffs are differently effective, their associated preferential OPT treatment is 'attractive' to varying degrees.

The effect of tariffs on trade can be shown to be less constraining and less distorting than that of quotas. This means that whenever the protective device used is a tariff, the incentive to use OPT is lower than if a quota were enforced.

Trade liberalisation in the textile and clothing sector

Being considered to be a 'sensitive' sector, T&C is subject to a specific regime of liberalisation which is slower than that scheduled in other sectors by the Europe Agreement. It is important to stress that trade

Table 4.1   Trade liberalisation schedule

Products	Obstacles	Interim agreements	Liberalisation path	Copenhagen	Elimination
Sensitive industrial products (Annex IIa)	Custom duties	Abolished at the end of the 1st year after the entry into force of the Agreement	Reduced by 50% in 1992		End 1992
Sensitive industrial products (Annex IIb)	Custom duties	Abolished at the end of the 4th year after the entry into force of the Agreement	Reduced by 20% per year	Abolished at the end of the 2nd year	End 1993
Sensitive individual products (GSP consolidation; Annex III)	Custom duties within tariff quota or ceiling	Abolished at the end of the 5th year	Annual reduction of 15%	Abolished at the end of the 3rd year	End 1994
Sensitive individual products (GSP consolidation; Annex III)	Quota or ceiling for the application of quota	Abolished at the end of the 5th year	Increased by 20% per year	Increased by 30%	End 1994
Agricultural products (Annex Xia)	Levies/duties quotas		Reduced by 60% increased by 10% from 3rd year	6 months earlier	
Textile products (Protocol 1)	Custom duties	Abolished at the end of the 6th year		Abolished at the end of the 5th year	End 1996
Textile products (Additional Protocol)	Quantitative restrictions				End 1997

Table 4.1   (*continued*)

Products	Obstacles	Interim agreements	Liberalisation path	Copenhagen	Elimination
ECSC steel products (Protocol 2)	Custom duties	Abolished at the end of the 5th year	1st reduction of 80% on entry into force	Abolished at the end of the 4th year	
Processed agricultural products (Protocol 3)	Custom duties				
OPT	Custom duties			Exemption as of beginning 1994	

Source: Official Journal of the European Communities, various issues. Own elaboration.

liberalisation in the sector takes place outside the framework provided for by the Europe Agreements, and within that of the multi-fibre arrangement (MFA). The fourth round of the MFA (negotiated under the auspices of the GATT) provides for quantitative restrictions imposed by the European Community on CEECs through bilateral agreements from 1987 to 1997.[97] On the basis of the conclusion of the Uruguay Round, it was decided to dismantle the MFA regime with the achievement of free access to EC markets as of 1 January 1998.[98] Quantitative restrictions have thus been increased in four waves: in 1987, January 1991 (for Czechoslovakia), April 1992, and December 1992.

Several studies have shown that quantitative restrictions have been significantly relaxed since the demise of the CMEA (Nagarajan, 1995; Corado, 1995). These studies are based on different indicators of the bindingness of EC quantitative restrictions imposed on CEECs' T&C exports. They reached the same conclusion: the significant liberalisation of constraints imposed on CEECs' exports since 1991.[99] There are, however, several problems with these indicators and their inter-pretation.[100] Most fundamentally, these indicators address only a narrow question: whether the *trend* of trade obstacles is geared toward more or less bindingness. Given that liberalisation is the general objective, these findings offer no surprises.

In his study on the impact of EU trade policy with CEECs, Messerlin brings in additional elements necessary to build a complete picture of the effects that the very process consisting in removing trade obstacles has on the *structure* of trade flows. (Messerlin, 1993). His argument is that enlarging quotas does not translate automatically into more 'free' trade. In fact, this can result in further biases in trade patterns.[101] For example, Messerlin highlights how controversial the interpretation can be of the Quota Utilisation Rate (QUR) indicator, whose low levels should not be taken as an unconditional sign of the unbindingness of quantitative restrictions.[102] In short, Messerlin's analysis makes clear that increasing quotas is not an innocent move merely aimed at lifting distortions. In certain sectors, and under certain conditions this can influence CEECs' trade performance. This shows

> the ability of the general architecture of the EC MFA regime to shape the Central European countries' export performance. (Messerlin, 1993: 47)

There follows a brief illustration of Messerlin's arguments applied to the case of the Czech Republic.[103]

Direct trade

There were until 1997 24 quotas imposed on direct trade from the Czech Republic, (there were 46 from 1991–93, and 26 in 1994). Originally, quotas on direct trade displayed regular growth rates over the 1993–97 period: quotas were supposed to increase at an average rate of 21 per cent, with lower peaks in the categories of woven fabrics (8 per cent only). However, following the entry of EFTA countries (notably Austria) into the EU as of January 1994, quotas were readjusted. Eventually, the actual average growth on the period from 1993–97 amounted to 61 per cent, with higher peaks of +109 per cent (in the category of men's jackets). As to the distribution of direct quotas, with the exception of two categories which are granted particularly high quantities (woven fabrics and stockings), this is relatively even.

There was one binding quota in 1994 (there were 12 in 1991), and QUR ranged from 8 per cent (men's suits) to 92 per cent (woven fabrics) in 1994, following a decrease almost entirely concentrated between 1991 and 1992. Overall, from a level of 71 per cent in 1991, the average quota utilisation rate stabilised at relatively low levels of around 45 per cent in the following years.

On the basis of this evidence, quantitative restrictions imposed on the former Czechoslovakia do not appear to have been significantly binding. However, before drawing definitive conclusions, their effect in relation to the structure of specific quotas imposed on OPT trade will be further investigated.[104]

OPT trade

If the liberalisation of 'normal' quotas on direct trade has been effective despite controversies, the specific OPT regime has been a source of additional potentially strong distortions.

Until 1991, subject to the 'autonomous' trade regime (i.e. provided for unilaterally at the level of each member state), OPT was for the first time included in bilateral agreements with CEECs in parallel with the conclusion of the more all-encompassing trade provisions of the Europe Agreements.[105] Specific OPT quotas, endorsed by the Community, were thus imposed as of 1 January 1992. Twelve of these were imposed on Czechoslovakia, then on the Czech Republic; no decrease in the number of quotas had been provided for.[106] The growth of OPT quota was substantially modified as a result of the membership of Austria. Whereas these were supposed to grow at an average rate of +31 per cent between 1993 and 1997, additional quantities granted over the 1995–97 period brought the figure to +52 per cent. This is lower than the increase characterising quota on direct trade (+52 per cent as opposed to +61 per cent). Of particular significance is the fact that the average rate of growth conceals some significant disparities (the strongest growth of OPT quota is +89 per cent for men's suits, the lowest is +36 per cent for men's shirts).

Another way to characterise the situation of OPT quotas is to compare OPT with direct quotas following the EFTA adjustment, for example, thanks to an indicator such as the proportion of OPT quotas in total quotas. OPT represented 55 per cent of total quota in 1993, and 51 per cent in 1997. OPT quotas thus underwent an average decrease of their proportion in total quota amounting to approximately –7 per cent over the 1993–97 period. The rate was broken down in the following way: –1.5 per cent from 1993 to 1994, and –4 per cent from 1994 until the abolition of quantitative restrictions in 1998. These average figures conceal very significant disparities. Category 12 (stockings), for example, displayed variations of more than 30 per cent in both directions with an overall share stable at around 30 per cent. On the face of it, the share of each category in total OPT quantitative restrictions remained relatively stable.

Studies on OPT found utilisation rates lower than those pertaining to direct trade. For example, the average QUR by Czechoslovakia in 1992 – which amounted to 47 per cent – was broken down in the following manner: the average QUR was 50 per cent on direct exports, and 36 per cent on OPT exports (UNECE, 1990). On the basis of figures expressed in tons, however, Messerlin found a utilisation rate of total quota amounting to 92.6 per cent, which divided into 48.7 per cent for OPT, and 105.6 per cent for direct trade (Messerlin, 1993: 79). The present study found different figures yet agreed on lower OPT utilisation rates in 1992: 38 per cent in average (from OETH sources) which compares with 44 per cent for quotas on direct trade. There was one binding quota.

Interestingly enough, in 1993 and 1994, OPT quotas were suddenly extensively utilised with average above 100 per cent. There were eight, then nine binding quotas on a total number of twelve quotas. Overall, quota utilisation rates increased at the rate of +9 per cent from 1993 to 1994. These figures compare with average utilisation rates of direct quotas which did not exceed 50 per cent in 1993 and 1994 (and even decreased by 4.5 per cent during the same period). Indeed, comparing the growth of licences and that of quotas from 1993 to 1994 (on the basis of figures expressed in tons) yields a straightforward result: whereas the former grew at a rate of +13 per cent, the latter recorded an increase of only 7 per cent (Corado, 1995).

However, it is the comparison between growth of OPT quotas and that of quotas on direct trade broken down on a yearly basis which is the most worrying. First, it appears that an increase of quantitative restrictions is concentrated between 1994 and 1995, as a result of the EFTA enlargement. What is more, there are large variations in the respective growth rates of OPT and direct quota; as a rule of thumb the former tend, on a yearly basis, to be higher than the latter. Overall, the structure of trade protection imposed, respectively, on direct and OPT trade provides significant incentives to undertake OPT at the expense of direct trade.

Sector-specific determinants: the structure of trade protection

A primary factor accounting for the peculiar patterns of OPT observed in T&C has therefore to do with the structure of trade protection: OPT in T&C increases markedly because restriction measures on direct trade are binding constraints. Having become fairly efficient and competitive, local firms with often important production capacities inherited from the Communist era, rapidly filled the quantitative protection measures still in place during the process of trade liberalisation. Thus, if they wish to enter EU markets, local producers have few other options than to engage in OPT partnerships with EU firms, a door purposely and acrimoniously left open to them. They can thus benefit from preferential market access in the form of additional 'specific' OPT quota.

In other sectors, conversely, the structure of trade protection constitutes much less of an incentive to undertake OPT. As a matter of fact, these sectors are subject to a system of tariff protection which is, as a general rule, less constraining and less irreducible than protection through quantitative protection. Whereas there is no – legal – way to overcome a filled quota, there is always the possibility of paying a tariff in full. What is more, tariffs have been rapidly decreasing whereas the above section reveals a relative resilience of quotas pertaining to normal trade. As time goes by, it thus proves to be increasingly rational to pay a small tariff as opposed to have to contend with cumbersome administrative tasks. One factor which made the arrangement more attractive in the specific case of CEECs is that the latter were granted particularly preferential treatment in the form of a *complete* tariff cut on OPT transactions (as against a reduction in the case of other countries).

Figure 4.1 summarises the respective incentive to undertake OPT depending on whether the good concerned is subject to quantitative or tariff protection. In part one of the figure, at $t = 0$, the gains obtained by undertaking economic OPT in sectors subject to quota, and that obtained by undertaking tariff OPT are ab, and a'b', respectively. There is no reason,

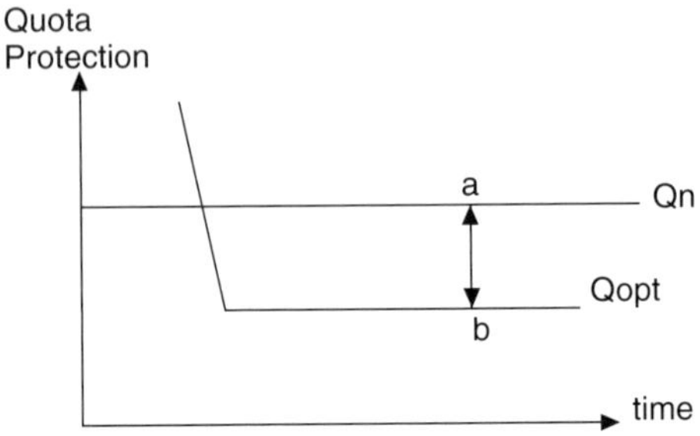

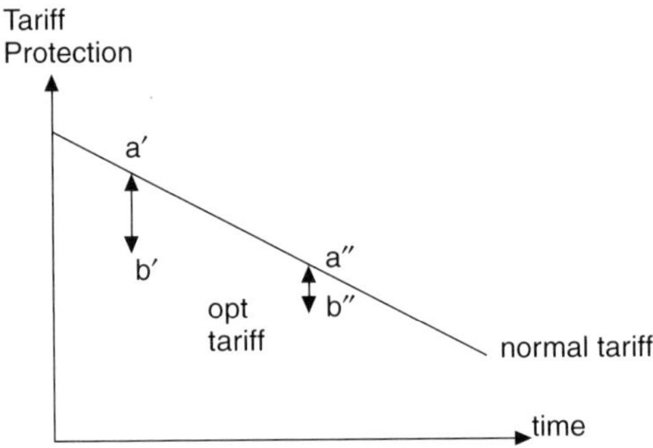

Figure 4.1   The liberalisation of direct and OPT trade in sectors subject to quotas; and liberalisation of direct and OPT trade in sectors subject to tariffs.

a priori, to think that one is superior to the other. As time goes by, however, with tariffs being progressively lifted, the gain pertaining to the tariff regime decreases from a'b' to a''b''. Eventually, whereas the structure of trade protection discriminates in favour of OPT until the very end, when quotas are suppressed, incentives to undertake tariff OPT diminish over time.

Vertical quasi-integration

The sector-specific feature characterising OPT in T&C is the bindingness of quantitative restrictions which makes recourse to the arrangement imperative. From the viewpoint of foreign partners, local firms' dependence on OPT places the former in an interesting position of power. The unparalleled merit of OPT in this respect is that it makes possible control without capital engagement. This is an important trait distinguishing OPT from other more traditional forms of contractual agreements which allow the exertion of a minor degree of control.

Binding trade protection measures favour the vertical 'quasi-integration'[107] of firms party to an OPT agreement in such a way that foreign firms can extend control over their local partners without engaging capital. In other terms, trade restrictions measures substitute for internalisation. Such a vertical quasi-integration is a sort of ideal medium term between normal subcontracting and foreign direct investment, combining at the same time the advantages of the two formula (i.e. the flexibility of entry and exit, and control over the partner, respectively) while attenuating the inconvenient (the uncontrolled spill-over of knowledge and financial cost, respectively).

Interestingly enough, these mechanisms are effective mainly with respect to the size of the firms party to an OPT agreement. In fact, large firms with important production capacities are the first to encounter binding quotas. They are therefore more likely candidates for vertical quasi-integration and for the eventual consolidation of OPT partnerships than their smaller counterparts.

Thus, the criteria of the size of the firm reinforces the respective effectiveness of the tariff and the economic OPT regimes: resorting to OPT is all the more imperative for large firms in sectors subject to quotas. On the contrary, small firms or larger firms in sectors subject to tariffs are less likely to be constrained by quantitative restrictions, and their decision to engage in OPT partnerships less influenced by measures of trade protection enacted by the EU/EC.[108]

The OPT mechanisms put in place by EU policy makers have therefore been effective in promoting use of OPT at the expense of other vehicles of integration in the T&C sector. By granting preferential access to *re*-exports, the OPT measure promoted relocation of EU firms' activities through contractual non-equity links rather than the development of FDI-related exports and 'independent' CEECs' exports, both of which are subject to normal protection measures (Corado, 1995). The outstanding proportions of OPT in CEECs' exports in textile and clothing, which is almost exclusively protected by quantitative restrictions, can be explained as follows: OPT-specific quotas were utilised in order to bypass normal quotas which were relatively restrictive and therefore rapidly filled.

Thus, OPT has forced the vertical quasi-integration of local firms into production networks controlled by EU firms, especially where the latter have a competitive advantage but are unable to access EU markets due to traditional protection measures erected by the EU. The recourse to OPT is made all the more imperative when local firms are competitive and trade protection measures particularly effective, OPT being indeed, in that case, the only option should local competitive firms wish to access EU markets.

Overall, the structure of trade protection, together with firm-level variables such as the size of firms party to an OPT agreement, account for the development – on the basis of OPT – of a durable vertical division of labour at the regional scale in the textile and clothing sector.

Transformed conditions of international competition: 'the use firms make of the OPT measure'

The above is a description of how OPT mechanisms discriminate between EU and CEECs' firms and between the different vehicles they have at their disposal, especially in the T&C sector. However, these biases are both 'de jure' and static in essence. Even though the arrangement contains such intrinsic discriminating mechanisms, in the end, the important thing is what firms actually make of it. In sectors other than T&C, where trade restrictions are not such a factor, rendering the arrangement particularly decisive for accessing EU markets, the potentials for quasi-vertical integration are lower and OPT is less effective in fostering the vertical division of labour on a regional scale. Hence, the story is a slightly different one.

Besides the 'institutional' determinants of OPT (the process of trade liberalisation), an alternative set of factors acquires a specific importance in the structuration of OPT relations between Eastern and Western Europe. These factors are ascribable to the transformation of the terms of competition in the world economy which forces firms to reorganise their production activities. The OPT arrangement, rather unexpectedly, has proved to be an adequate vehicle to cope with such transformations.

The following section will review factors in the world economy – constraints and opportunities arising from the transformed nature of international competition – that influence the way in which firms use an OPT arrangement. By making possible a correct interpretation of OPT developments identified in Chapters 2 and 3, this will demonstrate how OPT can be used as a 'learning' device and thus help CEEC firms and economies conform to the redefinition of the terms of international competitiveness.

New context: opportunities and risks

One central feature characterising the new conditions of international competition is that the division of labour in the world economy is less based on the exchange of final products and more on the (sub-)assembly of intermediate goods. This trend developed at the instigation of MNCs which are reconsidering the way they used to organise their production activities by increasingly carrying out the de-integration of the value-added chain at all levels.[109] The resulting 'International Production Networks'[110] are in fact 'organisational counterparts' of a change in the terms of international competition which corresponds to

> the shift in competition away from final assembly and vertical control of markets by final assemblers. (Zysman *et al.*, 1998: 5)

These developments are ascribable to – but not equated with – the greater emphasis placed on the *flexibility* of production conditions. In a first version of the flexible organisation of industrial production, flexible methods of production were (thought to be) best implemented by small and medium-sized entreprises (SMEs) in 'industrial districts' (Piore and Sabel, 1984). However, empirical evidence was limited to only a few cases,[111] with these mainly referring to trends that developed in the 1980s. On the face of it, Borrus and Zysman insist that: 'We are not entering an era of small and flexible firms' (Borrus and Zysman, 1998: 49).

In a recent reappraisal, an alternative form of flexible specialisation is considered to be initiated by MNCs (Herrigel, 2000). This is based on the integration (to varying degrees), of the two functions of conception and execution which were held separate in the Fordist system of production. This applies within firms (for example, in the development of teamwork) and *among* firms, in particular as far as suppliers are concerned.[112]

It is important to recast these broad trends sectorally and historically, however. The 'lean production' revolution was developed in the automotive industry in Japan by Toyota in the 1970s (Womack *et al.*, 1990). It diffused practices such as the 'modularisation' of production, in which the production process is divided between different tiers of suppliers. Suppliers in the first tier acquire greater autonomy and responsibility and become 'system suppliers' (Hancké, 1997). Volkswagen-Škoda in the Czech Republic, for example, adopted a so-called 'fraktalisation' strategy consisting of an energetic reorganisation and concentration of its suppliers.[113]

This model of industrial production was diffused to other consumer durable industries as well. 'Traditional' sectors embraced certain of the principles of production ascribable to 'lean' production methods. Indeed, the textile and clothing industry, too, has had to adapt to a change in the terms of international competition. With the mode of competition being no longer solely based on costs but on cost *and* creativity, this traditionally labour-intensive industry has become knowledge-intensive (Mytelka, 1991). This has been accompanied by many technological developments such as CAD (computer aided design) which enabled organisational changes such as a recent and intensive recourse to international sub-contracting and the organisation of suppliers into several tiers. In Central and Eastern Europe, the industry has, in the words of Graziani:

> started to adopt the 'lean' production system, that is, just-in-time deliveries, short runs, smaller orders, low inventories, and high quality. (Graziani, 1998: 252)

Borrus and Zysman suggest that present developments in the electronic industry in the US are deemed to mark yet another stage in the story of international competition. They contrast the 'lean' revolution still marked, in their interpretation, by vertical hierarchy, to 'Wintelism'. In this new paradigm, rather than vertical control, what is crucial is to set *standards*:

> firms located anywhere in the dis-integrated value-chain, can potentially, control the evolution of key standards and in that way define the terms of competition not just in their particular segment but, critically, in the final product markets as well. (Borrus and Zysman, 1998: 39)

In strict terms, Borrus and Zysman (1998) ascribe the above 'shift away from final assembly' to 'Wintelism'. However, whereas 'setting standards' will characterise the mode of competition in sectors other than the electronic industry remains to be seen, the diminishing importance of vertical control can already be shown to apply in different industries. The recourse to modularised systems of production in particular can be an interpretation of it.

Interestingly enough, while the trend towards de-integration of the production chain offers multiple opportunities for local firms to link-up into MNCs' sub-delivery basis, it can also provide conditions favourable to the development of innovative activities. The two forms of flexible organisation described above are indeed propitious to 'innovation' being defined as an 'interactive process' (Lundvall, 1988). In the second form of flexible organisation, interactions between suppliers and principals, if not rigidly vertical but more horizontal and flexible, can provide local firms with great potential to strengthen their technological capabilities.[114] Indeed, in the context of innovation-based competition where a premium is placed on the ability to learn and innovate (Mytelka, 1999b), what is at stake is not significant technological breakthroughs, but

> a continuous process of innovation that enables firms to catch up and to keep up as technology and the mode of competition change. (Mytelka, 2000)[115]

However, relying on MNCs' adoption of flexible practices to diffuse knowledge and foster local suppliers' competitiveness through 'learning by interacting' is not without risk. It might be that local capabilities are neglected, even eroded, instead of being 'capitalised' and updated. For example, Mytelka (1999b) argues that the entry of MNCs in local economies can disrupt existing ties between local suppliers and auto assemblers with resulting decreasing incentives to strengthen local R&D. The success story of the machine tool industry in Taipei has some relevance in this respect. It illustrates a successful strategy of relying on a gradual learning process consolidating competitiveness in 'niches' in the market of non-'Numerically-Controlled' machines. An important source of technology has indeed been original equipment manufacturer (OEM) production. However, this has not meant the

> replacement of local by foreign designs. Instead, foreign firms have often adopted and placed their own brandnames on Chinese Taipei products. (Mytelka, 1999a: 51)

In other words, local capabilities have been preserved even if control over the end product has been relinquished.

OPT in the context of 'global competition'

In this context, the OPT measure has been used as a vehicle for implementing methods of production complying with the requirements of international competition in terms of flexibility and quality. Indeed, the arrangement facilitates the decomposition of the production process into independent stages 'de-integrated' from one another and which can be geographically scattered. The arrangement thus contributes to the formation of production chains which are less linear and more horizontal than traditionally organised. In the T&C industry, OPT has offered the opportunity of developing automatisation of the production process, that new methods like CAD enable. Also, Just-in-Time methods of production have been applied in the context of OPT partnerships which make possible shorter delays and more rapid delivery. In the electrical machinery sector, OPT has also accompanied or even fostered the development of 'system suppliers' by enabling local competitive firms to join the ranks of second tier suppliers. In general, the arrangement could give rise to more equal 'two-way' relations between contractors and sub-contractors (Mytelka, 1995b).

Thus, OPT developments are to be connected with the rationalisation on a regional scale of multinational companies' strategies, followed with that of large firms among their first-tier suppliers. OPT has thus been used to – more or less directly – include local firms into MNCs' sub-delivery basis. If part of the OPT developments is also due to the 'workbench' strategies of smaller firms relocating their activities across the border in order to lower costs, this scenario is less representative of the general thrust underlying OPT in CEECs.

The fact that the measure has had the important effect of promoting the inclusion of local firms into MNCs' sub-delivery basis, especially in the electrical machinery sector, explain some of the results obtained through fieldwork. A 'traditional' strategy for local firms consists to of endeavouring to impose their own brand and recover autonomy. The alternative is to diversify partners and specialise in a supplier role. The main objective in this latter case is to try and establish a good reputation as second tier suppliers, more seldom in direct relations with original equipment manufacturers. In fact, this proved to be the strategy with the better chance of success. Producing independently would be a desirable outcome in an old traditional context, but less so if a premium is no longer placed on control of the entire production chain. Indeed, no case was recorded of a local firm successfully recovering *full* autonomy.

A mixed strategy is however also possible – that is, supplying at the same time a MNC and producing own-branded goods. This is because of the segmentation of product markets according to quality. Local firms specialise in lower quality segments as far as their own products are concerned, while producing according to higher quality standards for MNCs (or for a first-tier supplier) under the strict supervision of the latter.

Two additional factors have made possible the use of OPT as a vehicle for implementing new flexible production methods. Reduced distance acquires a renewed importance in this context. As the cost component of competitiveness shrinks, the application of 'flexible' methods of production also reduces the share of variable labour costs in total costs. This means that the labour cost saving derived from relocation is also reduced. Thus, geographical proximity – undertaking production activities in low-labour cost countries in the *immediate vicinity* of developed countries –

takes on new importance as it is a major condition of fulfilling the requirements of flexibility (Oman, 1994). Of particular relevance is the fact that transport is mostly organised by land (rather than by air or sea as in Asia), giving proximity an even higher premium (Zysman and Schwartz, 1998: 420).

Considerations pertaining to the proximity of partner countries are significant factors shaping OPT patterns.[116] They explain without contest the privileged relations that develop in general between Germany and its immediate neighbours, Poland and the Czech Republic, as well as Hungary. However, they can assume different specific significations. Proximity is clearly very important in the T&C sector where transport costs are a non-negligible factor. Large firms adopting JIT production methods need close and reliable partners. This is a powerful argument accounting for the fact that waves of re-relocation from the first fringe of CEECs further East to Romania or Bulgaria concern only the lowest VA activities.

In electrical machinery, instead, and particularly with regard to more sophisticated electronic components, distance is less important. In this respect, CEECs do not yet compare favourably with suppliers in Asia. However, the old-fashioned role of proximity is also a contributory factor for the quantitatively important and qualitatively diversified German OPT engagement in the former Czechoslovakia. This possibly developed at the instigation of smaller firms based in Bavaria. Geographical and cultural closeness here accounts for the development of German workbench activities across the Czech border.[117] Overall,

> The distribution and composition of OPT exports suggests that proximity is more important in determining the location in higher technology sectors, whereas low wage become more important in low-skill high labour intensity sectors. (Eichengreen and Kohl, 1998b: 36)

Time considerations are a second variable which also influenced OPT developments. First, CEECs' opening up occurred at a specific time, just when the redefinition of the terms of international competitiveness began to acquire a general and widespread relevance for certain firms and sectors. Second, they possibly account for the specifically favourable position of Hungary with respect to the development of OPT in the country. Hungarian firms benefited from an earlier process of opening up which enabled them to secure a first-mover advantage, particularly valuable in a time of heightened competition. It also accounts for the early involvement of major MNCs which chose the country as a basis from which to organise their regional strategies, and to conclude in this context many OPT agreements.

Finally, some case studies made clear the risks that playing the game of 'global competition' conceals. As illustrated by the two contrasting examples of Vilati and CKD-Elektrotechnika, there is a fine line between making the most of a supplier position and being subject to the severe pressure of a partner who possesses incomparably greater bargaining clout. The cases of CKD Tatra and Tesla suggested that competition to access international production networks is extremely tough. To win contracts, potential local candidates must first and foremost comply with a necessary condition, MNCs' expectations in terms of costs (with reference to the *diktat* of the quotation: 'world prices'). What is more, they have to respect a long list of stringent requirements, including such considerations as product specifications, delivery times, and so on.

To be successful, it is crucial that local firms take advantage of their position to learn new practices and know-how, and keep abreast of the development of new techniques so as to upgrade their capabilities. Local firms have indeed to play on this second range of assets so as to entice MNCs and render themselves indispensable. This is to secure, first, their contract on a long-term basis; then, eventually, to upgrade as far as possible along the value chain and maximise chances of moving up from one tier to another. Clearly, this does not require the deployment of radically new technical competencies but, more simply, the addition and improvement of many already existing practices, skills and assets. The case of Vilati shows how important is a combination of realistic expectations concerning ways to better withstand international competition, and a strategy building on existing technical capabilities which are continuously updated. Local firms should – and indeed could in certain cases – take advantage of OPT partnerships to engage

> continuous improvement in product design and quality, changes in organization and management routines, creativity in marketing and modifications to production processes that bring costs down, increase efficiency and ensure environmental sustainability (Mytelka, *et al.*, 1999).

This is a condition of primary importance to strengthened competitiveness in the context of knowledge-based international competition.

Does OPT help CEECs catching up?

The high proportion of OPT in CEECs' foreign trade has had important consequences for the terms under which East–West economic integration develops. However, such consequences are not necessarily those that OPT mechanisms would have led us to expect. The results of the fieldwork presented in Chapter 3 helped identify conditions under which local firms can actually take advantage of the arrangement. Much depends on the sector, but also on the host country concerned. This is of particular relevance for assessing progress achieved so far and the chances of for catching up process engaged in CEECs.

OPT inter-firm relations and market linkages

As testified by Chapter 2, OPT has played an important role in the process of CEECs' trade reorientation to the EU. What is more, the arrangement has proved to be a useful measure to help local firms in difficulty, either by helping them to engage in a process of modernisation or by paving the way for and smoothing an inevitable closure. Thus the arrangement has greatly contributed to easing costs arising from the necessary process of enterprise restructuring during transition.

Crucially, the arrangement has continued to impinge on the terms under which East–West patterns of interdependence develop after the initial period of the transition process. One remarkable feature characterising OPT developments in this respect is the highly varied outcomes the measure brings about. This is to say that any sort of generalisation is impossible.

As a rule of thumb, the adverse consequences of development of OPT that might have been feared on the basis of too literal an understanding of OPT mechanisms, or of similar examples of regional integration taking place between areas at different levels of development, did not materialise. The mechanisms of OPT have not promoted a *maquiladora*-type of economic transaction, locking local firms/economies into low wage specialisation patterns. Nor have EU (i.e. German) partners been taking advantage of the flexibility characterising the arrangement to 're-relocate' massively elsewhere (eastwards), thus putting at risk between 10 per cent and 25 per cent of CEECs' foreign trade. Even though the measure was explicitly designed at exploiting wage differentials, and although wages have been rising throughout CEECs, OPT partnerships have been, in fact, continuing. EU firms stayed committed to their local partners, and no massive withdrawal has been documented. Generally speaking, OPT has not simply constituted a footloose business subject to cyclical downturns and wage increases.

In fact, evidence presented in Chapter 2 and 3 indicates that the measure has, in certain circumstances, triggered a learning process within local firms. This is testified by two distinct developments at the aggregate level: the upgrading of OPT product structure,[118] and the respective and simultaneous strong dynamism of OPT and direct trade.

There are crucial country and sectoral distinctions to be made, in this respect. First, the shift of OPT product structure to more value-added goods has taken place in the first 'fringe' of CEECs, in particular in Hungary and the Czech Republic – as well as, to some extent, in the Baltic States (Estonia) – but *not* in Romania and Bulgaria. Second, the simultaneous dynamism of OPT and direct trade is restricted to the case of electrical machinery in Hungary and to a lower extent in the Czech Republic. The above developments on the transformation of the terms of international competition confirm what was proposed as an hypothesis in the earlier chapters: that this reflects the development of system suppliers in the Hungarian and the Czech electrical machinery sectors.

In T&C, OPT partnerships are also being prolonged, but under more 'traditional' terms. OPT takes place mainly among large firms, often at the instigation of MNCs but partnerships are more vertical and exclusive, leaving local firms in a more 'captive' and vulnerable position. This is the outcome of the combined effects of the effectiveness of the OPT mechanisms which foster the quasi-vertical integration of the partners party to an agreement and the transformations of the organisation of production in a sector which is going 'global'. As a result, local independent capabilities exports are not at all strengthened.

Other important findings concern the evidence of 're-relocation' eastwards principally in the footwear sector, but presumably in T&C as well. In footwear, foreign partners have put an end to their OPT partnerships in Hungary and Czech Republic, and relocated all the production process to Romania and especially Bulgaria. In the first fringe of CEECs, local partners have not been able to take over OPT production. This has had severe negative consequences for export performances in the sector. In T&C conversely, foreign partners have been adhering to their commitment and retaining higher value added operations in the Czech Republic and Hungary. They re-relocated or engaged new OPT agreements further east, but in lower VA activities (Eichengreen and Kohl, 1998). In short, this is evidence that OPT has thus followed and contributed to replicating the formation of different tiers in Europe.

Overall, this evidence testifies to the varying degrees of constraint presented by OPT mechanisms depending on the sector concerned, as well different 'learning capabilities' throughout CEECs enabling local firms to take advantage of the measure and strengthen their competitiveness. In particular in Hungary, and in the Czech Republic in the electrical machinery industry, there is evidence that firms are 'learning to learn', and this translates into sound export performances. In addition, both countries fare well with respect to the second indicator proposed to assess learning capabilities, that is, the shift toward more value added of their OPT product structure. The case of the Baltic States, in particular Estonia, is also promising. In Poland, instead, evidence is mixed, whereas Romania and Bulgaria present clearly more worrying cases.

Thus, although on the basis of different data and methods, the present study broadly agree with the conclusion by Freudenberg and Lemoine that:

> the scenario of an integration of the first wave of Eastern enlargement to the EU based on a 'residual' specialisation on down-market products, with its correlative adverse consequences for the catching-up is not supported by the evidence at this stage. (Freudenberg and Lemoine, 1999: 58)

Transforming heterogeneity into complementarity

In principle, the OPT measure, the raison d'être of which, is to deal with the increased degree of heterogeneity introduced by CEECs' opening up, can help achieve complementarity between Eastern and Western specialisation patterns in different ways.[119]

The arrangement can contribute to making rival specialisation patterns complementary through a sustainable vertical division of labour. Rivalry can thus be made complementary either in space (with the possible consolidation of OPT into FDI) or in time (with successive waves of relocation in conformity with the predictions of the Product Cycle Model, and the 'flying geese' analogy – see below).

In the former case, what is at stake is the level of the production chains within which local partners are included, and the prospects that the latter have to upgrade their position. In the latter case, much depends on whether local firms can take over OPT production on their own, and pave the way for indigenous autonomous development.

More interesting is when OPT helps transform heterogeneity into complementarity in a more horizontal manner. This is when firms party to an OPT agreement use the arrangement to implement new production methods in line with the redefinition of the terms of international competition. By contributing to the development of system suppliers in

CEECs, the measure promotes inter-firm linkages between local and foreign firms which are indeed less integrated (if at all), less vertical (in the sense that local suppliers can be included simultaneously within several production chains, and that they are responsible for broader and more complex tasks) and, as a rule of thumb, more flexible.

The available evidence speaks in favour of a mixture of the above avenues to achieve complementarity: (a) in space and vertically (quasi and total vertical integration especially in T&C); (b) in space and horizontally (the development of system suppliers); and (c) in time (with the relocation to Romania Bulgaria – and possibly to the Ukraine – of OPT activities in lower value added sectors). However, the present study found little evidence of cross-border transactions of the *maquiladora* type (Sander, 1996).

Horizontal complementarity achieved in space (system suppliers) conveys the most favourable prospects for the development of local capabilities, and the eventual movements up the market of CEECs firms and economies insofar as it is more conform to the redefinition of the rules of the game of 'global competition' and inasmuch as it gives better possibility to local firms to engage a *learning* process.

Are Germans network organisers?

The fact that the overwhelming majority of OPT in CEECs is actually of German origin, and that OPT was shown to be a potential 'learning instrument' in the hand of local firms suggests that the measure can, in certain circumstances, be used by German firms acting as 'network organisers', that is: organisations that act as promoters of trade, production and/or innovation linkages (Radosevic, 2000).

The evidence presented on the 'learning mechanisms' the instrument triggers at firm-level suggests that exchange of knowledge can take place within the production networks OPT contributes to develop. Even if it would be largely premature to equate the latter to 'technology networks', these can nevertheless be considered to offer first evidence on the contribution that international production networks in CEECs are making to the formation of local systems of innovation.

This relativises excessive fears of the 'germanisation' of CEECs. True, if local firms are unable to take advantage of OPT, the arrangement has the potential to become an instrument in the hands of German companies to exploit CEECs' cheap labour, and transform neighbouring countries into Germany's economic backyard. This could take the form of a border economy along the former iron curtain in a European version of the Mexican *maquiladora*. However, if local firms are integrated into the sub-delivery bases of MNCs based in Germany, and if OPT is used by the latter as a vehicle to implement new production methods with significant transfers of knowledge to local firms, this would enable the latter to upgrade their competitive position. German firms might then be regarded as exerting a 'benign hegemony,' offering CEECs the means to weather the challenge of knowledge-based competition. Evidence presented in this study support this hypothesis especially in the sector of electrical machinery, to a lower extent in the T&C industry, and mainly in Hungary and the Czech Republic.

Conclusion

EU and CEEC firms have utilised the OPT arrangement in a manner quite different from the way in which this measure was designed. This is because the context in which the measure was adopted has changed: OPT has been used by firms to respond to a different set of constraint and opportunities arising from conditions at work in the world economy. The OPT arrangement has thus certainly been effective in forcing local competitive firms into partnership with EU firms, especially where the latter represented a threat to Western interests. However, it has also served as a useful instrument to ease the cost of transition for the most vulnerable firms. More fundamentally, it has proved to be an unexpected vehicle for the application of new production methods in line with a redefinition of the terms of international competition, and a factor promoting the inclusion of local firms into MNCs' sub-delivery basis.

If the measure has the potential to entrench heterogeneity in Europe by locking local firms into low wage specialisation patterns, or by forcing them to integrate Western firms' production chains at their lower end, OPT can also be a factor contributing to the strengthening of local capabilities in the context of transformed conditions of international competition simply because it offers local firms the opportunity to 'learn by interacting' (Lundvall, 1995). From an instrument of exploitation, OPT can become a learning device.

In this respect, OPT developments provide evidence of the *varying abilities* of CEECs' firms to make the most of this arrangement. Clear dividing lines were found between countries (Hungary and the Czech Republic, at one extreme, Poland together with Estonia in an intermediate position, and Romania and Bulgaria at the other extreme) as well as distinctions between sectors (footwear, T&C and electrical machinery).

Two very important insights into the dynamics of regional integration in Europe are to be inferred from these evidence. First, the OPT developments suggest how uneven patterns of integration in an enlarged Europe are. Second, by illustrating different 'learning capabilities' throughout CEECs, they reflect the formation of different 'tiers' of countries with different chances of catching up.

5
The Politics of OPT

This chapter proposes to analyse the logic underlying the adoption of the OPT measure. The objective is to identify vested interests aligned in reaction to CEECs' opening up. Enshrining into law such an apparently anodyne mechanism – consisting as it does in discriminating between the imports of local producers and the 're-imports' resulting from the relocation strategies of Community producers – has actually given rise to a complex bargaining process. Debate has revolved around the long-running opposition between the advocates of protection and those who are favourable to free trade. It has involved numerous actors, and has taken place in various arenas: within domestic constituencies, between firms, federations of industry and labour unions, and at the European level, between virtually the same actors plus confederations of industries and of labour, member states and institutions of the Community participating in legislation-making at EU (Commission) level.

In the following discussion, an attempt will be made to reconstruct the process that led to the adoption of the OPT measure. This will offer some insight into the European 'mode' of integration, and pave the way for an identification of the system of governance of the economy which is developing in the context of the enlargement process.

Trade policy and the challenge of international competition

A major characteristic of OPT – its ambivalence – makes possible the conciliation of different policy objectives which are in principle contra-dictory. On one hand, OPT may be considered a useful instrument for preserving employment at home; on the other, the arrangement can be viewed as a window of opportunity for relocating production activities in otherwise highly protected sectors. It is therefore no surprise that there are numerous and conflicting interpretations regarding use of such an instrument of trade policy. Indeed, interests in presence are aligned according to many sectoral and national cutting lines. The present section identifies them.

The OPT raison d'être: protection versus relocation

The adoption of OPT as an instrument of trade policy was conceived in the context of competitive pressure placed on declining industries of developed economies by exports from low wage countries. An immediate policy response to such a threat is protectionism. There have been indeed different historical waves, to be distinguished according to the nature of the protectionist measure adopted. These include tariffs and non-tariff barriers (first among which were quantitative restrictions such as quotas), also more recent and innovative devices such as anti-dumping and countervailing duties. In the long term, recourse to a pure and 'classic' protectionist strategy is unsustainable in an increasingly interdependent world-economy. For example, one serious drawback of such protectionist measures is that, while protecting declining sectors as a whole, they also prevent the most dynamic home-based firms from taking advantage of opportunities on a global scale. Indeed, protectionism might imperil the complete or partial relocation of production activity to low-wage countries, a strategy which constitutes, an alternative means for weathering the competitive pressure pertaining to exports from these very same countries. It was noted that OPT proposes an ingenious device for resolution of this dilemma: to discriminate between 'direct' and 'temporary' trade flows on the basis of the motive of the transaction (further processing or direct sale), and the content of the products concerned (do 'imports' contain locally-sourced components, and/or material previously exported from the country of destination?).

Institutionalising a specific custom regime offers the most straightforward way to implement and monitor the distinction between permanent and temporary trade flows. Historically, it is the United States which first 'invented' and used such an arrangement.[120] On the European rim of the Atlantic, a version of the arrangement was adopted in 1975 under a substantially altered form (further discussion below).

Interestingly enough, the ambivalence of the arrangement as regards the trade-off between employment and competitiveness is made explicit in the European legislation that provides for the arrangement. Indeed, Preambles of the various texts providing for OPT at Community level state that the objective is to allow for adjustment of the EU T&C industry to 'the conditions of international competition'.[121] A further priority, however, that of preserving production within the Community, appears to be in clear contrast to this. In this respect, the Preamble of one of the first versions insists that the arrangement be restricted to producers with plants located *within* the Community whereas another version insists that levels of employment are to be preserved. Potentially conflicting raison d'êtres pertaining to the arrangement were already contained in the Preambles of the texts providing for OPT.

The OPT main features: sectoral and national variations

It has been shown that there are *two* OPT regimes. Indeed, a specific OPT arrangement corresponds to each of the two traditional protection measures, tariffs and quantitative restrictions. Hence, a distinction is made between 'Economic OPT' (applying to goods subject to quantitative restrictions) and 'Tariff OPT' (regulating the conditions under which tariff relief is authorised). This distinction depends both on the nature of the adopted protective measure and the sector where the latter is enforced. As a matter of fact, the textile and clothing sector is mostly protected by quantitative restrictions and almost all other sectors are subject to tariff protection. Sectoral variables are therefore a first criteria of primary importance in distinguishing between the two OPT regimes.

However, the above sectoral criteria also corresponds to another very important dividing line: the authority which is ultimately responsible for providing of the specific OPT preferential treatment. In principle, since trade matters are under the competence of the Community, OPT is subject to EU legislation. The first Community regulations dealing with OPT developed as of the mid-1970s with the very first comprehensive text adopted at the end of 1975.[122] It is worth stressing that it is a *directive*, that is, that it has to be translated into national legislation before acquiring its bindingness.

In practice, however, the prerogatives of the Community were effective only in the tariff regime. Indeed, the provision of quantitative restrictions being one of the few trade-related domains where national authorities preserved their prerogatives,[123] management of the economic regime tended to escape the control of the Community. In fact, member states enjoyed considerable room for manoeuvre while deciding whether and under what conditions to grant OPT specific *national* quotas. This explains why the economic OPT regime was characterised by sometimes different important *national* variations. Hence, beside the criteria of the nature of the trade restrictions pertaining to the concerned good, the distinction between 'economic' and 'tariff' OPT corresponds to two additional (overlapping) dividing lines:

1. the sector (most products in T&C are candidates for economic OPT, whereas the other sectors are eligible for tariff OPT);
2. the authority in charge of the *actual* provision and application of OPT legislation (national authorities in the case of economic OPT, and the Community in the case of tariff OPT).

Overall, the distinction between tariff and the economic OPT regimes depends both on the sectors to which they respectively apply, while differences *within* the economic OPT regime depend on the member state concerned.

Guiding principles at the Community level (sectoral variations)

The existence of two distinct protective measures (tariffs and quotas), and their associated OPT regimes, is reflected in Community law. Originally, however, the 1975 text applied to both cases and provided the basic principles of OPT without much refined detail as to the nature of the protection measure the arrangement was supposed to lift. The benefit of the arrangement was meant to consist of the partial or total suspension of tariffs; eligible products could be of whatever kind of origin; and the type of processing activities firms were authorised to undergo abroad was only loosely binding. As to the beneficiaries, they simply had to be a natural or a legal person established within the Community. Re-imports after processing could be carried out in any member state, and a transfer of ownership during the transaction was possible.

On this basis, the legislation on 'Tariff OPT' was adopted without significant debate and no substantial changes to the above rules.[124] Its 'technical' objective was to distinguish between a 'pure' form of OPT, and temporary exports and re-imports with a view to 'repairing' products (the so-called 'standard exchange system'). This second text defined eligible products more precisely as goods which are either of Community origin, or in free circulation.[125] It also referred to beneficiaries as being established in the Community *and* offering enough 'guarantee' to the relevant custom authorities. It is worth noting that no mention was made as to whether it would be possible to re-import such processed products in a different member-state than that which issued the OPT authorisation. This feature contributed to making the arrangement particularly open and flexible.

The legislation on economic OPT is much more complex and technical than its counterpart in the Tariff regime. Indeed, the 'Economic OPT' regime in textile and clothing gave rise to a far more tortuous process of legislation-making. The reason has to do with the contention of prerogatives between national and the supranational levels in the field of quantitative restrictions which make the definition of clear guidelines particularly difficult to achieve. Two texts were adopted, the first in 1982[126] and the second in 1994[127] in an attempt to 'harmonise' the different national OPT regimes. One consequence is that recourse to the economic arrangement is much more tightly regulated, with a clear resulting restrictive bias. For example, an attempt is made to define the level of authorised processing abroad more 'precisely',[128] as well as quantitative restrictions set at national levels.[129] Moreover, it is made clear that re-imports after processing must be geared back to the country of origin.

National variations

Different policy standpoints have been adopted throughout member states when applying Community guidelines concerning OPT in the T&C sector. Not only did national positions on OPT contrast widely from country to country; they also evolved sometimes dramatically in quite unexpected directions.

A first important divide took place between those member states which established liberal OPT regimes, and others which were rather reluctant to enshrine specific measures, if at all, adopting only very restrictive provisions. The first country to adopt specific OPT quotas was Germany. Two other countries followed: the Netherlands and France.[130] At the other extreme, the last country to provide for specific OPT quotas was the United Kingdom. Indeed, until 1986, not a single OPT quota had been released by the British authorities. What is more, British representatives in Brussels systematically voted against any establishment and increase of quantitative restrictions at the European level.[131]

Whether a specific OPT regime is provided for is one thing; whether a granted regime is more or less liberal is a second important feature differentiating member states. It is no surprise that the first countries to adopt specific measures dealing with relocation were also those which adopted the less stringent sets of rules. The German and the Dutch legislations were so loosely designed that they were almost not binding. One very important feature characterising these was their accessibility to all companies, irrespective of their actual economic status, be they established producers or retailers (an example being C&A) without production facilities. Conversely, Belgium and Italy established OPT legislations but attached quite stringent conditions of access to benefit from the arrangement. Not only had beneficiaries to be producers located within the Community, they also had to respect various thresholds of production levels maintained in the Community. In addition, a series of provisions was explicitly designed to contain an intrinsic bias towards job-exports proper to the arrangement. In Belgium, for example, there is a long-standing policy concern dealing with the detrimental impact of relocation on levels of employment.[132] Thus, the authorities decreed that OPT should be reserved for producers relocating less than 30 per cent of their value-added of their product in third countries, with a resulting employment level no lower than 90 per cent of the original position. Unions played an important role in this respect. Being strongly opposed to the OPT arrangement, they contributed to making the positions of governments and industry more difficult to harmonise.

As time passed, significant changes altered the above starting positions. On one hand, the United Kingdom – but also, albeit belatedly, Italy and Belgium – became convinced of the benefits of OPT; on the other hand, newcomers (especially Portugal, but also Greece and Spain) reinforced political forces opposing OPT. The United Kingdom witnessed the most dramatic change of policy objectives. In 1986, under the ruling of M. Thatcher, the official position of the British authorities underwent a sudden U-turn. OPT was subsequently embraced as a relevant restructuring strategy; if anything not to be hampered by restrictive trade policy measures. The official Italian position also evolved from a fundamentally wary perspective to a more openly positive approach and this was echoed by the Belgium authorities who progressively relaxed their initially very strong opposition to any preferential regime favouring relocation. It should be stressed that such evolution never truly led the concerned national authorities to reach positions as liberal as those of the Germans. For example, each of the three above-mentioned countries remained hostile to the idea of extending OPT arrangements to retailers.

Finally, the opposite tendency was registered as a result of the accession of new members to the Community. Overall, regarding the original opposition mainly organised around the British and German poles, the 1980s come to be characterised by a north–south divide, with southern newcomers hostile to OPT and northern members more prone to liberalising the OPT regime.

Policy-making at the Community level

Necessary harmonisation

Recourse to the European level in OPT matters was necessary because trade policy matters come, in principle, under the exclusive competence of the Community. What is at stake is to *recapture* control in a field where member states had unduly extended their competence. The first text on economic OPT, adopted in 1982, was therefore primarily intended to monitor the way national authorities were granting specific quantitative restrictions besides normal quotas. At the beginning, when the first countries started to impose specific OPT quotas (Germany, followed by the Netherlands and France), the Commission was endorsing the authorisation adopted at a national level virtually automatically.

There were three groups of concerned host countries at this time: North Africa (Morocco and Tunisia), Yugoslavia, and the then Centrally Planned Economies, all of these being classified at the lowest level in the hierarchy of preferences granted to the Community's trade partners.[133] However, from 1980 onwards, the Commission began to slow down the pace of quotas attribution. This was because trade conditions with this latter group of countries looked as if they might become less restrictive than those with other countries supposedly benefiting from preferential treatment. Legislation at Community level was thus made necessary in the Commission's view, in order to curb what it saw as an excessive degree of autonomy enjoyed by member states. The decision to control OPT quotas at Community level had logically to be accompanied by an homogeneous definition of the specific conditions of eligibility that distinguish an OPT regime from a regime on direct imports.

The 1982 text, in turn, had to be revised. This time, the objective was to eliminate any potential degree of autonomy accruing to member states that could prove incompatible with the objective of the Single European Act. As a matter of fact, being seriously imprecise on several key points, the first version left significant room for manoeuvre in its interpretation. Contrary to its intention, the text was thus applied very differently by member states. With the coming into force of the Single Market in 1993, such divergence of trade conditions in the different member states could no longer be tolerated. Indeed, with the complete removal of internal trade barriers, the risks was that all OPT activities would be concentrated in the most liberal member states which would subsequently re-export 'exceedingly' competitive products to other more restrictive countries. The Commission had therefore to endeavour once more to harmonise the different national positions. Once again, the legislative exercise consisted in defining guiding principles as precisely as possible in order to avoid potentially diverging interpretations. And yet, once more, the exercise was only partially successful. After two years of negotiations, a text was adopted in 1994 which contained several ambiguities, as will be discussed below.

However, two absolute prerequisites of a technical nature were, at least, fulfilled. First, quotas on OPT, like all other quantitative restrictions, were no longer to be broken down into member states' shares; rather these were fixed at Community level.[134] Second, re-imports after processing had to be allowed in any member states, regardless of who issued the OPT authorisation. Finally, it is worth noting that the text achieved, as expected, achieved the formal task rendered necessary by the conclusion of 'Europe Agreements' with Central and Eastern European countries.

The whole raison d'être of the economic OPT arrangement is, therefore, very much ascribable to the harmonising endeavour under-taken in the context of the workings of Community institutions. In this view, the initiative of the OPT decision-making process essentially belongs to the Commission, whose objective is the smooth functioning of the Single Market. However, it was the initial decision taken by individual member states to grant specific OPT quantitative restrictions that actually triggered the whole process.

Harmonisation in practice

The above description of the content and principles regulating the arrangement underplays the outstanding degree of controversy which was aroused during the process of legislation-making. Every single provision was subject to controversy. A glimpse into these rather arcane developments is therefore useful in identifying the presence of vested interests.

First version of the community legislation

(a) Reserving OPT to producers: the actual victory of the Germano-Dutch authorities: The provision concerning Community production is in principle made more restrictive in the 1982 text than in the 1975 version. Here, it is not enough that beneficiaries of the arrangement be established in the Community, they should also be producers.[135] This precision was intended to satisfy the vested interest of the clothing sector whose European federation, ECLA, was strongly opposed to allow retailing firms to benefit from the arrangement. Had the provision been properly applied, the Dutch and German governments, which were subject to very heavy pressure by large retail chains' lobbying activities, would clearly have been among the losers. However, not only was a derogation formally provided for, but also interpretation of the rule was relatively loose throughout member states. As a result, the main European retailing companies could benefit from this arrangement.

(b) the case of 'similar products': the formal victory of national authorities: This is yet another illustration of the failure to exclude retailers from benefits of the arrangement. Indeed, to render the principle more binding, the 1982 text provides that producers can benefit from the arrangement only if, in their Community plants, they produce goods that are 'similar' to those they re-import after processing. However, the definition of a 'similar' product is left unclear. Indeed, shortly after publication of OPT legislation in the Official Journal of the European Communities, the Commission issued a regulation of application which failed to provide any clarification on the matter.[136]

Here lies the main factor explaining why the principle of primacy of producers was actually applied very differently throughout member states: the latter could interpret the notion of 'similar product' more or less restrictively, according to their own priorities. Thus, as opposed to the case of the very principle of the exclusion of retailers from the arrangement, there are no winners and no losers. To be precise, there are *only* winners: national authorities as opposed to supranational entities, be these Euro-groups or the Community itself.

The mechanisms for reaching such an outcome are quite uncommon. The latter is not obtained through negotiation, exercise of power, concessions and agreement, but through the absence of confrontation and the *deliberate* impression of certain crucial provisions.

(c) The origin of fabrics used in the transaction: the say of Euro-Groups: One area where European federations have voiced their position and influenced the outcome is within that of the origin of goods eligible for the arrangement. Indeed, for the textile lobby, as represented through the channel of COMITEXTIL, the European Confederation, the principle is that eligible products be of Community origin. In this way, the arrangement was intended to be a very powerful instrument for promotion of the textile sector. On the face of it, the clothing industry argued forcefully in favour of an unrestricted use of fabrics of whatever origin. A final agreement was eventually reached. As a concession made by the textile to the clothing interests, a derogatory clause was introduced: in the case of shortage of Community textile,[137] it was made possible to incorporate goods of non-Community origin in the temporarily exported goods up to 14 per cent of the total value of the latter. In exchange to concession made by the textile sector to the clothing interest, the arrangement was restricted to producers alone. To obtain the principle that the arrangement be reserved to fabrics of Community origin, COMITEXTIL traded off its other objective of extending benefits of the

arrangement to retailing chains and distributors. It is as if COMITEXTIL conceded the production orientation of the arrangement together with the 14 per cent clause to the clothing lobby, as this latter sector had the most to lose from OPT in terms of levels of employment.

Even though provisions concerning the origin of fabrics used in OPT transactions appear to have been designed as a result of the political activity of Euro-groups, they do not necessarily illustrate the pre-eminence of European federations in OPT decision-making. Indeed, the diverging positions of the two Federations tended to weaken their respective positions as opposed to reinforcing and combining their bargaining power.

(d) Assessment of the text and of its application: Overall, it can be said that the Community legislation of 1982 missed its objective of harmonising conditions for undertaking OPT throughout member states. As might be expected, Germany favoured the most liberal interpretation, with almost no restriction being effectively enforced. As in the Netherlands, for example, it was legally possible for traders to undertake OPT activities provided they 'symbolically' acquired a producer, responsible for carrying out OPT activities.[138] Conversely, the Italians and Belgians imposed strict controls on OPT operations.[139] Other areas where member states made quite distinct, if not diverging, interpretations of the text were those of the relation between levels of Community production and of authorised processing abroad. The further south in the Community you look, the more the two were correlated.

Second version of the community legislation

Besides the necessity of preserving the Community competence in trade-related matters, the coming into force of the Single European Act made even more unacceptable the diverging conditions for undertaking economic OPT in the different member states, resulting from the imprecision of the 1982 text. The objective of the 1994 text was therefore to harmonise positions on four points of contention raised by the 1983 legislation:

- the definition of 'similar' products;
- the definition and admission of beneficiaries to the arrangement;
- the restriction of the arrangement to producers located within the Community;
- management of the 14 per cent derogation clause.

(a) 'Similar products': The most notable achievement of the 1994 legislation is that it finally provided for the definition of the highly

controversial notion of 'similar' products. These were goods which fell into one of three categories defined in an annex.[140] Concerning conditions of eligibility, the text introduced precisely defined rules. For example, the tasks that beneficiary producers should perform within their EC factories were specified, and consisted in 'sewing and assembly, or knitting'. Furthermore, a time limit was imposed on the period during which processing tasks are supposed to take place in third countries.

(b) The case of newcomers to the arrangement: An important novelty presented by the Regulation is the distinction it operates between past beneficiaries and newcomers. The underlying logic is to make the legislation more precise for newcomers, while preserving the rights of past beneficiaries. Interestingly enough, however, a number of deroga-tions tend to mitigate the divide between the two categories. This is so, for example, for firms in new member states entering the Community which are allowed to benefit, under certain conditions, from the previous national regime (Austria, most notably). Most importantly, provisions extending the arrangement to retailing companies already engaged in OPT activities before the 1982 regulation are re-conducted. This constitutes, indeed, a serious infringement of the principle of restriction of the arrangement to producers alone. This is at the core of concessions made in the course of OPT negotiations. Those who obtained satisfaction were countries particularly prone to a liberal interpretation of the arrangement. It is also no coincidence, that these countries are ones where large retailing companies are based: Germany and the Netherlands.

(c) The definition of 'Community production': A fundamental innovation in the text is the provision stating that, in the case of newcomers and past beneficiaries asking for additional authorised amounts, the value of goods that undergo processing abroad should be inferior by 50 per cent to the value of Community production of the former. In addition, the concerned EU producer should have used at least 50 per cent of the amount previously authorised, or (re)exported 80 per cent of the products which had undergone processing abroad.

The problem is that a definition of 'Community production' is not given. This indeed seems like *dejà-vu*. Like the 'similar product' issue, the provision on Community production is crucial to the whole edifice of the text. The same mechanisms as those which obfuscated plain interpreta-tion of the 1982 text were thus at work in the 1994 text as well.

A Commission Regulation was therefore rendered necessary; and the fate of the whole text (its degree of bindingness) would depend on it. It was adopted in December 1995, that is, around five months later than the Commission had been hoping. The objective of defining the meaning of Community production was eventually achieved.[141] However, some minor issues remained undetermined. This is also true of the provision concerning reduction of authorised amounts in the case of decreasing employment levels in Community plants proportional to the undertaking of processing activities abroad. In addition, in the case of preferential treatment granted to CEECs, the regulation of application makes necessary the granting of a prior authorisation. However, the procedures that should be followed in such cases are not provided for.

(d) Assessment of the text and of its application: The introduction of the notion of 'Community production' and its failed definition is a major pitfall, serious enough to consider the whole endeavour to be a failure. Indeed, besides clarifying old rules, the legislation elaborated new ones which were not necessarily better designed. They did not put an end to the indeterminacy of the text. What is more, apart from the politics of deliberate vagueness, another reason rendering the text and its application regulations far from satisfactory has to do with its high degree of technicality. The very cumbersome procedures that must be followed are likely to dissuade would-be candidates; it is indeed realistic to believe that firms will prefer to face rapidly decreasing trade restrictions as opposed to dealing with complex and time-consuming administrative tasks.

An important aspect of the new text is that of its apparently restrictive drift. However, any definitive conclusion in this respect should be avoided. First, if it is indeed more difficult for firms to resort to the arrangement, this does not appear to be the result of a deliberate intent. In other words, this does not correspond to an objective of industrial policy adopted by the Commission such as slowing down the relocation of production activities outside the Community so as protect its levels of employment. It is rather a direct and 'neutral' consequence of the harmonisation process, defining every single measure as precisely as possible in order to make diverging interpretations difficult, if not impossible.

Second, the question as to whether the text is actually 'more' restrictive should be gauged by comparing the latter not with its predecessor at Community level, but with the national regimes of application previously enforced in different member states. A German firm, for example, will find it much harder to resort to OPT under the new text than before 1993; on the contrary, for Italian firms, precisely the opposite is true. Third, and more importantly, the legislation would indeed be made more restrictive were it not for the introduction of a highly controversial provision concerning the beneficiaries' level of Community production (the 50 per cent issue).

The winners and the losers

Member states, and in more general terms the national level of policy-making, went through the process unchallenged by any overt threat of sovereignty transfer at the supranational level. It is important to make a distinction: it is not a case of some member states obtaining satisfaction at the expense of some others. The Germans, let us say, did not impose their view upon the Portuguese. Such a fact, indeed, would indicate that the integration process is effective since, on the contrary, the German *and* the Portuguese national authorities obtained satisfaction as both of them could eventually implement the policy that best suited their priorities. The mechanisms for obtaining such an outstanding outcome consist in *obfuscating* a plain interpretation of the legislation, supposedly providing for the harmonisation of diverging national positions. Whether deliberately maintained, or simply an unintended consequence, the result is the same: ambiguity makes possible different interpretations according to the particular interests at stake in the negotiation. In short, whenever a provision is more or less irreducibly obscure, it is a sign of the failure of the harmonisation process and consequently, of the centralisation of competence at the supranational level.

On the face of it, supranational entities appear to be clear losers of the game. The Commission, for example, was not only unable to take advantage of a potentially powerful instrument of industrial policy, that is, to *actively* impose its own objectives, it was also unsuccessful in carrying out the more neutral process of harmonisation. In fact, the position of the Commission could have been much stronger. The initiative to provide for OPT legislation at Community level does indeed emanate from the Commission. A 'technical committee' within DG XXI in charge of Custom Affairs submitted a proposition endorsed in principle by the Commission to the Council of Ministers (providing the latter agrees on a favourable opinion). This empowered the Commission for the detailed application of the proposal, while maintaining its prerogatives on the broad lines of the text. The Committee set up by the Commission was then in charge of the application and the proposition is further elaborated as it goes back and forth between the Committee's group of experts, and COREPER.[142] In the case of the 1982 revision, however, the Committee did not reach the qualified majority necessary for adopting the proposal and the latter was returned to the Council of Ministers.

One possible (partial) explanation for the weakness of the Commission is its lack of internal coherence. There has been indeed potential rivalry between the different Directorates General in charge of OPT legislation. Although the Commission supposedly acts as a collegial body with a unitary position, DGI (external affairs), DGIII (industrial matters), and DGXXI (Custom matters) held distinct positions. DGI was more concerned with the potentially positive effect of OPT on the competitiveness of declining European industries, whereas DGIII was particularly sensitive to the adverse consequences OPT may have had on the level of employment in these sectors.[143]

Such an internal division within the Commission is due to the fundamental dilemma characterising use of OPT as an instrument of industrial policy. In this debate, DGXXI has a somewhat intermediary position as it tries to achieve a compromise between the antagonism of the other DGs.[144]

Euro-groups did not prove to be much more efficient either. Generally speaking, the two federations representing the textile industry and clothing sector at European level, COMITEXTIL and ECLA,[145] were weaker than their national counterparts. Traditionally, however, COMITEXTIL benefits from having quite strong bargaining clout, particularly at Commission level.[146] On the OPT issue, COMITEXTIL did indeed agree on a common opinion which was favourable. However, the traditional influential weight of COMITEXTIL was seriously limited because of controversy with ECLA over the restriction of the arrangement to sole producers. ECLA was already traditionally weaker than COMITEXTIL for the simple reason that the industry resorts to more diversified and internationalised adjustment strategies; hence a lower degree of consensus is attainable. The conflict with COMITEXTIL certainly did not improve the situation. Indeed, ECLA did not reach a common position on the latest revision of OPT legislation undertaken by the Commission.[147] In this context, a more thorough accord between ECLA and COMITEXTIL presenting a unified front on the OPT issue, is quite unrealistic.[148]

The respective position of the two groups evolved over time, however. Even though ECLA remained partially unsuccessful in defending the interests of the European clothing sectors as a whole, the Federation has substantially strengthened its grip over policy matters. The European federation's strong original aversion for offshore processing activities was watered down and a liberal approach to OPT has been consolidated, even though it continued to insist that OPT be reserved for *producers*.

Conversely, the European textile industry, through the voice of its European federation, has continued to favour a restrictive interpretation of the OPT arrangement. In particular, it remained determined to prevent OPT from applying to fabrics which do not originate in the EC. For COMITEXTIL, OPT has been a device to limit the use of fabrics imported from third countries.

Overall, the effectiveness of business representation through the channel of the two European federations has not been warranted. Firms, and the national industry associations of both textile and clothing, had to rely on their respective government, to have their interests represented in Brussels. A problem presented by this mode of representation is when there is no alignment between the positions of the national industry and that of the concerned member state's government. In Portugal, for example, the industry's position is favourable to the liberalisation of the access conditions to OPT, whereas the Portuguese government is openly against the arrangement. Therefore, Portuguese industry had to go directly to Brussels to defend its view. Another consequence of the imperfect endorsement of industry positions by respective governments is that it renders negotiations in Brussels significantly more complex.

Relevance for theories of European Integration

As shown above, adoption of the OPT measure interfered both with Community institutions and arrangements. In the textile and clothing sector, where national governments have traditional prerogatives in the provision of quantitative restrictions, the necessity of harmonising diverging national regimes potentially strengthened the competence of the Commission. However, the definition of a common position on OPT proved to be extremely difficult to formulate. In the other sectors subject to a system of trade protection already agreed at Community level (the Common External Tariff), the centralisation of competence at the European level was in principle already a reality.

In fact, no effective centralisation of competence occurred, either because the potential was not seized (in T&C) or because the Commission did not use the competence it was endowed with (in the other sectors). Thus, even if it was part of its natural development, the OPT policy did not contribute to the deepening of the European integration process. Overall, what is at stake in the whole endeavour is the effective 'Europeanisation' of the framework of constraint and opportunity within which European firms adopt their OPT strategies.

Launching the policy-making process

The above empirical account is telling insofar as the factors triggering the whole process of OPT legislation-making in T&C are concerned. This is useful in differentiating between contrasting approaches to European integration. Two paradigms are pertinent in this respect. In very rough terms, whereas a neo-functionalist interpretation would put forward the notion of 'spill-over' for explaining the extension of Community competence, and therefore the definition of new supranational policies at the expense of national policy-making,[149] neo-realism believes that the involvement of the supranational level of decision-making is always carried out in harmony with the interests of member states, if not at the very instigation of the latter.[150]

The above evidence demonstrates that the intense legislative activity at European level is mostly ascribable to the *necessity* of harmonising diverging national regimes. It is the existence of a Common trade-policy and the objective of the Single European Act which rendered the Commission initiative necessary. This very much recalls the nature of the integrative mode highlighted by the neo-functionalist school. In this interpretation, Community institutions and arrangements already in place inevitably give way to the further strengthening of competence at the supranational level in related areas. Thus, the advance of integration in the field of trade policy, as embodied in the provision of a Common External Tariff and the implementation of the Single European Act, spilled over to the connected area of adoption of specific quantitative restrictions.

It is worth noting that the very origin of the OPT story at European level has to do with the adoption by national authorities of incompatible and competing policy stances on how to challenge international competition, with the resulting strong risk of competition between different OPT regimes[151] at work throughout EU countries. One possible interpretation is that certain member states favoured adoption of the Community harmonisation policy in order to reduce the threat of being taken over by the Germans in the promotion of industrial competitiveness (and the subsidisation of job exports). They thus accepted the erosion of their competence with the objective of turning the Community arrangement into an instrument for keeping the policy orientations of their German partners under control. Thus, an intergovernmentalist flavour complements the above straight neo-functionalist interpretation: in the last resort, harmonisation was rendered necessary by factors making sense at a national level. If the process was actually able to take place, it is because member states were willing to accept it.

This is not to say that the process was *deliberately* triggered at the instigation of member states, however. If member states attempted to turn the process in their favour, they did not necessarily and deliberately trigger it. Confronted with the necessity of harmonisation, member states did their best to render the process compatible with their own policy priorities. It was therefore after harmonisation had taken place that member states went to Brussels with the intention of using the European forum for dealing with the risk of regime competition. Recourse to the European level is thus not the result of an initial deliberate intent of member states. Thus, intergovernmentalist and neo-functionalist explanatory patterns should be carefully handled and viewed in combination.

Developing the process

The way the process actually develops once triggered is another story. The above empirical explanation shows that member states actually managed to preserve most of their prerogatives in stark contrast to the predictions of a neo-functionalist approach. Hence, for some reason, and at some point, an initial neo-functionalist starting point notwithstanding, the process emerged as developing in conformity with the interests of member states. The 'technical' account for such an outcome may be found in a description of the legislation-making procedures. Here, the politics of 'deliberate vagueness' consist in maintaining (if not favouring) the unintelligibility of certain provisions in order to put at risk the very harmonisation the Commission was set up to foster.

Theoretical approaches to the European integration process help us go beyond the mechanics of such an outcome, to its actual meaning. The way the OPT story develops gives credit to both the interdependence and the intergovernmentalist schools which consider that the European integration process eventually profits member states. However, the above empirical approach demonstrates that none of these offers a truly satisfactory account of the reality. According to proponents of the interdependence school, for example, the way in which national authorities take advantage of the European integration process carries a price in terms of the preservation of their competence: they actually irredeemably lose certain of their prerogatives which may be recaptured, under an altered form, only at a second-best supranational level. On the face of it, in the intergovernmentalist model, the national level of action is indeed, in the last resort, considered to be adequate: acting at the supranational level is instrumental in serving national authorities' interests. In other words, according to the intergovernmentalist analysis, the national level of action is eventually strengthened whereas the interdependence paradigm emphasises the effectiveness of the centralisation of competence, even if this results from the express objectives of member states.

On this simple basis, one would conclude that the intergovernmentalist account fares better than an interdependence explanation. Indeed, the latter is characterised by a double shortcoming:[152] not only is a lack of competence extended at the supranational level, there are also not many prerogatives lost at the national level either. Instead, the intergovernmentalist is closer to the point concerning the final outcome, that is, the strengthening of the national level at the expense of the Community development. However, even the intergovernmentalist approach is imperfect. First, as previously suggested, soliciting a Community level of action does not result from member states' autonomous initiatives. They do not appear to go voluntarily into the Community arena to recapture what they have hypothetically lost at the national level. What is more, nothing much happens in *effective* terms at the Community level. Whether pulled unintentionally or whether they consent, member states do not, properly speaking, *use* the mechanisms of European integration in their favour. They simply block the development of such mechanisms at an early stage.

The overall lesson to learn from the above analysis concerns the partial irrelevance of theories of European integration. Each of these contains a nugget of relevance, each of them are in a large part, inadequate for relating the OPT story. The interdependence explanation is the most easily discarded. Its pertinence in the case of OPT consists (only) in accounting for an ideal state of affairs, that would have occurred, had the process developed as expected. Indeed, centralisation of competence at the European level is one solution to growing economic interdependence.

The most serious candidates are thus the neo-functionalist and the intergovernmentalist models. However, none of these provide a satisfactory explanation. This is an invitation to pick up and combine the most pertinent parts of each approach. This has to be done carefully, however, as the two paradigms are, indeed, in principle incompatible. One way to distinguish between them is to refer to the direction of the process of competence devolution. In the words of Hollingsworth, an intergovernmentalist process corresponds to 'the upward delegation' of competence from the national to the supranational level. Thus, in a dialectical vein, sovereignty is sacrificed in order to be restored. On the contrary, staying according to Hollingsworth's perspective, the neo-functionalist interpretation illustrates the 'downward authoritative modification of national regimes, by international regimes' with harmonisation[153] the instrument for implementing mandated convergence (Hollingsworth *et al.*, 1994: 292).

The OPT example reveals that there is a strong premise ascribable to the latter logic, but that the actual outcome is in fact in conformity with the former approach. Factors initiating the OPT policy-making process at Community level are clearly identified by a neo-functionalist approach, but intergovernmentalism rightly predicts the way in which the process eventually benefits the national level of action.

What happens in between is better grasped by a sui-generis interpretation of the OPT case. Greenwood's 'disaggregated approach to the study of interest intermediation' seems particularly adequate for tackling the difficulty (Greenwood *et al.*, 1992: 18). The OPT developments would be appropriately accounted for by notions such as 'multi-level policy-making',[154] or 'multi-level system of governance' (Marks *et al.*, 1996). They would indeed fit with the injunction to distinguish between a series of 'policy communities'[155] at the European level (Greenwood and Ronit, 1994: 35), and give credit to Streeck's developments on 'disjointed pluralism' and 'competitive federalism' in Europe (Streeck, 1991).

Process achievement: a potential industrial policy at the European level

What is at stake in the above account is the missed opportunity to design an industrial policy at European level. Indeed, the OPT case offered potential for placing in the hands of the Commission a powerful instrument of industrial policy. To be sure, the OPT arrangement was originally supposed to satisfy trade policy imperatives. However, as illustrated above, the first regulation dealing with economic OPT already contained certain overt elements of industrial policy. This is so, for example, regarding the necessity for eligible products to be of Community origin, a provision introduced by the 1982 legislation which is indeed loaded with important industrial implications.[156] The same may be said of the necessity that producers have facilities located within the Community. Subsequent negotiations destined to harmonise the application of the regulation throughout member states served to accentuate these nascent elements of industrial policy. As a matter of fact, opposition between member states using the OPT text as an instrument to foster international competitiveness and those willing to use the arrangement for preserving employment levels in the Community placed issues of industrial policy at the core of the debate. Thus, from being a typical trade policy measure, OPT has come to be an instrument for choosing between two objectives the relevance of which has clearly to do with industrial policy matters.

That trade measures might be used intentionally as instruments of industrial policy, or simply that trade measures entail unintended consequences for the organisation of industrial activity is nothing new. What is particularly interesting in the OPT case is that the process is coupled with a simultaneous potential transfer of competence from the national to the supranational level.

However, here the *potential* was not seized. Whereas member states were particularly aware of the underlying implications of the legislation in industrial-policy terms, the Commission remained exclusively focused on the objective of harmonising trade conditions in strictly technical terms.

Conclusion

Tracing the decision-making process that led to adoption of the OPT measure provides an interesting picture of the vested interests aligned in the process of enlargement. It appears that the legislation on OPT is the product of two series of bargains, between firms and national authorities, and between states. On the face of it, representation of business interests through supranational associations proved to be relatively more marginal. It is therefore member states' preferences that have constituted the fundamental motor of the legislation-making process. The main players have been Germany, backed by the Netherlands, pressing for as liberal as possible a regime (with the inclusion into the arrangement of distributors) versus. the UK, later overtaken by Southern European countries, determined to keep under tight control the potentially disruptive consequences of OPT on employment in the clothing sector.

A bone of contention between the advocates of relocation to foster international competitiveness and firms' profitability, on the one hand, and those backing protectionist measures in order to preserve domestic employment and to gain foreign exchange, on the other, means that the arrangement achieves the remarkable outcome – *not* of reconciling widely antagonistic interests, but of making their coexistence possible. Rather than leading to the centralisation of competence at the Community level, the flexibility of the arrangement's interpretation made possible the simultaneous satisfaction of member states' diverging policy orientations.

6
Theories of Regional Economic Integration Revisited

Besides testing theories that examine European integration in its political aspect, the OPT example offers an opportunity to apply a further set of literature to the case of CEECs' transition economies. This is comprised of international trade and international production theories and, in general, theories of regional economic integration. Whereas International Trade theories provide – in principle – an answer as to *why* OPT develops in CEECs, International Production theories are better apt at answering *how* OPT is chosen by EU firms to extend their activities to CEECs. As for as theories of regional integration are concerned, these should offer an explanation to account for the contribution of OPT to the dynamics of regional integration in an enlarged Europe.

This chapter undertakes the task of comparing the OPT empirical features presented in Chapters 2 to 4 to theories capable of predicting OPT's developments. It will reveal the limitations of these various bodies of literature, thereby highlighting the very 'sui generis' nature of OPT developments.

On the limited appropriateness of International Trade theories

Textbooks traditionally distinguish between four main theoretical frameworks of international trade theories (IT). Three of these – the Ricardian theory, the Heckscher–Ohlin model (HO), and the specific factor model – belong to the neo-classical paradigm, and are the objects of long-established traditions of research. A fourth current emerged more recently and is comprised of heterogeneous contributions. The common point of this latter strand of research is that studies all depart from the assumption of perfect competition. Mention should also be made of the neotechnology approaches to international trade. These consist of two different versions:

the technology gap model (first analysed by Posner in the 1960s), and the product cycle model (Vernon, 1966), which more resemble empirical generalisations of the world economy than properly predictive theories.

Overall, two broad sets of determinants are considered to give rise to trade flows: (1) comparative advantages and (b) economies of scale (increasing returns). The question at stake is: which of these market mechanisms underpin OPT trade between CEECs and Western Europe? The selection between contending models of international trade to account for OPT in CEECs has to be conducted on the basis of their respective pertinence, first, concerning the particular case of CEECs' foreign trade, and second, taking into consideration the specific features of OPT.

The explanatory power of International Trade theories in the case of OPT in CEECs

The basic opposition between comparative advantages and economies of scale as a source of trade flows rests on a fundamental antagonism. This concerns the issue of whether it is differences or, on the contrary, similarities between economies that trigger trade. In the first perspective, international differences in factor costs are considered to be the primary determinants of trade; comparative advantages materialise due to either technological differences, or distinct factor endowments. As to the second paradigm, it developed more recently in response to empirical evidence revealing the intensity of trade between industrialised countries, despite their being characterised by similar factor endowments. Intra-industry trade, caused by economies of scale and product differentiation, has been identified as the explanation for such an anomaly with regard to traditional theories (Greenaway and Milner, 1986).

A recent and promising approach proposes a further alternative view. Coming from a different perspective (the economics of technical change), it embraces the possibility of increasing returns posited by the 'new' theories of IT but places greater emphasis on their dynamics, 'particularly those associated with production technology and innovation' (Dosi, Pavitt and Soete, 1990: 2). International patterns of trade – or to be more precise, their *evolution* – are thus explained by differences of technological capabilities and innovation, together with dynamic 'learning' features.[157]

There is traditionally, a 'paradigm specialisation' by country, in which the HO model and the Ricardian model are thought to account for the foreign trade of developing countries. Models assuming imperfect competition are reserved, meanwhile, for developed market economies (Greenaway,

1991: 157). In HO terms, trade develops due to differences of factor endowments; it is therefore between economies which are most dissimilar that HO trade is most likely to occur. This argument applies to CEECs' trade with 'developed' Western economies, since the period of centralised allocation that CEECs underwent stamped its mark upon their production structure, as well as their level of development, rendering them significantly different to their immediate Western neighbours.

Can the HO model account for OPT in CEECs on this basis? Put simply, the HO theory affirms that a country enjoys a comparative advantage in (and will therefore export) the good whose production is relatively intensive in the factor with which that country is relatively well endowed. Thus, one might expect that the trade specialisation (and division of labour) resulting from OPT would take place along the lines of comparative advantages. The fundamental conclusion achieved by application of the HO theory to the OPT case is straightforward: if OPT trade takes place along the lines of a comparative advantage based on labour, then as wages increase OPT trade will decrease. Such a conclusion is far too simplistic to account for the complex reality of OPT developments depicted in previous chapters. It is worth briefly explaining why.

The HO model is in fact characterised by two main general short-comings. The first is that comparative advantage is a static notion. The HO model claims to explain trade patterns at a point in time, not to predict future trends.[158] The only (compromise) solution consists in adopting the HO model as a starting point, and complementing it with dynamic considerations. Future trends are indeed commonly merely inferred from current comparative advantages, even if this is clearly a usurpation of the theory. Theoretically sounder, Balassa (1979a) proposed a 'stage-approach' to comparative advantage. He relates changes in comparative advantage to changes in factor endowments, and considers that the structure of exports changes in line with the accumulation of physical and human capital. Eventually, comparative advantages move along a scale, progressing from the most labour-intensive products to the most capital-intensive goods. In simple terms, the question is therefore to determine whether the referred to economies are characterised by hidden or latent assets such as, for example, a skilled labour force. The Asian newly industrialised countries (and Japan at an earlier stage) are often considered to be cases in point in this respect, as comparative advantages shifted away from unskilled labour-intensive products to more capital and technology-intensive goods. As far as OPT is concerned, the lessons to be drawn from such theoretical developments are clear: will the factor endowment of CEECs' economies upgrade, yielding a lower labour content of trade? If the conclusion is yes, how might this impact on OPT trade?

The second problem of the HO model in accounting for OPT developments concerns the treatment accorded by HO to trade in intermediate goods. In the words of Ballance:

> patterns of trade and product specialisation entail much more than the processing of indigenous raw materials into final goods which are either consumed at home or exported. Instead, they are highly interdependent processes whereby some countries produce and export raw materials to others, which process the materials into intermediate products for export to third countries for yet further processing. The degree of interdependence, the number of processing stages, and the international location of these stages will vary among industries. (Ballance, 1988: 16)

International vertical chains of production processes can, indeed, overlap in association with intricate patterns of comparative advantages. As a result, the simple predictions of the HO model, for which two trading partners are defined by well-determined comparative advantages, are obscured. More importantly, Ballance's apparently innocent remark suggests that countries do not specialise so much in products, but rather in stages of production. There have been attempts to formalise semi-finished goods into the HO model. However, these do not strictly correspond to OPT features inasmuch as they adopt a view in which products undergo a *continuum* of processing stages. The circularity proper to OPT trade is therefore not taken into consideration. It thus seems more sensible to consider that countries 'specialise in a particular stage of the internationalised production process which corresponds, in terms of factor intensity, to their relative factor endowment' (Nagarajan, 1995).

Overall, the above theoretical shortcomings of the HO model make it difficult to account for OPT. It would be quite naive to believe that it is comparative advantages *per se* which are the determinants of OPT. In fact, out of a peculiar irony, OPT trade takes place along the lines of comparative advantages because this is where trade protection is. In other words, OPT trade develops where policy makers *think* CEECs' comparative advantages lie. That OPT trade develops effectively along the lines of comparative advantages as defined by neo-liberal IT theories simply reveals that policy-makers have a good command of their IT textbooks!

Are the 'new' theories of International Trade better, then, at explaining OPT developments? It was noted in Chapter 2 that CEECs are characterised by a growing importance of intra-industry trade. Besides, CEECs participate in a regional integration process and it is often presumed that preferential, as opposed to multilateral, trade liberalisation is more likely to bring about intra-industry specialisation as opposed to inter-industry reallocation.[159] One might argue that these 'new' theories of international trade (already) provide a pertinent framework for analysis especially as, with the passage of time, structures of the respective economies converge.

Furthermore, the developments OPT gives rise to are quite akin to intra-industry trade. Indeed, OPT brings about a two-way trade which is most often classified within the same category of the combined nomenclature at 2-digit level. What is more, it corresponds clearly to a sub-category of intra-industry trade (IIT) as identified by those very scholars who pioneered its study. Grubel and Lloyd (1975: 114–18), for example, cite the case of the processing activities of multinational enterprises (where goods are sent abroad to undergo processing before being imported back) as a source of IIT. Such processing activities were considered by other early scholars of IIT to be a fully-fledged category classified in the typology of different types of IIT. Gray (1973) described it as belonging to category 'C', that is IIT in components, whereas Helleiner (1973) provided a number of examples of commodities involved in assembly activities abroad as an illustration of the rise of IIT.[160] Finally, Willmore (1979) distinguished between three distinct kinds of heterogeneous goods that give rise to IIT specialisation: goods produced with the same machines and skills, but belonging to different and narrow ranges of product lines; goods with different factor input requirements, and; differentiated goods exchanged between monopolistic competitors, the second category corresponding to processing activities.

Interestingly enough, these early studies on IIT often referred to the specific custom regime contained in the US Tariff Schedule under which import duties are levied only on the value added abroad. Indeed, these studies use trade data resulting from this specific custom treatment as evidence of intra-firm trade (this is almost taken for granted in Gray, 1973; Helleiner, 1973; Grubel and Lloyd, 1975; and Helleiner, 1981). These are sometimes even associated with intra-firm trade. Helleiner (1973), for example, uses American customs figures as evidence of the extending reach of US multinational firms' activities. Balassa, on the contrary, notes that vertical (as well as horizontal) specialisation is not necessarily of an intra-firm nature. He goes even further, actually stressing the declining importance of US multinationals for organising the vertical integration of production processes on an international scale. In turn, the symmetrically increasing role of contractual agreements demonstrates the growing independence of US partners abroad (Balassa, 1979b: 261–65).

Later formalisations further clarified the specificity of IIT. Its determinants are not comparative advantages, but economies of scale or product differentiation (Greenaway and Milner, 1986). In this respect the use of IIT theories to account for CEECs' trade is an improvement, allowing for the fact that CEECs participate in the international division of labour. In the case of OPT, this approach would also align more closely with what is an important feature of the arrangement, that is, its 'quasi intra-firm' nature. Finally, the double upgrading processes characterising OPT developments within firms as well at the aggregate level (OPT product structure) would, in principle, be explainable.

In fact, there is some confusion regarding the real meaning of 'intra-industry trade' and some controversy concerning its statistical expression. In straight statistical terms, OPT has the appearance of IIT. However, it is in fact 'just' the manifestation of the international splitting up of a value-added chain which IIT theories *do* purport to account for. This has already been well summarised in Grubel and Lloyd (1975), who considered that the development of processing activities invites traditional theories to take account of two previously ignored factors, namely, the role of transport costs and of information in determining trade patterns. For the rest, however:

> International assembly and finishing, which give rise to intra-industry trade because they involve the import and export of goods which often are reported in the same statistical category, are consistent with the Heckscher–Ohlin model since they represent the exploitation of comparative advantage in the production of certain services. (Grubel and Lloyd, 1975: 118)

This therefore brings us back to the problem of the difficult treatment of intermediate goods in IT theories.

The latest theoretical developments in terms of technology gaps are broadly inappropriate to account for the specificity of OPT in CEECs. on the grounds that many of its developments are for the moment restricted to the case of 'developed' economies (Dosi *et al.*, 1990). However, these approaches help shed some light on the real issues at stake in OPT developments. For example, their overarching conclusion seems to fit with OPT evidence. Indeed, the international composition of trade by countries within each sector appears to be essentially explained by technology gaps while comparative advantage mechanisms appear to be of lesser importance. (Dosi, Pavitt and Soete, 1990: 11)

What is of specific interest here is the emphasis that these approaches place on the dynamic learning mechanisms that trade entails. In the words of Grossman and Helpman,

Countries that trade in world markets invariably learn a great deal about innovative products and about the novel methods that are being used to produce older goods. (Grossman and Helpman, 1991: 238)

This is particularly germane in the case of CEECs to enable an assessment of CEECs' chances of catching up (Hotopp and Radosevic, 1999). For the OPT story, one finding proves especially relevant. This is that:

changes in trade performance are more strongly associated with changes in innovative activities than changes in relative labour costs. (Dosi, Pavitt and Soete, 1990: 12)

Interestingly enough, the OPT example, can, in return, correct what appears to be the weakness of this approach. It indeed makes explicit what these learning mechanisms consist of. The key in this respect is that the trade flows we are concerned with take place within a network of firms which are interacting with one another; this offers many opportunities to learn. To return to the above quote of Grossman and Helpman, it is not so much countries that learn, but *firms*. Unfortunately, trade theories still consider firms as 'black boxes' – a major drawback, as far as OPT is concerned.

Limitations

Generally, IT theories miss the point that the mode and speed of trade liberalisation have a direct influence on patterns of trade specialisation. Rather than 'taking place along the lines of CEECs' comparative advantages', OPT trade is determined by the structure of trade protection still in place between the EU and CEECs.

The second and more fundamental drawback of traditional – and less traditional – IT approaches to account for OPT developments is their neglect of corporate variables. As suggested in the above remark by Ballance (Ballance, 1988), the irreducible unit of analysis of IT theories, that is, *national markets*, does not appear to be the most appropriate in the case of intermediate goods. Indeed, division of the production process is organised within networks of firms participating in the internationalisation of production. In the case of OPT this is particularly relevant since, depending on the nature of an OPT partnership, the measure can have very different impacts on aggregate trade flows. Thus, acknowledging the fact that OPT is the product of firms' decisions, rather than mere transactions taking place between markets characterised by different factor endowments, is likely to make more complex the actual determinants of OPT and their likely consequences.

In conclusion, the fundamental shortcoming of most IT approaches in accounting for OPT is that they fail to acknowledge the connection between firms' international production activities and international trade flows. This is a serious drawback in a world economy where a growing proportion of international trade is attributable to firms' international production activities. The point has now been reached where theories of International Production addressing organisational factors as well as market forces must take into account a trade-centred analysis.

The partial relevance of International Production theories

The conclusion achieved by an approach in IT terms is that it is necessary to bring into the picture the *network* of firms within which OPT takes place – as indeed OPT is a matter for firms' decisions. Although highly diversified, International Production (IP) theories pose the question as to *how* (and to a lesser extent *where* and *when*[161]) national firms decide to go abroad. It is thus natural to turn to these to see what they have to say on the specificity of OPT strategies. It might be, however, that rather than providing a complete and ready-made explanatory pattern for OPT, the exercise will display some of the weaknesses of IP theories.

The foundations of International Production studies

International Production theories form a disparate set of various theoretical contributions. Perhaps as a reflection of the complexity of the object they describe, they are highly diversified and sometimes contradictory in nature. Different strands correspond to the different theoretical backgrounds from which they are derived. For example, internalisation theories draw on the traditional theory of the firm based on the Coasian distinction between firm and market. Alternatively, the school initiated by Hymer in his seminal dissertation owes much of its substance to Industrial Organisation concepts (Hymer, 1976).

Dunning's merit consists in bringing together the various contributions in an appropriately named 'eclectic' framework for analysis. Briefly summarised, his argument is as follows: a firm invests abroad when it has an 'ownership' advantage at its disposal that it can internalise (Dunning, 1979). Ownership advantages can be of various sorts: deriving from the privileged possession of an income-generating asset; enjoyed by a branch firm as compared to a greenfield plant; resulting from geographical diversification.[162] As to internalisation advantages, these arise either from risk, from the ability of firms to exploit economies of scale, or, alternatively, from the existence of a benefit associated with the transaction which cannot be taken into account in an externalised form (Dunning, 1988). The ownership and internalisation advantages ('O' and 'I') answer the 'how' question of international production theories, that is, which would be the best route for servicing foreign markets. Finally, locational advantages ('L'), explain *where* international production activities will take place, that is, where firm- and country-specific advantages coincide. This latter series has much in common with (if it is not directly adapted from) international trade theories. The only difference is that, when combined with the two other determinants of international production, the latter allow for the introduction of government intervention, as well as the existence of intermediate goods.

Applying an eclectic theory to the case of non-equity forms of international production requires, first, an understanding of the rationale underlying internalisation decisions. An understanding of the reasons why firms do not actually resort to internalisation is also necessary. Two distinct sets of factors bring about internalisation. Buckley and Casson, who were the first to make an explicit association between the notion of internalisation and that of market imperfections in an international context, adopt a Coasian approach: that is, that there are imperfections on markets of intermediate products resulting from transaction costs. This explains why firms resort to *vertical* international integration (Buckley and Casson, 1976). Conversely, Hymer's interpretation of internalisation has more to do with market power than with intrinsic market inefficiency: by internalising, certain (large) firms are in a position to raise barriers to market entry, thus generating a rent. This second approach is more appropriate when addressing the *horizontal* dimension of international integration. Beyond this distinction, determinants of internalisation have broadly to do with market failures. The choice of the most appropriate vehicle for international production (foreign direct investment or licensing) is mainly made on the basis of firm-specific assets: internalisation is not necessary when these latter are 'easily identified and vested in exclusive and freely transferable property rights' (Buckley and Casson, 1985:52). Other related factors are relevant, such as the degree of standardisation of the concerned products, and the extent of segmentation of the markets for goods and factors. A final important factor favouring non-equity forms of international production, consists of obstacles to internalisation erected by government policy measures (Oman, 1984).

Overall, in an eclectic paradigm, the account of non-equity forms of international production is relatively neglected. The reason for this is ultimately ascribable to the conditions under which IP theories were born. In fact, the raison d'être of IP theories is a refutation of the basic assumption of IT theories, that is, the immobility of production factors. As opposed (in addition) to a world where only goods are mobile, the IP paradigm takes into account the possibility of capital transfers. Removing the unrealistic assumption of capital immobility is indeed a necessary step toward a more faithful account of the world economy.[163] The problem is that almost by reaction, international production activities tackled by IP theories tend thus to become synonymous with integration.[164] Hence the opposition between international trade theories dealing with market transactions, and international production theories concerned with transactions taking place within firms.

The result is that intermediate forms of international production hardly fit into such a rigid division of labour between IT and IP. As illustrated by the above analysis, the only way to address non-equity co-operation is in second-best terms: being that internalised transactions are considered to be optimal forms of international production, incomplete integration might nevertheless be justified when the former are not necessary or are difficult to achieve.[165] As a rule of thumb, however, it is considered that a higher degree of *control* results from integration. Consequently, higher returns are achieved (Anderson and Gatignon, 1986).[166] What is more, the mere opposition between licensing/ investing[167] is evidently insufficient to account for the variety of international production forms (Stopford and Strange, 1991: 67). This shortcoming is itself related to the failure of the theory to acknowledge distinct objectives of international production.

The study of the relocation of international production activities

A first series of approaches simply ignores tricky internalisation issues. The main focus of these is on the objective pursued by a firm when undertaking international production activities. From a situation where the search for markets was a dominant rationale for going abroad, current developments rather correspond to the necessity of finding advantageous production sites. In Delapierre and Michalet's terminology, the tendency to shift from 'relay-subsidiaries' to 'workshop-subsidiaries' drives the current globalisation of production activities (Delapierre and Michalet 1976).

Thus, some studies address the specific question of the *relocation* of economic activity abroad. They offer a definition which indeed corresponds to the OPT case: in its broadest interpretation, international relocation occurs when a production unit closes in country A, and reopens in country B.[168] As a direct consequence, trade flows take place between A and B. The problem with the debate over relocation, however, is that it is dominated by the question of how restricted the definition of relocation should be. In short, what is at stake are taxonomic issues. Due to this bias, the study of relocation presents poor analytical validity in addressing OPT. Their explicit objective notwithstanding, such studies are nevertheless interesting in that they adopt a perspective which reveals the inseparable nature of the relocation of international production activities and its related trade flows: if firms go abroad aiming to take advantage of superior production locations, international production activities necessarily entail one trade flow ('re-imports'), if not two (preliminary exports).

Efforts made to address sub-contracting activities in an international setting are also of interest for understanding OPT. According to a minimal definition of International Sub-contracting (ISC), a foreign firm awards the injunction to local firms to perform certain tasks according to a blueprint provided by the former (Germidis, 1980). What (implicitly) differentiates ISC from licensing is that output is not geared to local markets, but is instead re-imported. Approaches to ISC all resort to some extent to the double reference to international production and its related international trade flows. Michalet, for example, proposes a typology which places emphasis on the nature of the relations between contracting partners (Michalet, 1988). This typology is deprived of explanatory power. However, it makes two essential points. First, relocation is simultaneously ascribable to the two logics of international production and of international trade. Second, IP-related trade flows can be of an intra-firm nature or they may take place at arms' length. The issue is, after all, of secondary importance since what really matters is that in both cases they occur within firms' networks and as a result of firms' initiatives.

In fact, an early theoretical development on sub-contracting activity in a *national* context might prove as relevant, if not more so, in the case of OPT. At the end of the 1950s, Houssiaux, later followed by Blois, considered that sub-contracting was akin to the 'vertical quasi-integration' of the firms concerned (Houssiaux, 1957).[169] While bypassing integration, vertical quasi-integration substitutes for markets achieving an intermediary position (op. cit: 221). In this view, sub-contracting is:

> a device for economic integration, not within a firm, but within the group made of a big firm and its sub-contractors. (Houssiaux, 1957: 222)

If extended to a national context, this definition might prove particularly accurate in describing OPT developments.

Approaches to non-equity forms of international production activities

Further developments in the world economy forced attention back on to the difficult question of internalisation. In response to converging empirical evidence, renewed attempts to address the question of co-operative ventures considered the latter to form a fully-fledged category between market and hierarchy. Two empirical developments in the world economy eroded the centrality of the internalisation notion, putting increasing strain on traditional second best approaches.[170]

First came the recognition in the 1970s of so-called 'new forms of investment' (NFIs).[171] These new forms of investment were defined as joint ventures; licensing agreements; management contracts; franchising; turnkey agreements; 'product-in-hand' contracts; production-sharing and risk-service contracts, and last but not least; international sub-contracting (Oman, 1989: 834). There is something 'new' about this first wave; what exactly this is, however, is not completely clear. Oman evokes the increasing importance of co-operative ventures in the relatively untraditional setting formed by the developing countries (Oman, 1989: 384). In this view, what Germidis calls 'non-investment'[172] responds to the complementary objectives of host states and investing firms. These are: to secure technology and access to markets while preserving sovereignty on the one hand, and to minimise risks taken in an uncertain environment on the other hand.[173]

A second wave of contractual agreements was identified in the late 1980s as the development of 'co-operative ventures' (Contractor and Lorange, 1988) or 'cross-border non-equity collaborative ventures'. As opposed to the NFI of the 1970s, this second wave was more clearly innovative. To the list of forms previously identified are added alliances between multinationals that pool resources in areas such as R&D.[174] Such alliances take place in developed economies of the northern hemisphere and tend to occur between firms of similar production profile and size which are, so to speak, on a more equal footing. They often take place in order to rationalise the activities of firms that move into global operations. Of course, the development of strategic alliances and, to a lesser extent, of contractual agreements remains marginal if compared, for example, to the unprecedented series of mergers and acquisitions that took place at the same time. The rationale put forward for explaining why firms increasingly resort to externalised forms of international production has shifted away from a second-best logic to arguments departing more openly from 'mainstream' international production (IP) theories.

An interesting feature of approaches aiming at an optimum (first-best) account of co-operative ventures is their emphasis on mutations at stake in the world economy, in particular, to changes in the modalities of international competition which is becoming 'global'. In the words of Stopford and Strange 'global competition' refers to:

> the outcome of how individual firms have reacted over time to the changing balance of opportunity and threat' at work in the world economy. (Stopford end Strange, 1991: 65)

Implications are numerous and have not yet been appropriately addressed in an all-encompassing framework for analysis;[175] but, what is at stake is the old Fordist model. These changes apply at different levels. First, they involve a new organisation of the production process with the development of flexible methods of production,[176] all carried out in the context of de-integration of the production chain. Second, they imply new assets as the basis of firms' competitive advantages: technology and, furthermore, knowledge, is becoming an increasingly important factor in determining the terms of competition between firms (Stopford and Strange, 1991: 34, 71). Finally, whether through cause or consequence, the changes refer to new conditions of demand, which is becoming increasingly volatile (Oman, 1989: 387). Overall, the new conditions of competition are bringing about inevitable consequences for the modalities whereby firms relate to each other, that is, in the ways they compete and co-operate. In the words of Contractor and Lorange, a firm is now to be viewed as: a coalition of interlocked quasi-arm's-length relationships' (Contractor and Lorange, 1988: 5).

These trends invite reconsideration of the traditional primacy of the notion of internalisation (Delapierre and Michalet, 1989). New patterns in conditions of international competition call for more flexibility and adaptability, rendering co-operative agreements particularly attractive. These changes require

> a general view of international competition to account for the various forms of international economic relations as different modalities for organising production on a world-wide scale. (Ravix *et al.*, 1989: 38)

However, besides the appropriateness of non-equity agreements for acquiring flexibility, there is an obvious difficulty in theorising the determinants of such forms of international production. A pertinent question in this respect is how far non-equity forms of international production can be treated together.[177] In other words, some doubt exists as to whether co-operative ventures really form an homogeneous category. This in turn questions the validity of the double reference to market and integration to account for their forming a fully-fledged category of international production activities (Delapierre and Michalet, 1989: 27).[178] For instance, Contractor and Lorange, who pioneered the study of co-operative ventures, offer a good example of how difficult it is to use the intermediary position between market and hierarchy as a sufficiently discriminative criteria. They begin by defining a spectrum of possibilities that goes from 'spot transactions' to 'complete merger' (Contractor and Lorange, 1988: 5), then evoke the 'two extremes of full integration and purely contractual relationships' (op. cit., 1988: 16). Does this bring us back to our starting point? Are co-operative agreements alike to arms' length transactions?

In fact, the main shortcoming of a view resting on the prominence of commonality of non-equity agreements (i.e. their rejection of complete internalisation) over their differences, is that it neglects the *rationale* of such forms of international production. This approach suffice if the question at stake is 'which is the best route for servicing foreign markets', but not if it is 'how best to combine different vehicles of international production to simultaneously achieve a wide range of different objectives'. Faced with this multiplication of variables, what is at stake is therefore the possibility of a comprehensive and exhaustive theory of international production.

Appropriateness and limitation

Thanks to IP theories, firms are no longer 'black boxes'; they are finally considered to be fully-fledged actors in the determination of international economic exchanges. The problem is that in contrast to IT approaches, by attempting to address a higher degree of complexity, IP theories lose something of their predictability.

The main difficulty is that while these present a wide range of potential explanations for the way in which firms go abroad (thus answering the 'how' question of international production), they tend to neglect reasons as to 'why' they do so. Thus, IP theories have a fundamental difficulty in addressing inter-firm relations that are not internalised. As a result, they fail to account for the consequences that different types of partnerships may give rise to for the respective partners. In fact, IP theories tend to revert to IT theories to explain inter-firm linkages which take place between legally independent firms.[179]

IP theories allow us to determine reasons why EU firms approach CEECs using OPT, rather than invoking other vehicles for organising international production. In other words IP theories are, in principle, useful when seeking to identify reasons why OPT transactions do not occur within internal, but on external markets;[180] that is, why internalisation does not occur in such situations. In particular, IP theories claim to address the specific issue of the *control* that one firm may, or may not, extend over its partner. They also examine the reasons why an OPT foreign partner does not need to extend control over its partner, that is, why do they not engage capital?

Several possible responses are offered by IP theories. Only one of these – and this is not, strictly speaking, a theoretical explanation – applies to the actual OPT developments as described in Chapters 2 to 4. It has to do with recent developments relating to the transformation of modes of international competition which require an adaptation of the way firms organise production. Several studies highlight the transformation of the traditional sub-contracting relation, in both national and international settings: from dependence to partnership,[181] sub-contracting is more and more characterised by a 'two-way' relationship (Mytelka, 1995b). OPT developments would be rightly seen in this light as the response given by EU firms to the necessity of acquiring more flexibility, or of reaping economic opportunities on a global scale. Thus, OPT responds to constraints imposed by the development of new methods of production, and new patterns of demand.

Other explanations put forward by older versions of IP theories are more ambiguous, if not clearly inappropriate. In very 'eclectic' terms, for example, OPT firms do not undertake internalisation because there is no 'appropriability of proprietary assets'.[182] In other words, there would be no transfer to operate because products concerned do not contain a high content of firm-specific advantages. However, this does not fit with the statistical evidence presented in Chapter 2. The evidence demonstrated that a process of upgrading of the OPT product structure is taking place, although this is currently restricted to a first fringe of CEECs. What is more, and this is a more serious drawback, such a line of argument rules out any possibility of *evolution* of OPT partnerships: either a partnership continues to be based on the exchange of very rudimentary products in the absence of firm-specific assets, or it terminates as such. Again, this contradicts findings that OPT partnerships can indeed undergo a process of upgrading at firm level as OPT can either give way to FDI, or be the first step in the transformation of local firms into system suppliers. Fundamentally, 'mainstream' IP theories bypass the learning processes that inter-firm partnerships might trigger. This fails to account for one of the main theses proposed in this study that OPT offers the means to *learn*, and that this is a form of upgrading of firms' capabilities which does not necessarily translate in statistics concerning the value-added content of exports.

At the other extreme, IP theories are unable to account for 'institutional' OPT determinants – the pace and speed of the process of trade liberalisation – highlighted earlier. They miss the fact that, contrary to its very flexible appearance, OPT might actually offer a powerful instrument for foreign firms to extend a very high degree of *power* over local partners. Indeed, evidence in Chapter 3 made clear that, in sharp contrast to the IP prediction, OPT may be associated with an extensive degree of control, even in the absence of capital involvement. In other words, the risk with IP theories is that they fail to acknowledge means of extending control outside those of internalisation and capital involvement. There are, of course, notable exceptions. Oman (1989: 391), for example, notes that it is not equity that makes investment, and that, vice versa, it is possible to have an equity involvement without the usual consequences associated with FDI. For example, control can be acquired through the use of bargaining power, or by the enforcement of contracts (see Buckley and Casson, 1985).[183]

OPT indeed illustrates yet another means for acquiring control. This consists of 'exogenous' institutional factors in general, and trade restrictions in particular. The above empirical evidence made clear that the latter render the arrangement particularly compelling, yielding a degree of integration which can compare with full internalisation. They create an ideal situation where foreign contracting firms find themselves in a very strong bargaining position. In the last resort, it is an institutional design that actually brings about the effects normally associated with internalisation. In short, institutional factors substitute for internalisation.

Overall, IP theories might well account for the different vehicles firms have at their disposal to move operations abroad. However, apart from the theoretical difficulty in addressing non-equity forms of involvement, their major drawback, as far as OPT is concerned, is that they tend not to address the nature – the 'content' – of the co-operation established between firms. In particular, this leads them to neglect the learning process that inter-firm partnerships can trigger and therefore, the possibility of evolution of the latter.

Theoretical contributions on regional integration

There are several topics addressed in the literature on regional integration which can provide useful insights into some of the issues at stake in the OPT story. Broadly speaking, there are two strands of approaches. The first is concerned with the different possible forms regional integration can take, while the second has more interest in the consequences of the latter. Of course, the two series of developments are not exclusive.

In the following, a literature review will select the most relevant approaches and assess the insights they bring to the OPT story. As in the case of similar previous exercises, it will be shown that by confronting OPT empirical evidence with pertinent theories, much can be learnt from OPT.

Different stages and arrangements

A predominant approach considers economic integration to be a process rather than a state; a first question has therefore to do with its different *stages*, and the evolution from one stage to another. In fact, initial analyses were taking place in parallel with the formation of the European Community, the underlying normative principles of development of which – mainly formalised in Jean Monnet's doctrine – inevitably influenced the former. In 1961, Balassa proposed his dynamic approach to regional integration, with the identification of at least four forms representing various degrees of integration: free trade areas, the custom union; a common market; and the formation of an economic union. Eventually, the process is posited to yield complete economic integration (Balassa, 1961: 2). It is not made explicit, but Balassa treats these different forms of regional integration as if they were taking place in a chronological order. After having progressed through these disparate stages, the process would then culminate in an all-encompassing political integration translating into the enforcement of the principle of supranationality.

A slightly different interpretation of the stage approach to regional integration consists in distinguishing between positive and negative integration (Tinbergen, 1954: 77). Indeed, integration can be more or less strong depending on the degree of centralisation of economic policies. Whereas during the 'negative' phase of integration all barriers to exchange are removed, the 'positive' stage is characterised by the implementation of common economic policies. This second view corresponds to Balassa's account of the opposition between 'liberalist' and 'dirigist' ideals of economic integration. The former is limited to trade liberalisation, the latter has to do with co-ordination (Balassa, 1961: 7).

Finally, emphasis in an additional version of a stage approach to integration rests on the distinction between 'shallow' and 'deep' integration (UNCTC, 1993). In this case, the difference between integration of trade and that of international production activities is referred to. Although it is now acknowledged that the two go hand in hand (Julius, 1990), there might be a short lapse of time with trade integration preceding the development of interpenetration of production activities on a regional basis.

More recent developments tend to place a different emphasis on chronologically ordered stages. As a result, stress is placed, rather, on the difference between various forms of regional integration schemes, characterised by distinctive substantial traits that do not necessarily evolve towards a homogenous outcome. One area of research is, for example, the difference between free trade areas and custom unions.[184] This is a prerequisite that paves the way for addressing the other big issue at stake in theories of economic integration: the welfare consequences of integration.[185]

Locational issues

Some attempts have been made, at the margin between international economics and economic geography, to address locational issues in the context of regional trade liberalisation. Krugman and Venables, for example, examine the integration of peripheral low-wage countries into a core of larger and more developed countries (Krugman, Venables, 1990). They propose a model for determining the effect of such a process on the competitiveness of the periphery's industry, where outcome varies according to the degree of trade liberalisation. When trade barriers are high, industries can be marginally relocated to the periphery, with the sole objective of accessing local markets. When trade is being liberalised in the face of sustained barriers, industry is likely to remain in core countries in order to take advantage of higher economies of scale. It is only when trade is completely liberalised that industries are relocated to the periphery in order to take advantage of lower wages. This example is quite unusual in relating the *form* of trade liberalisation to changes in the location of economic activity within an integrating area. Trade liberalisation is indeed often taken for granted, with barely any distinction being made between the process and its result: trade liberalisation is usually identified with its outcome, that is, free trade.

Regional integration and regional development

Alternative approaches to regional integration, rather, emphasise the dynamic dimension of economic integration without significant reference to the institutional setting within which the latter takes place.

A precursor of these approaches was the product cycle model. Its primary objective was to account for innovation by predicting trade patterns, without resorting to the notion of comparative advantage (Vernon, 1966). Here, new products are first launched on domestic markets (usually characterised by strong demand and high wage levels), irrespective of questions of cost. These then mature and are exported as demand also increases abroad. Finally, the production process becomes standardised and can be relocated to where labour costs are more favourable. There are many problems with this model, not the least of these being, in particular, the paucity of empirical evidence with which to validate it.

Subsequent studies are more relevant; in particular, those developed on the basis of the empirical observation of the Asian regional model of integration. Conceptual tools have been put forward, such as the 'flying geese' analogy in which the regional division of labour is based on the replication of the national model of development of one leading country – Japan as a 'core country'.[186] Applying Vernon's product cycle model to the Asian regional context, this approach focuses upon the relocation of production migrating in successive waves according to the maturation process of products and the stages of development of host economies. This scenario thus implies the structuration of a region into several 'tiers' at different stages of development. It predicts the promotion of autonomous local capabilities, and the development of import-substituting industries.

An interesting counter-argument has been developed on the basis of the notion of cross-national production networks (CNPN). In Ernst's definition, these are:

> the organization across national borders of research and development activities, procurement, distribution, product definition and design, manufacturing, and support services. (Ernst, 1999).

The development of CNPN is thus connected to the transformation of the conditions of international competition. They boost non-equity and non-arms' length inter-firm relationships in which entire business functions may be outsourced. From the perspective of host economies, CNPNs enable access to technology through backward linkages between foreign and local firms.

Bernard and Ravenhill, utilise the notion of production networks to account for the process of regional integration in Asia (Bernard and Ravenhill, 1995). They argue that the driving force of this process is the globalisation of production networks, increased intergovernmental disputes over bilateral economic relationships, and the rapid pace of technological change. Rather than the migration of products across national economies, the Asian development pattern would produce:

> a new regional division of labour that is based not on national economies but on regionalized networks of production. (Bernard and Ravenhill, 1995: 206)

Bernard and Ravenhill thus reject the 'flying-geese' analogy on three different grounds. First, the flying geese analogy makes very restrictive assumptions regarding the maturation of products; second, it erroneously predicts the development of import-substituting industries in countries where production has migrated and finally, it incorrectly accounts for 'reverse exports' (i.e. from low labour cost countries to originating countries).

One important feature of regional integration through CNPN is that it is specific to areas characterised by high levels of heterogeneity. Thus, there is more to CNPN than economies of scale spurring intra-industry trade, together with comparative advantages which are considered to be the motor of inter-industry trade. However, empirical evidence on CNPN has been, until now, mainly confined to the example of the electronics industry.

Finally, another possibility is the development of workbench activities, these being characteristic of the Mexican *maquiladora* industry model (Sander, 1997). Such cross-border transactions are certainly primarily designed to take advantage of low labour costs, but the proximity of a new production locus is the decisive factor which determines the ability of home firms to shorten delivery delays and, more generally, to apply 'flexible' methods of production.

Adopting 'flexible' methods of production reduces the percentage of variable labour costs in total costs. It therefore also reduces the labour cost savings derived from relocation. On this basis, Oman predicts the decreasing importance of traditional offshore activities, and the increasing importance of activities undertaken in low-labour-cost countries in the *immediate vicinity* of developed countries (Oman, 1994). Oman offers this as one of the reasons for regional sourcing, as opposed to 'global sourcing', as being more likely to occur.

OPT in the light of regional integration theories

The depiction of the contribution of OPT to economic interdependence between Eastern and Western Europe proposed in Chapters 2 to 4 provides many direct answers to certain distinctions and predictions proposed in the regional integration literature, as briefly sketched above.

The fact that the location and distribution of economic activity can be, to a large extent, institutionally and therefore politically underpinned has important consequences as far as the basic distinction between 'liberalist' and 'dirigist' approaches to regional integration is concerned. The fact is that it questions the pertinence of the position held by proponents of regional integration limited to free trade as opposed to more interventionist developments. The validity of the distinction between *positive* and *negative* integration is thus at stake. The empirical evidence demonstrating how OPT affects CEECs' trade specialisation and the division of labour between CEECs and the EU thereby anchors the view expressed by Balassa in concrete terms; in his words, it would be a

> great error to believe that the decision to create regional unions would re-establish the conditions of an economic liberalism extirpating with one stroke all the so-called dirigist policies. (Balassa, 1961: 9)

An additional channel through which the institutions implementing regional integration alter economic outcomes is therefore identified.[187] The OPT story invites us to focus upon the locational consequences of trade liberalisation within a regional context. It shows that institutional factors like the form and speed of trade liberalisation are an important source of alteration of market determinants.

Moreover, the OPT example questions the distinction between shallow integration (limited to trade) and deep integration (which also encompasses production activities). In fact, the institutional background shaping the trade specialisation resulting from trade liberalisation resorts primarily to trade policy instruments. However, its ultimate impact is to be gauged through the organisation of international production activities throughout Europe. In this sense, OPT mechanisms can be viewed as 'investment-related trade measures'; these illustrate how integration through trade and integration through international production activities can occur simultaneously, the two being different dimensions of the same phenomenon.

Finally, the OPT example illustrates the shortcomings – the inappropriateness, in fact – of the product cycle model to account for current developments of international production in the world economy. Apart from the paucity of empirical evidence validating such a model,[188] the problem as far as OPT is concerned, is that the latter does not account for trade in intermediary products.[189] Its inadequacy in dealing with OPT is therefore straightforward.

Of particular interest are the OPT findings for highlighting specificity of the European model of regional integration, in contrast with alternative examples in the world economy. Neither the Asian experience – be this in its 'flying geese' interpretation or in the production network version – or the Mexican case offer entirely appropriate comparisons. OPT evidence supports the formation of different tiers of countries in an enlarged Europe. However, these do not seem to be chronologically and geographically ordered as in the case of the Asian model of integration – or in the interpretation the 'flying geese' analogy makes of this. What is more, the division of regional labour does not replicate the model of development of a core country – Germany.

At the same time, OPT evidence testifies to the development of system suppliers in CEECs in the wake of MNCs' rationalisation strategies on a regional scale, that is, to a certain extent to the formation of 'cross-national production networks' in Europe. However, the OPT evidence illustrates only one dimension of CNPN – supplier–principal relations – and more evidence is needed to substantiate the hypothesis of the formation of CNPN in Europe. That said, some tentative hypotheses can be proposed here. In particular, the reach of European nascent CNPN seems far more limited than in the Asian case, and their evolution more problematic. Findings made in the first chapters suggest that OPT is not really a *first* stage in the formation of more complex forms of production networks. Partnerships captured in the OPT picture have great potential for upgrading at the micro-level. However, they seem to rather reflect a *stable* state of division of labour at the regional scale. If this interpretation is correct, evolution is bound to take place *within* the present structure of regional division of labour. Finally, evidence of *maquiladora* developments were found to be only marginal, restricted to certain countries and sectors; in particular, footwear.

Conclusion

One of the most interesting insights of the OPT example concerns the very differentiated patterns of economic interdependence the arrangement can yield.

The fact that these patterns developed at the instigation of two radically opposed sets of factors, these being highly institutional and politicised on the one hand, and ascribable to the forces of globalisation on the other, makes their comprehensive formalisation in theoretical terms extremely difficult, if not impossible. A common underlying problem with the different theories reviewed above in the case of OPT concerns the fundamental assumption made as to the separability between the two domains of politics and economics. The fact that institutional determinants such as the process of trade liberalisation can seriously impinge on the free development of market forces, and that, in turn, corporate variables make significant sense of both market and political factors renders OPT developments particularly difficult to explain. Another general drawback of the above theories is their common difficulty in grasping the possible different directions in which OPT can develop. In this respect, only an *evolutionary* perspective would enable the capture of what is one of the fundamental features characterising the implications OPT has for the terms under which East–West interdependence develops: the potential of the arrangement to become a 'learning instrument' in the hands of local CEEC firms.

7
Conclusion

An analysis of the development of OPT in CEECs is particularly heuristic in the sense that it provides extremely rich material from which insight into different aspects of the dynamics of regional integration in Europe can be inferred. Different findings were presented in the previous chapters which concern CEECs' chance of catching up in the context of the regional integration process, as well as implications for policies conducted in the EU and in CEECs. In this chapter, it is proposed to pull this evidence together and draw some wider conclusions concerning the exercise of the governance of the economy in an enlarged Europe.

Dynamics of regional integration and CEECs' chances of catching up

The major analytical insight offered by the present study on OPT consists in shedding some light on the dynamics of regional economic integration in Europe. One of its particularly important aspects is re-appraisal of the contribution – in both its quantitative and *qualitative* dimensions – that OPT has been making to the development of economic interdependence between the EU and CEECs.

A first feature, widely documented in Chapters 2 to 4, is the quantitative importance of OPT in East–West patterns of economic integration. In general terms, the arrangement played an important role in the early years of the transition helping CEECs reorient their trade towards EU markets. Furthermore, it continues to occupy a persistently high proportion of CEECs' foreign trade.

Another important feature is the many asymmetries that characterise OPT developments. From the perspective of the home countries, the OPT story is a very German – and to a lesser extent, Italian – story. Many divergences were also detected among CEECs; first, with respect to the amounts of transactions involved, and second, with regard to the product structure of OPT exchanges. A first tier of CEECs attracts the bulk of EU OPT, tending to do so in higher value-added products. By contrast, in a second fringe – in fact, mainly in Romania – OPT transactions concern less elaborate products.

What is of specific relevance is that contrary to a common expectation (for example, Lemoine, 1998; Hamar, 1999), while very dynamic in CEECs' second tier, OPT relations continue in fact to increase in the first tier, too.[190] This demonstrates that if waves of re-relocation take place from a first to a second tier, it is not to the detriment of OPT in the first tier. One important exception is the footwear sector. Apart from this case, OPT can it has been demonstrated give rise, in some cases, to stable partnerships.

The case studies presented in Chapter 3 were intended to investigate the more qualitative nature of these partnerships. It was suggested that different 'learning mechanisms' apply at firm level, which translate at the aggregate level. Two favourable developments were detected in Hungary, and to a lesser extent in the Czech Republic: the upgrading of the OPT product structure away from textile and clothing in favour of electrical machinery, and the *simultaneous* growth of OPT and direct trade in this latter sector.

In the T&C sector, it was found that OPT relations have been evolving towards vertical integration, sometime culminating with FDI. One main reason put forward for this, was OPT mechanisms themselves, which favour the 'quasi-vertical integration' of the two partners party to an OPT agreement. In the electrical machinery sector, instead, local firms were sometimes able to diversify partnerships and ascertain their simultaneous integration within several more horizontally organised production chains. They took advantage of the measure to become system suppliers. There was only mild evidence of these developments in Poland, whereas none of the above two indicators were registered in the cases of Romania and Bulgaria.

It is worth noting that the different 'tiers' of countries thus identified are relevant as far as CEECs' chances of catching up are concerned as, indeed, they attest to the different learning capabilities of firms in the concerned countries. However, recourse to this notion does not imply the replication of different models of development, as with the 'flying geese' analogy applied to the Asian model of regional development. In fact, the European case is more complex as there are important distinctions *within* countries in the first tier and, generally speaking, strong country specialisations.

The findings of the above chapters provide a direct response to studies (even the most optimistic) which still consider OPT to be a minor vehicle for integration, especially when compared to FDI. It is argued here that OPT has the potential to yield spillovers which are different from those traditionally associated with FDI but which are nevertheless as valuable – if not in certain cases, even more so. Provided this potential is seized – in particular, if local firms develop the capacity to engage their own sourcing strategies – OPT then promotes forms of international production which are particularly adequate in the context of a redefinition of the terms of international competition. Non-equity links are indeed a preferred option for implementing flexible methods of production. They can also be shown to favour learning processes. Correspondingly, this study has demonstrated that recovering autonomy has little chance of being a successful strategy engaged by local partners. The presented evidence thus helps relativise both the high expectations which are too often solely placed on equity links, and the traditional view, difficult to eradicate, that what matters is control over end products.

If this is so, then there should not be too much concern over whether: 'local firms can stand up to international competition once OPT ends' (Graziani, 1998: 242), or regarding the fact that, '. . . OPT may do little to encourage the development of products with brand recognition' (Eichengreen and Kohl, 1998b: 40).

Taking into account the changing terms of international competition and the centrality of knowledge and innovation as a source of competitiveness also relativises fears that OPT might contribute to locking CEECs into low value-added sectors. In fact, if what matters in a catch-up phase are continuous, gradual learning processes, the objective is not so much to achieve a general movement up-market; or, at the microeconomic level, to realise technological breakthroughs. Instead, 'learning to learn' is a process local firms need to engineer so as to, for example, find 'niches' where world demand is particularly dynamic. Indeed, recent studies have emphasised how even allegedly 'traditional' sectors can become an important source of growth and achieve dynamic performances with regard to foreign trade (Mytelka *et al.*, 1999). The results presented in this study thus contrast with Eichengreen and Kohl's opinion that:

> Because technologies involved in assembly and processing tend to be less sophisticated, OPT has relatively little impact on production technology. (Eichengreen and Kohl, 1998b: 40)

To be more precise, the evidence presented here suggests that this can be the case, but not *necessarily* so. It is appropriate to stress the positive potential the measure contains because of its being widely neglected elsewhere. However, it is also important to remain aware of the detrimental effects such a measure can bring about should this potential not be seized. In short, things are complex, especially in Europe. Thus, in general, the OPT evidence suggests how qualified must be an answer to the question as to 'which form of integration [complementary production or least cost strategies] will become prevalent' (Zysman *et al.*, 1998: 9).

Overall, OPT is not simply a transient phenomenon destined to be washed away as wages increase in CEECs. Rather than 'losing ground' after having made an initial positive contribution to the transition process engaged in CEECs (Hamar, 1999), the OPT developments are symptomatic of an enduring form of regional division of labour in an enlarged Europe. They took place in the context of the rationalisation of MNCs' strategies on a regional scale, and reflect the inclusion of local firms into MNCs' sub-delivery basis – most likely in the second tier of suppliers. The measure has been used *in certain circumstances*, that is, by certain firms in some countries, to implement flexible methods of production, offering local firms the opportunity to 'learn by interacting' (Lundvall, 1995), and providing German firms with the means to become 'network organisers' (Radosevic, 2000).

The OPT evidence thus reflects different 'learning capabilities' throughout CEECs which are relevant in assessing the respective chances of CEECs to catch up – and eventually to become 'viable' members of an enlarged EU. It illustrates highly differentiated national trajectories of development throughout CEECs,[191] and confirms, if need be, the unevenness characterising patterns of integration in Europe. In this way, it corroborates a view in which:

> the modes of involvement of the CEE[Cs] into the world economy do not proceed in a linear manner i.e. along one mode of adjustment but represent a combination of several patterns. (Hotopp and Radosevic, 1999).

EU and CEECs' policies in an era of 'globalisation'

The OPT case is also very useful from a policy perspective. It makes possible an understanding of the ambiguous role played by EU policies, and the policy options left to CEECs. In fact, it offers a rare opportunity to dissect the mechanisms whereby globalisation influences economic activity in general, and policy making in particular. It thus enables the carrying out of a detailed and empirical investigation of the *microfoundations* of 'globalisation'.

EU policies

The OPT story illustrates how a policy instrument has been diverted from its original purpose partly as a result of 'globalisation'. The original purpose of the OPT arrangement was the exploitation of wage differentials. In fact, as demonstrated at length, the actual outcome has been that the arrangement could be utilised as a vehicle to implement flexible methods of production and as a 'learning instrument'. This is because firms have used the OPT measure to weather an alternative set of more impelling challenges than constraints presented by EU policies. In fact, *the mode of competition* applying in a given sector has influenced the use firms have made of the measure.

It is therefore necessary to distinguish between three different levels for analysing the OPT developments under its policy aspect: the EU rhetorics (establishing free trade); its actual intent (where the process of trade liberalisation is used to shape trade and production specialisation); and the eventual outcome (unintended consequences of the type evoked above).

That trade liberalisation aims at free trade is without contest. However, this study invites us not to exchange the process (liberalisation) with its outcome (free trade). Indeed, trade liberalisation does not take place all at once, thereby suddenly freeing market forces: trade policy measures left in place during the transition period in which trade is being liberalised *do*, in fact, matter. The OPT case is an example of how this happens. By forcing firms, especially large competitive ones, into vertical production chains controlled by EU firms, the OPT arrangement is an ingenious device favouring Western producers through exploitation of CEECs' comparative advantages at the expense of local firms. It is a very effective tool for discriminating between products, firms and sectors, thus affecting patterns of East–West trade specialisation in a way that serves the EU's interests. It creates the basis for compatible patterns of trade specialisation and industrial organisation in sectors which are typically a potential source of threat, that is, where local actors would have the best chances of developing their own competitive positions in the so-called 'sensitive' sectors.

Depending on whether emphasis is placed on that part of trade relations which is being liberalised, or upon that which continues to be regulated by trade measures, the OPT arrangement achieves the real 'tour de force' of – apparently – bringing together the advocates of free trade and those of protection. Indeed, and this is very important for the EU rhetoric, the arrangement can be presented as an opportunity offered to Eastern producers to access EU markets. It thus reflects the fundamental ambivalence characterising the EU stance towards Eastern Europe: on one hand, this takes the form of liberalisation and openness; on the other hand, there is an irrepressible temptation to protect and exploit what amounts to an incomparably higher bargaining clout. Overall, the OPT story demonstrates that the form and speed of trade liberalisation, far from being neutral, is expected to influence trade specialisation and the division of labour on a regional scale.

However, actual consequences of the OPT measure are not necessarily the ones expected. Indeed, the OPT story is full of unexpected developments. First, firm-level variables were shown to be important factors altering the institutional determinants set by the OPT measure. As argued in Chapter 4, it is, indeed, the size of the firm that makes sense of the bindingness of trade restrictions, which in turn substitutes for internalisation, and favours 'vertical quasi-integration'.

Second, and most fundamentally, the impact of the measure depends on the use firms actually make of the arrangement. It emerged that not only was it German firms that availed themselves on a massive scale of the preferential treatment granted by the measure, but also, the implications the measure has for the division of labour depend on the underlying logic governing firms' OPT strategies. These, in turn, are determined by conditions at work in the world economy. In this respect, the arrangement has helped European firms re-organise their production process along more de-integrated, value-added chains, a decisive feature in the context of a redefinition of the terms of competitiveness. Thus, even though EU policy makers might not have fully envisaged the reach of the measure, the fact is that OPT offers unanticipated solutions to weathering the challenge of 'globalisation'. That firms across countries and sectors were differently able to take advantage of this potential, and that this is contributing to the formation of different tiers in Europe, is yet another unintended consequence. Overall, much depends on 'the use firms make of the arrangement'. EU policy measures thus assume their significance at firm level.

All this demonstrates the relative inappropriateness of the EU's past policies towards CEECs. First and foremost, as argued in Hölscher *et al.* (1996: 45–9), free trade alone cannot secure convergence among countries party to the liberalisation process. What is more, the OPT example shows that the process of trade liberalisation has been used to influence trade and production specialisation patterns in a way that favours the EU's interest. The good news is that, out of a peculiar irony, actual developments extend far beyond Brussels policy-makers' initial intent. What is decisive, in the last resort, is firms' capacities to make the most of the framework of constraint and opportunity in which they take strategic decisions.

Policy implications in CEECs

The fact that firm-level variables are such important determining factors in the OPT story suggests some lessons for policies in CEECs. The empirical evidence proposed in Chapters 2 to 4 reveals that it takes little for OPT to either relegate local firms to a position of true 'structural dependency', or to promote the development of local firms' capabilities. Much depends on whether local firms are ready to learn, not by deploying radically new technical competencies but, more simply, by adopting new practices and improving old ones, and by keeping abreast of the latest technical developments. In this respect, the long neglect of OPT by the academic community in general, and by CEECs' policy makers in particular, is rather perplexing. The resulting 'laissez-faire' policy attitude does nothing to correct the inherent danger that the measure locks local firms into the lower end of Western firms' production chains. Perhaps, worse, it ignores the potential that the arrangement has to become an instrument in the hands of would-be Western 'network organisers' to help build local technological capabilities.

This has a general validity concerning the role of international production networks in strategies of development engaged in CEECs (Lorentzen, 1998: 17). It is indeed important to be aware of the simultaneous great potential and risk that a strategy relying on IPN represents. While offering multiple opportunities for local firms to link up into IPN, the practice of de-integrating the production chain also transfers the burden of the cost adjustment onto local suppliers. Being under enormous cost pressure, local suppliers have only very limited scope for taking advantage of their partnerships. Especially if these are in the second tier of MNCs' suppliers, the risks are real that they will be relegated to a position where there is no opportunity for them to learn new competencies. In short, if getting into IPN is an instrument for learning, such learning is an imperative for local firms to get the most out of their partnership with MNCs.

Thus follow some important policy implications. First, policies to attract FDI are simply not enough. Their role should definitely go beyond the objective of attracting FDI in a narrow sense, and policy attention should shift towards IPN *in general*. Measures and programmes adopted, especially in Hungary and more belatedly in the Czech Republic, which aim at promoting backward linkages between MNCs and local firms, are moving in the right direction.[192]

More fundamentally, CEECs' policy makers need to foster the 'structural competitiveness' of their economies (Stopford and Strange, 1991: 63) and contribute to the creation of an action framework favourable to learning as this is the *sine qua non* condition for making the most of the presence of foreign firms (Mytelka, 1998; Radosevic, 1998; Myant, 1999). Thus, CEECs governments should engage in 'sustained investments in building an educated society' (Stopford and Strange, 1991: 13) as 'their role in fostering education and R&D assumes a far greater proportion than hitherto in conditioning their success in attracting those foreign firms who might assist in achieving national aims' (op. cit., 1991: 56). In this respect, governments should learn to learn, and to unlearn as well (Mytelka, 1998, 1999b; Maskell and Malmberg, 1995).[193]

The governance of the economy in an enlarged Europe

In the last resort, the OPT story is relevant for understanding a broader set of issues relating to the governance of the economy in Europe in an era of 'global competition'. As noted by Friis and Murphy,

> To date, the governance approach [to European integration] has not been directly applied to studies of the external role of the EU. (Friis and Murphy, 1999: 212).

What is more, if these two authors remedy the situation and put forward a convincing framework for analysing EU governance in the light of the enlargement process, their attention is focused on the *politics* of enlargement, not on its economic dimension. One – last! – lesson of the OPT story is that the enlargement process also calls into consideration a traditional concept of governance of the economy which underlies the process of European integration. The OPT case is indeed a straightforward illustration of the politicisation of economic activity. Yet, because actual politicisation has not necessarily been as expected, the OPT example illustrates the shortcomings of a system of governance of the economy which appears to be inadequate within the dual context of enlargement and fast-developing mutations in the world economy.[194]

Transposition

The OPT arrangement was originally devised according to a traditional conception of governance of the economy which applies at a national level. This conception of governance is strongly rooted in a traditional view of the proper exercise of political authority over economic matters. Its mechanisms rest on the assumption of the congruence, over a bounded territory, between political competence and the structuration of economic activity.

Ironically, the measure has in fact been adopted as a result of a crisis in governance of the economy at national level. As illustrated in Chapter 5, its raison d'être was to solve the dilemma between firms' international relocation strategies and the objective of protecting employment in declining sectors at home. Hence, the mismatch needed to be adjusted between the scale of firms' outlook, and the national framework within which economic policy is effective.

This process developed in several steps. First, an OPT policy in the textile and clothing industry was devised at national level. OPT was a compromise solution making possible corporate strategies in conformity with the requirements of globalisation, while maintaining the process under tight political control. The national framework was still the uncontested reference. However, in the face of the constraints presented by Community institutions and arrangements, OPT had to be 'european-ised', that is, centralised at Community level. It thus testified to the attempt to transpose the national model of governance of the economy, without altering its mechanisms.

In this traditional view, the centralisation of political competence in economic matters is accompanied by a necessary adjustment of the scale at which the competence of the newly centralised authority applies to that referred to in economic calculations. This is to restore congruence between economics and politics, as in the national model. In this interpretation, therefore, the enlargement of the Community is a necessary corollary of its deepening process.

This illustrates how the European integration process, in both its widening and deepening dimensions owes part of its raison d'être to the establishment of a system of governance adopted in response to globalisation. It enlarges the territorial constituency in which a central-ised authority is expected to reward different social and economic interests.

Failure

If this interpretation of the OPT story is correct, that is, if the OPT developments are ascribable to the tentative establishment at the

European level of a system of governance which has traditionally applied at the national level, then the findings presented in Chapter 5 are nothing more than the illustration of the failure of such an attempt. First, the centralisation of competence in OPT matters at Community level is only partially achieved. The harmonisation of national regimes was unevenly successful in the 'economic' OPT regime. Even in the 'tariff' regime, where a harmonised position was already achieved at Community level, no centralisation of competence effectively occurred.

Moreover, it was demonstrated that the ultimate features characterising OPT relations between the EU and CEECs and their impact on the terms of East–West economic interdependence are largely beyond the control of Brussels's policy-makers. If what is at stake in OPT policy is to keep the regional division of labour under (political) control, then the objective is only partially satisfied. For there is an irreducible indeterminacy concerning the effect of trade liberalisation due to the importance of firm-specific variables.

Hence, the process consisting of rolling back boundaries in the hope that the enlarged constituency thus created would give rise to a system of governance newly congruent with the scale of economic activity is partially ineffective. Recovering political control over economic interdependence is not to be expected from a mere shift in the scale of application of political activity. To the 'lack of "fit" between membership, territory and function in the EU' noted by Friis and Murphy in the political sphere (1999: 213), corresponds a mismatch between the new territorial scale adopted through enlargement and economic calculations. Indeed, 'the jurisdiction of the European Community extends only to part of the world economy' (Hollingsworth *et al.*, 1994).

This illustrates the relative ineffectiveness of the reference to a bounded territory in the structuration of economic activity whether at national or at Community level. The growing irrelevance of the notion of bounded territory means that: 'there is not much left of a territorial basis for authority' (Strange, 1996: 45).

This is not to proclaim, however, the disappearance of boundaries.[195] It is just to make clear that the latter are justified by factors which are in essence economic. In the words of Bernard and Ravenhill,

> While transnational networks organize production in ways that do not correspond to the boundaries of formal political communities, they still exist *concurrently* with the inter-state system. (Bernard and Ravenhill, 1995: 184–5)[196]

Implications for the governance of an enlarged European economy

We are thus far from a system of market management where the economic outcome is structured in harmony with social and political objectives centralised within a single political authority and formulated in a territorially defined constituency. The conceptual implications of this for the enlargement problematique are far-reaching. The fact that the mechanisms of governance of the economy applying in an enlarged Europe cannot be those designed at the national level has considerable implications as far as the enlargement problematique is concerned.

First, departing from a territorially-based conception of governance in which a centralised authority manage the economy does require discarding the principle of congruence between economic and political constituencies. In other words, it implies that the widening and the deepening dimensions of the European integration process must be disconnected. Both the enlargement and the deepening processes need to be defined and grounded on alternative and distinct rationale of a political nature. Second, if not in a traditional mode, an enlarged European economy must still be governed in some way. How, then? Which new mechanisms of governance apply in an enlarged Europe in a context of the globalisation of economic activity?

The OPT case invites reconsideration of the nature and role of the actors party to the game. First, it is worth stressing that the competence that could not be wrested away from member states' authority is, by definition, still in the possession of the latter. In this sense, although with differing political clout in Community negotiations, member states continue to exert an important influence on the corporate strategies of their domestic firms. However, this in no way corresponds to traditional patterns of state intervention in the economic sphere. States are engaged in developing functions such as negotiating agent and 'gate-keeper', thereby engaging into a bargaining process with other states. Indeed, international agreements such as the multi-fibre agreements – and the OPT case in particular – can be interpreted in this light; a co-ordinated approach at the international level adopted to recover competence the existence of which is challenged at the national level by world-wide economic interdependence:

> National states in response to the pressures of regime competition and the 'tyranny of external effects' resulting from internationalisation under nationally fragmented governance, may try to defend their 'sovereignty' by collective action through international organisation. (Hollingsworth *et al.*, 1994: 291)

In this respect, the effort of co-ordination carried out among Western states, and the lack of it among CEEC states, is a potentially important source of asymmetry between EU member states and Applicant countries.

In fact, the above bargaining process also involves the business sphere. In a game of 'triangular diplomacy', states bargain with other states, but also with firms (Stopford and Strange, 1991). The OPT case is indeed a tripartite confrontation taking place within the forum provided by Community institutions.[197] This also applies to CEECs where the bargaining process between national governments and MNCs in particular, concerning application of the 'acquis', is concerned is a privileged domain where such state–firm bargains develop.[198]

Even more importantly, policy implications that were inferred from the OPT story from CEECs' perspective, suggest that states are cast with the role of 'good landlords' (Strange, 1998). Thus, CEECs policy makers have little choice but to strengthen the 'structural competitiveness' of their domestic economy and provide a favourable action framework in which firms make their decision (Porter, 1990). In this interpretation, the weak capacities of CEECs' states are therefore not a feature specific to CEECs. This is in contrast to the Asian experience, for example (Eichengreen and Kohl, 1998). It does not only result from a reaction to decades of authoritarianism in CEECs, but also and more essentially from the specific 'competitive moment' in which CEECs states have to devise development strategies. Conditions at work in the world economy are simply not the same as when Asia entered the 'development race' and currently when CEECs are doing so.

In the face of the weakening of states's capacities, firms appear to be players of primary importance in the game. It is not only because they are increasingly endorsed with prerogatives until now left to states. It is also and especially because it is their strategies which give their full significance to political and institutional determinants. In this respect, German firms which control their local OPT partners' production chains are powerful 'by being there' (Strange, 1996: 26), that is, by taking advantage of a set of constraints and opportunities which they partially contributed to shaping.[199] The power German firms thus exercise in CEECs is more 'diffuse', more 'impersonal'. In one word, it is more 'structural' (Strange, 1994b and 1996).

In particular – and this is crucial – German firms are powerful because they possess the *knowledge* that is going to be decisive for the development of local firms and economies. This is telling regarding the way in which firms are increasingly a privileged locus where knowledge is created, developed and diffused – or not. In the words of

Mytelka: Knowledge replaced capital as the basis for control by large MNCs' (Mytelka, 1999a).

This is a feature of tremendous relevance for the identification of an important source of structural power in the world economy nowadays. It is the respective mastering of *knowledge*, a decisive resource in the context of redefinition of the terms of international competition, by different firms in different countries, which ultimately decides on the terms of economic interdependence.

Overall, the OPT story illustrates power asymmetries between states, as well as a growing imbalance in the respective capacities of states and firms, as the former depend increasingly on the latter for their access to knowledge. It is a story in which firms are *empowered* by policy-makers in the determination of the outcome. It testifies to the 'diffusion' of the exercise of power in economic matters in general, and to the fact that it is market actors in particular who benefit most from this diffusion (Strange, 1996). This illustrates a shift in the privileged locus of the exercise of power away from the traditional political arena to the market.

Notes

1. The EU Commission has only belatedly decided to launch a campaign to promote enlargement. See *Financial Times*, 2 February 2000.
2. On a PPP basis.
3. Zysman *et al.* evokes the 'misdevelopment' of CEECs' (1998: 15).
4. Moreover, there is some evidence demonstrating that these funds proved relatively ineffective in bringing about convergence between the regions of existing EU member states. See Fagerberg and Verspagen (1996).
5. That is, those region regions with a GDP/capita which is 75 per cent below that of the average of the EU qualify for funding.
6. There are different methods for estimating the cost of extending the system to applicant countries. See Ellison (1999), Grabbe and Hughes (1998).
7. Interestingly enough, however, the sums involved are, from a Western perspective, relatively small in terms of the overall EU budget.
8. Indeed, CEECs' membership will lower the EU average. Consequently, many regions will become ineligible for the funding scheme.
9. Besides the system of funds, two other major reforms are to be engaged which extend beyond the remit of this book. These concern the Common Agricultural Policy, and institutional procedures related to the decision-making process.
10. Hence, two alternative strategies are discarded: a drastic change in the mode of integration in Europe to allow for, accept, and perpetuate heterogeneity; and, choosing between deepening and widening.
11. A principle of 'asymmetry' applies to the trade liberalisation process, i.e. that liberalisation takes place faster from a Western perspective.
12. This is reinforced by the difficult pan-European cumulation of rules of origin (ROOs).
13. The Associated countries of Central/Eastern Europe benefit from a particularly favourable treatment as tariffs are entirely removed. By contrast, the OPT measure, when it applies to other trading partners, provides only for a partial suspension of tariff restrictions. Hence, the measure introduces a geographical bias favouring (OPT) transactions between the EU and CEECs to the detriment of exchanges with third trading partners.
14. See Ellison (1999: 274).
15. There are a large number of studies on the evolving trade specialisation patterns of CEECs. For a short overview see Freudenberg and Lemoine (1999).
16. However, this is not necessarily so if FDI figures are measured against population and GDP. For example, with respect to FDI per head, Hungary comes just after France, Spain and the UK, and is ahead of Portugal. See Estrin *et al.* (1997).
17. FDI is expected to make up for a notorious lack of domestic capital, thus easing budgetary constraints, reducing debt burdens and providing cash receipts for privatisation (see the Hungarian case in particular).

18. Borrowed from the title of the 1993 World Investment Report.
19. There are some exceptions: Eichengreen and Kohl (1998a, b), Graziani (1998), Lemoine (1998), UNECE (1995), Naujoks and Schmidt (1994).
20. Respectively, the Czech Statistical Office (CSU) and Kopint Datorg.
21. According to the Economic Bulletin for Europe, proportions of OPT in total Hungarian Czech and Polish exports to the EU amount to 21–25 per cent (UNECE, 1997).
22. As will be made clear in the following chapters, a decrease of OPT is partly due to a statistical effect resulting from the progressive and eventual final dismantling of trade barriers between the EU and CEECs. OPT temporary exports and re-imports are indeed differentiated from normal trade so that re-imports do not face protection measures when re-entering EU markets. Without these trade measures, there is no (custom) reason to keep trace of OPT flows.
23. Emphasis added.
24. See also '... the criteria for competitiveness are derived from [firm's] capabilities to draw synergies from the interplay of technology, organisational, marketing and financial competencies' (Widmaier and Potratz, 1999: 23).
25. MNCs are increasingly driving the dynamics of international economic relations. The 1995 and 1996 Issues of the World Investment Report estimated that 66 per cent of total world trade are shaped by transnational corporations through FDI and other inter-firms relations within production networks.
26. Borrus and Zysman (1998) propose different criteria to distinguish between International Production Networks: open versus closed, horizontal versus vertical, regionalised versus bilateral. These different forms taken by IPN bring about differentiated impacts on local economies. Note that this taxonomy is not a classification of the *strategies* MNCs can adopt. For an interesting review of the latter in the case of CEECs, see Lorentzen (1998).
27. See Myant (1999: 12).
28. Porter's classic analysis (1990) proposes an alternative stage approach to consolidate the competitive advantage of nations which is both factor-driven and product-centred (the exploitation of raw material endowments or a cheap labour force, followed by an investment-driven, and subsequently an innovation-driven stage). This approach, however, is too linear and general. In this respect, the approach proposed in Ernst *et al.* (1998) is better suited to account for highly differentiated situations within and among countries, as well as the pervasive requirement of innovation – under all its forms – made necessary by the changing terms of international competition. For an application to Korea and for policy implications, see Mytelka (1998).
29. As opposed to 'learning by doing' which requires a less active stance.
30. Central to the NIS analysis is the notion of 'agglomeration economies' first developed by Alfred Marshall. Agglomeration economies result from the clustering of firms which favours the establishment of linkages between them.
31. There is a public element of knowledge which is codifiable and a tacit component, which is non-tradable and firm-specific. The latter corresponds to the ' technological capabilities' of a firm. See Ernst *et al.* (1998).

32. As a matter of fact, interactions and linkages are supposed to best develop in a national context as they are strongly favoured by proximity. Hence, the possibility of trans-national or cross-national clusters is considered – if at all – only on a second-best basis. This is rather unfortunate in the case of countries which are newcomers in the development race at this present moment of international competition (the approach is also too Western-centred as far as the privileged national unit of analysis is concerned).

33. Other such network organisers are domestic firms, domestic business groups, design institutes and foreign trade organisations. See Radosevic (2000).

34. The traditional notion of technological transfer is not sufficient to cover the complexity and the multidimensional aspects of such a learning process. Ernst (1999), for example, prefers to elaborate on 'cross border knowledge emigration' while Ernst *et al.* (1998) decompose two distinct processes: absorption (at firm-level), and diffusion (broader impact on the local economy). Likewise, the simple measurement of R&D intensity is not sufficient to 'measure' innovation (Lorentzen, 1998: 10).

35. This is a call to correct an all-too-common internalist bias of most approaches to the firm. Evidence from 'industrial districts', for example, shows that interactions leading to innovation occur between independent firms.

36. There are a host of studies that cannot be fully referred to here, their main focus differing from the main concern of the present study. For an evaluation of the effect of increased trade with CEECs on the EU, especially with regard to the EU labour market, see Rollo and Smith (1993); Baldwin (1994); Drabek and Smith (1995); Landesmann and Dobrinski (1995).

37. See Winters, (1992a, b); Collins and Rodrik (1991); Daviddi (1992); Rollo and Smith (1993); Erzan and Holmes (1992); Graziani (1994); Nagarajan (1995), Fieleke (1990), among others.

38. Product maturity and standardisation are notions that both refer to product cycle theory. Whereas the former is defined according to the level of skill required in the production of the good, the latter classifies industries according to their low or high rate of product development. An example of new industry is machinery; whereas clothing, footwear and glassware are mature industries.

39. These are: high tech goods intensive in human capital, goods intensive in human capital but using little physical capital, goods intensive in unskilled labour and using little capital, goods intensive in both labour and capital, and goods intensive in both human and physical capital.

40. For example, chemicals, office machines, software, and electrical machinery.

41. For example, non-electrical machinery, motorcars, optical goods.

42. Notable shifts are registered in electrical machinery in the Czech Republic, and in the automotive industry in Hungary.

43. UNECE (1998) also found a general trend towards higher value added exports, while Hotopp and Radosevic (1999) confirm and refine the notion of 'despecialisation' by elaborating on distinctions between the scale and scope of CEECs' trade product structure (see below).

44. As opposed to similar goods differentiated on the basis of variety.
45. Hotopp and Radosevic (1999) offer a short review of the main conclusions reached in studies by Landesmann, Guerrieri and Kubelias. The latter, for example, looks at the distribution of technological capabilities to explain differences in 'trade behaviour' between CEECs.
46. Two learning mechanisms are identified: learning based on scope economies (increase in the number of market situations as a result of increases in numbers of exported products) and learning based on scale economies (based on the link between cumulative output and learning by doing).
47. It is only mentioned on p. 38 of Freudenberg and Lemoine (1999) as taking place in the 'traditional' T&C industry.
48. As opposed to 'complementary' specialisation, this 'least cost approach' towards production transfer to the East does not imply the reorganisation of production activities in the West (Kurtz and Wittke, 1998).
49. Quantitative restrictions imposed on textile and clothing were dismantled in January 1996, and tariffs pertaining to other manufacturing sector were lifted in 1998 (see Chapter 4). In principle, therefore, there are no incentives to declare OPT transactions after these dates. In fact, as will be shown, OPT transactions are still recorded.
50. In the following, all the statistical data presented will be extracted from the EUROSTAT COMEXT database.
51. It is chosen, in the present study, to look at *re-exports* after processing (from the CEECs' viewpoint) as they arguably reflect the OPT phenomenon more accurately (imports risk, indeed, to be diverted from their supposed use and sold locally, for example; what is more, re-exports into the EU are likely to be monitored more carefully due to fears that they might be in contravention of trade measures enforced by the Community). Hence, in the following, 'OPT trade' actually stands for 'CEECs OPT re-exports into the EU'. In addition, the years 1996 and 1997 have been chosen as a reference to make possible a static comparative view while minimising the above 'statistical effect'.
52. In the following, 'CEEC4' refers to the Czech Republic, Hungary, Poland and Slovakia; 'CEEC6', to Bulgaria, Romania, the three Baltic States and Slovenia; 'CEEC10' are the two groups together.
53. In fact, the difference in magnitude between the T&C sector on the one hand, and the electrical machinery sector as well as others can be – partly – explained by the structure of trade protection – see Chapter 4.
54. Such figures probably reflect the activities of a limited number of firms, if not that of one unique company.
55. This is the case also for firms from the United Kingdom but they are responsible for almost irrelevant absolute levels.
56. The sector of edible preparations is rather marginal from the Polish viewpoint, but here again, it attracts the vast majority of EU OPT in the sector.
57. It is actually Slovakia which is responsible for this figure: the OPT proportion in the Slovak sector amounts to 38 per cent.
58. The formula used is the following, for OPT re-exports (OPT) and total exports (tot), between 1991 and 1996:

$$\frac{(\text{OPT96} - \text{OPT91})}{(\text{tot96} - \text{tot91})}$$

The main advantage of this indicator is that it corrects dynamic trends by the absolute levels concerned.

59. The indicator identifies correlations, not causations – see below.
60. To be more precise: not to *declare* OPT transactions as such. See the methodological *caveat* above.
61. The formula this time is, for OPT re-exports in sector i (OPTi), and total exports (tot):

$$\frac{(\text{OPTi96} - \text{OPTi91})}{(\text{tot96} - \text{tot91})}.$$

62. The contribution ratio offers a *quantitative* assessment of the role played by OPT. It does not mean that this role has actually been 'positive' or 'negative' (see Chapters 3 and 5). Similarly, one should regard the word 'contribution' in a neutral way, without the usual positive connotation that is associated with it in common parlance.
63. The contribution of the sector to the growth of total exports between 1993 and 1998 is 15 per cent, and the sector accounts for 13 per cent of total exports in 1998. The other sectors, by order of importance, are: the car industry, mechanical machinery and, after electrical machinery in third position, T&C.
64. The contribution of the sector to the growth of total exports between 1991 and 1998 is 26 per cent, and the sector accounts for more than 20 per cent of total exports in 1998.
65. In both cases, Germany was responsible for between 80 and 90 per cent of OPT in the sector.
66. A difference between the Czech and the Hungarian case, however, is to be found in the mechanical machinery sector: a stable share in the Czech Republic, the sector is promoted in Hungary but in the context of negligible levels of OPT dependence (2–3 per cent, whereas in the Czech Republic, the sector (used to) be more OPT-dependent beyond 10 per cent).
67. However, because of the 'adverse selection' phenomena, it can be argued that the profitability conditions of OPT, if compared to those attached to direct exports, are not, after all, so unfavourable.
68. See Chapter 5.
69. See Chapter 2.
70. Similarly, OPT decreases accompanied by matching increases of direct trade do not necessarily mean that foreign partners leave and that local firms take over OPT production on their own. First, the two developments are not necessarily connected. Second, and according to a similar reasoning, it might also reflect a transformation of the OPT partnership which are no longer recorded as such. See Chapter 4.
71. The proportion becomes 70 per cent versus 30 per cent if CKD's sales to Czech firms (such as Škoda) which are then exported by the latter are considered as (indirect) exports.
72. CKD, which is one candidate for the Czech Government Revitalisation Programme.

73. Vilati was privatised after complex exchanges of ownership in July 1997, and it was not until October 1998 that the firm assumed its present and definitive form.

74. Interestingly enough, although not in direct contact with Vilati, Mercedes sent observers to inspect conditions in the Hungarian firm.

75. Vilati supplies APAG with parts which are then assembled in Audi's plant in Ingostadt.

76. Vilati's manager himself underlined that the capacity requirements made by Siemens far exhausted those of the Hungarian firm: the relation mentioned was one to ten.

77. Wages were said to amount to around 400 DM per month.

78. A sharp reduction of the workforce: from 1250 in 1991, to 300 was due to take place.

79. Raba's activities do not correspond to OPT since there is no international transaction. They give rise to what may be called 'internal' OPT.

80. One factor that may hamper the desired upgrading of the local firms' capabilities is the bad profitability of OPT contracts. If the OPT business does not offer the means for investing, then the lifespan of a local firm is limited to duration of the co-operation (see, for example the case of Fekon). By contrast, Vilati stressed how important is the long-term commitment of its partners making possible to planify and undertake necessary investments.

81. These are not *categories*. It is worth stressing the permeability and blurred character of the boundaries between the cases, since firms can switch from one status to another rather swiftly. This has wider – epistemological – implications.

82. Here a pessimistic view is adopted regarding the prospect that OP has to be successful in the strategy it has chosen – for reasons that will be put forward in following chapters.

83. See EC Regulation 1765/82. A main peculiarity of this regime has to do with the definition of particularly restrictive anti-dumping laws.

84. The reason was politically motivated. See, for example, Benavides in Maresceau, 1992.

85. The system, *de facto*, ceased to exist in January 1991 when transactions started to be carried out in 'hard currency' and at world price. *De jure*, the system was officially dismantled in March 1991.

86. The PHARE programme is a joint initiative of the EC Commission and the G24 (OECD members).

87. New Europe Agreements were signed separately with the Czech Republic and Slovakia after the partition in October 1993.

88. Political co-operation, general principles, free movement of goods, movement of labour, movement of capital, economic co-operation, cultural co-operation, financial co-operation.

89. In December, and May 1993 for Bulgaria and Romania, respectively. The Interim Agreements are in JO L114, 30/04/1992 for Poland, in JO L115, 30/04/1992 for Czechoslovakia, JO L116, 30/04/1992 for Hungary,

90. As a matter of fact, they are 'mixed agreements', i.e. they must be signed by the Council of Ministers and each member state.

91. Together with the White Paper, the other two are the Phare programme, and the Structured Dialogue.

92. In particular structural reforms and financial issues.
93. Trade liberalisation, as provided for by the Europe Agreements, took place at a slower pace for 'sensitive' goods than for other products. For example, EU imports import tariffs for basic industrial products were removed by the beginning of 1995 for the Czech Republic, Slovakia, Hungary and Poland. However, tariffs on steel products were not eliminated until 1997 and quantitative restrictions were still enforced until 1999 for textile and clothing goods (UNECE, 1998: 88).
94. See Interim Agreement OJ L 115, 30.4.92, Protocol 1, Art 3.
95. In fact, OPT transactions are still recorded as shown in Chapter 2.
96. For the detail of the provision, see Chapter 5.
97. Initially limited to the 1987–91 period, the MFA IV regime was successively extended to December 1992, then to December 1993 and eventually to 1 January 1998.
98. Additional Protocol on T&C in OL L 123, 17.5.94, Agreed Minute No. 5.
99. These indicators are: the trade coverage ratio of quotas imposed by the EC on CEECs' T&C exports, the number of 'binding' quotas – i.e. that have an utilisation rate of more than 90 per cent (see Erzan and Holmes, 1992), the average Quotas Utilisation Rate (QUR), 'variation coefficients', and finally, a more synthetic indicator, the amount of exports which are actually bounded by quota compared to total exports.
100. For a technical account of the difficulties that are associated with the interpretation of such indicators, see also Nagarajan (1995).
101. The argument goes that attention should be paid to the sector where the increase takes place, and to equivalent preferences granted simultaneously to other CEECs. The share of one country in the quota granted by the EU to CEECs is also an important variable influencing the effect of quota increase. If the share is very large, it invites the beneficiary to take advantage of the associated market power rather than filling the quota. Conversely, very small quota shares generate dissuasive transaction costs. In both cases, the result is a low quota utilisation rate. Other factors influencing the outcome associated with quota increase have to do with the industrial structure of the concerned sectors. Everything else being equal, comparatively small outlets may favour a lower fulfilment of quota, thus yielding lower QURs.
102. The question is of importance since further quota increases are negotiated on the basis of past utilisation.
103. Due to seriously limited data made available by the Commission, the following analysis will take the Czech example as a case in point, showing how the structure of trade protection can impact on the decision to undertake OPT.
104. What is more, there can be possible distortions arising from other sources related to some characteristic intrinsic to the concerned products like quality problems. See, for example, *Business Central Europe* (April 1994: 21). Concerning the low utilisation of quota on farm products, see the *Financial Times*, 5 July 1995.
105. One of the main differences is that OPT can be subject to negotiation.
106. For Czechoslovakia, in OJ L 45, 20.2.92.
107. The term was first coined to denote sub-contracting activities in a national context (see Houssiaux, 1957). See Chapter 6.

108. Unless a small firm produces items that are constrained, as, for example, when a large firm has already fulfilled the available authorised quantities.
109. As defined by Porter, the value chain is a collection of activities that are performed by the firm to design, produce, market, deliver and support a product or service (Porter, 1985: 36).
110. IPN are defined as a '... mix of contract and FDI and a balance of internal and external management' (Zysman *et al.*, 1998: 45).
111. In Baden-Württemberg and in some regions in the centre/north of Italy.
112. This second form of flexible specialisation is thought to be superior to the industrial district model insofar as it offers superior problem solving mechanisms, and better chances of transferability as it does not rely so much on trust (Herrigel, 2000).
113. It is not argued here that these practices are homogeneously diffused throughout firms and economies. These are common trends that undergo considerable variations from firm to firm and country to country; they are not 'best practices'. This issue refers to the wider debate on the 'variety of capitalisms' (Hancké, 1997).
114. It would indeed be worth including them in the 'networks of users-producers relationships' identified by Lundvall (1988). See on this point Mytelka (1999b).
115. Another factor proposed to account for this success story is the 'extensive sub-contractor networks' which favoured the diffusion of technological knowledge. Although it is more akin to the 'industrial district' model of flexible organisation, this example illustrates the learning potential associated with principals–suppliers relationships.
116. Hotopp and Radosevic (1999) suggests that it is in fact levels of development which are more important explanatory factors.
117. Recall that the fieldwork found several examples where German supervisors were actually physically present on the production site.
118. This is confirmed in UNECE (1997).
119. Note that the fact that firm-specific features like the respective size of OPT partners are an important intervening variable in the determination of OPT trajectories, implies that the terms of the complementarity achieved through OPT take actually their full significance at firm level making any generalisation very difficult.
120. These provisions were enforced in the 1930s in the then US Tariff Schedule: Items 806.30 assesses a duty on the foreign value added of US metal products, whereas 807.00 grants duty-free entry to other US material and components. These are now HTS US 9802.00.600, and 902.00.800.
121. Rather euphemistically, the 1975 Preamble states that OPT would allow Community firms to take advantage of 'appropriate technical facilities, or the exclusive use of a patent' in possession of foreign firms. Needless to say, it is low wages that are of interest here.
122. Council Directive of 18 December 1975, in OJ L 24, 30.1.76.
123. At least until 1993.
124. Council Regulation of 24 July 1986, OJ L 212, 2.8.86.
125. Op. cit. Art 1, 3, b. Goods that are under the 'free circulation' regime were imported into the Custom territory of the Community and discharged from the incoming import tariff.

126. Council Regulation 636/82, 16 March 1982, OJ L 76, 20.3.82.
127. Council Regulation, 3036/94, 8 December 1994, OJ L 322.
128. Council Regulation 636/82, 16 March 1982, Art 2, 2, (d). Namely, 'processing from woven or knitted fabrics'.
129. Op. cit. Art 2, 2, (b), and Art 3, para 1. It is interesting to note that introducing specific OPT quotas should not entail overall increase of the quantities allowed to penetrate EU markets. It implies, therefore, that 'direct' quotas be reduced proportionately. See op. cit. Art 2, 3, para. 3.
130. French OPT business was very active in Northern Africa. There were no quotas, however, and no figures. As a rule of thumb, due to national disparities in OPT statistics, and as the Commission did not centralise OPT-related information, there is no way of tracing the evolution of OPT back to its origin.
131. It is worth stressing that member states' initial positions in the OPT debate do not necessarily conform to what common wisdom considers to be the traditional divide between free traders and protectionists within the Community. The most conspicuous examples in this respect, are the United Kingdom and Ireland: these are both considered to hold relatively liberal views on trade issues, although both actually opposed substantial pressure against liberalisation of the OPT arrangement.
132. The main concern of the government finds another more direct expression in the 'Plan Textile' openly designed to salvage employment in the T&C sector.
133. In the hierarchy of EU trade relations, centrally planned economies were positioned last, after MFA countries, and countries benefiting from a preferential regime. Under the 'autonomous regime' that was supposed to regulate such trade relations, OPT quotas were provided for unilaterally. With the conclusion of the Europe Agreements between CEECs and the EU, OPT quotas became subject to bilateral negotiations. To be precise, direct quotas were not included in bilateral negotiations until 1979, and OPT quotas until 1992.
134. Council Regulation, 3036/94, 8 December 1994, OJ L 322. Art 3, 1. See also Council Decision of 20 December 1993, in L123, 17/05/1994 for actual quotas with CEECs.
135. Council Regulation 636/82, 16 March 1982, OJ L 76, 20.3.82. Art. 2, 2 (a).
136. The regulation is merely concerned with the form of the so-called 'Prior Authorisations' necessary for benefiting from the arrangement. See Commission regulation 1828/83, 30 June 1983 (in OJ L 180, 30.7.83).
137. Interestingly enough, the alleged shortage is assessed on the basis of estimates made by Textile Industrial Federations.
138. This explains the OPT strategies of C&A, Kaufhof, Karlstadt.
139. In Belgium, for example, producers were not allowed to devote more than 30 per cent of their value added to OPT operations. What is more, they could not decrease levels of employment in their plant by more than 90 per cent.
140. Council Regulation, 3036/94, 8 December 1994, OJ L 322. Art 1, 4 (e), and Annex I. The three categories are: Outwear, Underwear and Others; each of these corresponds to a list of MFA categories. It is also specified that such similar products must be at the same stage of production as those relocated.

141. Art 2, 4. It is 'calculated on the basis of the normal ex-factory exclusive of VAT' of products listed in an Annex.
142. 'Comité des Représentants Permanents' – in principle, the procedure should also involve the respective competent ministers.
143. One can thus imagine possible coalitions between DGs and member states. For example, DGIII is closer to member states like Portugal, whereas DGI shares very much the same concern regarding international competitiveness as Germany.
144. The problem with the identification of DGs' respective alignment is that this comes up against a paucity of systematic evidence.
145. Mention should be made of the existence of a third federation, MAIEU-ROPE, representing the European knitting industry separately. The existence of MAIEUROPE does not, correctly speaking, further the divisiveness of European T&C representation as it works closely with the powerful COMITEXTIL. What is more, according to Cable, it has succeeded in transcending the substantial differences of interest between the export-oriented Italian industry and others, including British industry (Cable, 1983: 199).
146. By contrast with the positions of COMITEXTIL at the Council of Ministers.
147. That ECLA did not reach a consensus whereas COMITEXTIL did is not that surprising: it is probably due to the additional divide between retailers and producers in the Clothing sector.
148. EURATEX, which is formed by ECLA and COMITEXTIL, is indeed conspicuous for its inactivity.
149. The founding reference is Ernst B. Haas's *Beyond the Nation-State* published in 1964.
150. For the 'scanning' of the neo-realist approach, see Marks *et al.* (1996: 3).
151. The notion of 'regime competition' is controversial if anything because of the indeterminacy characterising that of 'regime'. See Strange (1994c).
152. The interdependence interpretation would rather correspond to an hypothetical state of affair.
153. What might seem inappropriate in the OPT case is that harmonisation is considered to be at work only in the second mode of competence shifting. On the contrary, the proponents of the first view could very well integrate the notion in their explanatory account. They could also argue that harmonisation comes only second after the decision of member states to resort to the supranational level.
154. Puchala, quoted in Wallace *et al.* (1983: 406).
155. Heritier uses a similar argumentation but another terminology: 'policy networks'. See Heritier (1993), Peterson (1995), and Scharpf (1993), quoted in Risse-Kappen (1996).
156. By contrast, recall that the tariff OPT concerns all goods placed in free circulation, irrespective of their origin.
157. One fundamental feature distinguishing this approach from the 'new theories' of international trade is that it is evolutionary in nature inasmuch as it assumes that '... firms with different technologies and organisation traits interact under conditions of persistent disequilibrium'.
158. In this respect it is interesting, in passing, to note the irony of the above-mentioned paradigm specialisation whereby the very static HO is reserved for *developing* countries.

159. The case for a causal relation between intra-industry trade and the liberalisation of trade in a regional context mainly rests on empirical findings, commencing with the example of European integration and its subsequent outburst of – unforeseen – intra-industry trade (Greenaway and Milner, 1986: 2). There is controversy, however.

160. Gray (1973), Willmore (1979) and Helleiner (1973) are all quoted in Balassa (1979b).

161. This is valid for the so-called neo-technological theories of the 1960s, of which Vernon's product cycle theory (vernon, 1966) is an outstanding example.

162. In Dunning (1976), quoted in Dunning (1988).

163. Mundell (1957)

164. Tellingly, Dunning defines international production as that which is 'financed by foreign direct investment and undertaken by multinational enterprises' (Dunning, 1988: 1).

165. In IP literature, licensing is almost always considered to be more expensive than internalisation. This is posited to be due to both the danger of knowledge dissipation and the difficulty of partners in reaching agreement on price(s). A further contributory factor is considered to be the important 'policing' costs associated with enforcement of contracts (see Buckley and Casson, 1985: 53). Contractor identifies four categories of costs that are higher when licensing: sunk research costs; general administration costs; marketisation costs; and opportunity costs (Contractor, 1984).

166. Interestingly enough, Anderson and Gatignon briefly evoke the possibility that control can be secured by other means than integration (Anderson and Gatignon, 1986).

167. Three ways of 'servicing foreign markets' are taken into consideration in early IP literature: FDI, licensing and exports.

168. See Sachwald (1995), or Lahille (1995: 3), Mouhoud (1993).

169. The analysis was restricted to the national setting, though.

170. See Michalet's arguments on the development of a contractual phase in the process of globalisation (Michalet, in Mytelka, 1991).

171. See Oman, 1984 and 1989; Buckley and Casson (1985).

172. See Germidis (1980: 37)

173. For an empirical illustration of this point in the case of German investing firms, see Pollak in Oman (1984: 264–8).

174. Delapierre and Michalet (1989: 2) distinguish between alliances and Association agreements. The latter roughly correspond to the above-described NFIs; they facilitate the organisation of MNF in the form of a network of contractual relations.

175. An interesting attempt is made in Ruigrok and van Tulder (1995).

176. See, for example, Altersohn (1992: 102).

177. 'Alliances' and co-operation agreements are most often studied together; but, however implicitly neglected, their distinctive features often appear clearly in such studies. Whereas alliances are concluded between firms that keep their separate identity, agreements are concerned with the reorganisation of MNEs into 'multinational network firms' (Delapierre and Michalet, 1989: 28). Michalet (1988: 272) distinguishes between co-operative ventures by ordering them on a spectrum of possibilities that goes from market transactions to complete organisation.

178. See also Rullière and Torre who argue in favour of a distinction between horizontal and vertical types of co-operative ventures. There are converging opinions which consider the hybrid position between market and hierarchy to be a valid criterion in the case of vertical arrangements alone, whereas horizontal co-operative ventures would be governed by a logic of their own. See the above paper by Rullière and Torre (1995), as well as Delapierre (1991: 146).

179. An example is Lassudrie-Duchêne's framework for analysing the 'International Division of the Production Process' (IDPP). Three modalities for carrying out segmentation of the production process are identified: association (i.e. co-operative agreements), integration and 'impartition' on the market mode. Disappointingly, however, ISC has been classified within the latter category (See Lassudrie-Duchêne, 1982).

180. The terminology is used in Buckley and Casson (1976).

181. See, for example, Baudry (1993: 51 and 1994). Altersohn, among others, relates the development of more equal partnerships between contracting and sub-contracting firms to the characteristics of a post-Taylorian economy (see Altersohn, 1992: 95).

182. See Contractor (1984).

183. The literature on International Sub-Contracting activities also has something to offer in this respect. In fact, it is considered that while materialising through international trade flows, ISC nevertheless brings about 'economic dependence', whether through contractual or ownership links.

184. For example, A.O. Krueger (1978), who analyses the implications as far as use of rules of origin is concerned.

185. The definitive reference in this respect, is Jacob Viner who elaborated the 1960s on the seminal distinction between notions of trade creation and diversion. De Melo and Panagariya, for example, consider the respective welfare effects of the different possible regional integration arrangements (De Melo and Panagariya, 1993).

186. The 'flying geese' analogy was developed, among others, by Bruce Cumings in 1984.

187. Four are already defined by De Melo and Panagariya (1993). These are the functions of 'purchase-commitment'; 'preference-dilution'; 'preference asymmetry' and of the 'institutional-design' of regional integration.

188. See on the matter Vernon (1979).

189. Another issue challenging the model regards the 'shortening' of the product cycle due to fast technological changes.

190. It is important to bear in mind the problematic reliability of OPT data. As suggested in Chapter 2, OPT decreases are partially due to the dismantling of trade protection measures, i.e. that these are ascribable to a 'statistical effect'. As to 'real' decrease, this can reflect the cessation of relations between former OPT partners, or transformation of the terms of their partnerships. The issue at stake is thus the correct interpretation of these trends. See Chapter 4.

191. In this respect, it is worth noting for example that the above evidence does not necessarily mean Poles are not 'learning', but simply that they are not learning *by interacting with foreign firms*.

192. In 1999, CzechInvest, the Government agency promoting investments in the Czech Republic, has launched a programme to help local firms become

suppliers of MNCs established in the country. This follows efforts already engaged by Hungary along the same lines.

193. See, for example, the past hesitations of the Czech experience with FDI: it was not until 1998 that the Czech authorities adopted an incentive scheme to promote FDI.

194. One attempt to connect the themes of governance and globalisation applied to the European case is developed by Snyder. For a first approach, see Snyder (1999).

195. See Friis and Murphy (1999) for a different and illuminating account of the link between boundaries and governance in Europe.

196. Emphasis added.

197. The direct access of multinational companies to the Commission is one piece of evidence suggesting a shifting system of governance, which need to be acknowledged more thoroughly. See, for example, Coen (1996) and Cowles (1996).

198. A topic in need of further research.

199. This confirms that control or bargaining power rather than ownership or profit are the key variables for understanding the structuration of value added chains, or in the words of Gereffi, 'commodity chains'. See Gereffi and Korzeniewicz (1994).

Bibliography

Aggarwal, V.K., 1985, *Liberal Protectionism – The International Politics of Organized Textile Trade*, London: University of California Press.

Anderson, E. and Gatignon H., 1986, 'Modes of Foreign Entry: a Transaction Cost Analysis and Propositions', *Journal of International Business Studies*, 1–25, Fall.

Altersohn, C., 1992, *De la Sons traitance an partenariat industriel*, Paris: Harmattan.

Anderson, K. and Blackhurst R. (eds), 1993, *Regional Integration and the Global Trading System*, Hemel Hempstead: Harvester Wheatsheaf.

Balassa, B., 1961, *The Theory of Economic Integration*, London: Allen & Unwin.

Balassa, B., 1965, 'Trade Liberalization and "Revealed" Comparative Advantage', *The Manchester School of Economic and Social Studies*, 23, 99–124.

Balassa, B., 1967, *Trade Liberalization among Industrialised Countries: Objectives and Alternatives*, New York: Mc Graw-Hill Book Company.

Balassa, B., 1979a, A Stage Approach to Comparative Advantage, in I. Adelman (ed.), *Economic Growth and Resources*, London: Macmillan Press – now Palgrave.

Balassa, B., 1979b, Intra-Industry Trade of Developing Country in the World Economy, in H. Giersch (ed.), *On the Economics of Intra-Industry Trade*, Tübingen: J.C.B. Mohr.

Balassa, B., 1979c, The Changing Pattern of Comparative Advantage in Manufactured Goods, *Review of Economics and Statistics*, May.

Baldone, S. and Sdogati, F. (eds), 1997, *EU-CEECs Integration: Policies and Market at Work*, Milan: Franco Angeli.

Baldwin, R.E., 1994, *Towards an Integrated Europe*, London: Centre for Economic Policy Research.

Baldwin, R.E., Haaparanta P. and Kiander J. (eds), 1995, *Expanding Membership of the European Union*, Cambridge: Cambridge University Press.

Ballance, R.H., 1988, Trade Performance as an Indicator of Comparative Advantage, in D. Greenaway (ed.), *Economic Development and International Trade*, London: Macmillan Press – now Palgrave.

Baudry, B., 1993, Partenariat et sous-traitance: une approache par la théorie des incitations, *Revue d'Economic Industrielle*, 66, 4° trim.

Baudry, B., 1994, Segmentation du marché du travail et de la sous-traitance, *Revue d'Economie Politique*, No. 1 Janv–Fev, 77–95.

Benacek, V. *et al.* 1999, The Determinants and Impact of Foreign Direct Investment in Central and Eastern Europe, mimeo.

Bernard, M. and Ravenhill, J., 1995, Beyond Product Cycles and Flying Geese: Regionalization, Hierarchy, and the Industrialization of East Asia, *World Politics*, 47 (2), January.

Bertsch, G. and Elliott-Gower, S. (eds), 1991, *The Impact of Governments on East–West Relations*, London: Macmillan Press – now Palgrave.

Bertsch, G.K., Vogel, H. and Zielonka, J. (eds), 1991, *After the Revolutions: East–West Trade and Technology Transfer in the 1990s*, Boulder, CO: Westview Point.

Biemans, W.G., 1992, *Managing Innovation within Networks*, New York: Routledge.

Black, S.W., 1997, *Europe's Economy looks East*, Cambridge: Cambridge University Press.

Borrus, M. and Zysman, J., 1998, Globalization with Borders: The Rise of Wintelism as the Future of Industrial Competition, in J. Zysman and A. Schwartz (eds), op. cit.

Brander, J.A., 1981, Intra-industry trade in identical commodities, *Journal of International Economics*, 111, 1–14.

Brenton, P. and Di Mauro, F., 1998, Is there any Potential in Trade in Sensitive Industrial Products between the CEECs and the EU?, *The World Economy*, Vol. 21, No. 3, May.

Buckley, P. and Casson, M., 1976, *The Future of Multinational Enterprises*, London: Macmillan Press – now Palgrave.

Buckley, P. and Casson, M., 1985, *The Economic Theory of the Multinational Enterprise: Selected Papers*, New York: St. Martin's Press – now Palgrave.

Caporaso J. (ed.), 1987, *A Changing International Division of Labor*, Boulder, CO: Lynne Rienner Publishers.

Casson, M., 1979, *Alternatives to the Multinational Enterprise*, London: Macmillan Press – now Palgrave.

CEC, 1975, Council Directive of 18 December 1975, OJ L 24, 30.1.76.

CEC, 1982, Council Regulation 636/82, 16 March 1982, OJ L 76, 20.3.82.

CEC, 1986, Council Regulation 2473/86 of 24 July 1986, OJ L 212, 2.8.86.

CEC, 1986, Council Regulation 4136/86, 22 December 1986, OJ L 387, 31.12.86.

CEC, 1986, Council Regulation of 24 July 1986, OJ L 212, 2.8.86.

CEC, 1987, *Improving Competitiveness and Industrial Structures in the Community*, Luxembourg: Office for Official Publications of the European Communities.

CEC, 1990, Council Regulation 3832/90, 20 December 1990, OJ L 370, 31.12.90.

CEC, 1990, *Industrial Policy in an Open and Competitive Environment*, Com (90) 556, 16 November 1990.

CEC, 1992, Council Regulation 369/92, 19 December 1991, OJ L 45, 20.2.92.

CEC, 1992, Additional Protocol, OJ L 410, 31.12.92.

CEC, 1992, Custom Codes, Council Regulation No 2913/92, OJ L 302, 19.10.92.

CEC, 1992, *European Commission Guidelines on the Future Relations between the EC and CEE*, Europe, December, No. 1814.

CEC, 1992, Interim Agreements, OJ CEC, L116, 30.04.1992.

CEC, 1992, Interim Agreements, OJ L114, 30.04.1992.

CEC, 1992, Interim Agreements, OJ L115, 30.04.1992.

CEC, 1993, *A Concise Overview of the EC Trade Policy*, European Economy, 52.

CEC, 1993, Council Decision, 20 December 1993, OJ L 123, 17.5.94.

CEC, 1993, Council Regulation 3030/93, 12 October 1993, OJ L 275, 8.11.93.

CEC, 1994, *An Industrial Competitiveness Policy for the EU*, Communication from the European Commission to the Council, Com (94) 319 final 14.09.94.

CEC, 1994, Council Regulation, 3036/94, 8 December 1994, OJ L 322.

Centre for Economic Policy Research (CEPR), 1990, *Monitoring European Integration: the impact of Eastern Europe*, London: CEPR.

Centre for Economic Policy Research (CEPR), 1994, *New Trade Theories – a Look at the Empirical Evidence*, London: CEPR.

Cerny, P.G., 1990, *The Changing Architecture of Politics – Structure, Agency, and the Future of the State*, London: Sage Publications.

Chesnais, F., 1995, National Systems of Innovation, Foreign Direct Investment and the Operations of Multinational Enterprises, in B.Å. Lundvall (ed.), op. cit.

Cline, W.R. (ed.), 1983, *Trade Policy in the 1980s*, Washington DC: Institute for International Economics.

Cline, W.R., 1987, *World Trade in Textile and Apparels*, Washington DC: Institute for International Economics.

Coen, D., 1996, *The Large Firm as a Political Actor in the EU: an Empirical Study of the Behaviour and Logic*, PhD thesis, Florence: IUE.

Collins S. and Rodrik D., 1991, *Eastern Europe and the Soviet Union in the World Economy*, Institute for International Economics, Washington DC.

Contractor, F.J., 1984, Choosing between Direct Investment and Licensing: Theoretical Considerations and Empirical Tests, *Journal of International Business Studies*, 167–88, Winter.

Contractor, F.J. and Lorange, P., 1988, *Co-operative Strategies in International Business*, Toronto: Lexington Books.

Corado, C., 1995, Textile and Clothing Trade with Central and Eastern Europe: Impact on Members of the EC, in R. Faini and R. Portes (eds), op. cit.

Cowles, M.G., 1996, German Big Business: Learning to play the European Game, *German Politics and Society*, Vol. 14, N(3).

Daviddi, R., 1992, From the CMEA to the Europe Agreements: Trade and Aid in the Relations between the European Community and Eastern Europe, *Economic Systems*, Vol. 16, No. 2, October, 269–94.

Daviddi, R., 1994, Integrazione e cooperazione nella 'nuova Europa' – Il quadro istituzionale e gli ostacoli principali, *Europa/Europe*, No. 3.

De Melo, J. and Panagariya, A., 1993, *New Dimensions in Regional Integration*, Cambridge: Cambridge University Press, and Centre for Economic Policy Research.

Deardoff, A.V., 1980, The General Validity of the Law of Comparative Advantage, *Journal of Political Economy*, 88, 941–57.

Deardoff, A.V., 1982, Testing Trade Theories and Predicting Trade Flows, in R.W. Jones and P.B. Kenen (eds), *Handbook of International Economics*, Vol. 1, Amsterdam: North Holland.

Dehousse, R. and Majone G., 1994, The Institutional Dynamics of European Integration: from the SEA to the Maastricht Treaty, in S. Martin (ed.), *The Construction of Europe – Essays in Honour of Emile Noel*, Dordrecht: Kluwer Academic Publisher.

Dehousse, R. (ed.), 1998, *An ever larger Union? The Eastern Enlargement in Perspective*, Baden-Baden: Nomos.

Delapierre, M., 1991, Les accords inter-entreprises, partage ou partenariat? Les stratégies des groupes Européens du traitement de l'information, *Revue d'Economie Industrielle*, 1° trim. 135–61.

Delapierre, M. and Michalet, C.A., 1976, *Les implantations étrangères en France: stratégies et structures*, Paris: Calmann-Levy.

Delapierre, M. and C.A. Michalet, 1989, Vers un changement des structures des multinationales: le principe d'internalisation en question, *Revue d'Economie Industrielle*, No. 47, 1° trim. 27–43.

Delapierre, M. and Mytelka, L.K., 1998,' Blurring Boundaries: New Inter-firm Relationships and the Emergence of Networked Knowledge-Based Oligopolies, in M. Colombo (ed.), *The Changing Boundaries of the Firm – Explaining Evolving Inter-Firm Relations*, London: Routledge.

Dobrinsky, R. and Landesmann, M., 1995, *Transforming Economies and European Integration*, Aldershot: Elgar.

Dosi, G., Pavitt, K. and Soete, L., 1990, *The Economics of Technical Change and International Trade*, New York: Harvester Wheatsheaf.

Dunning, J.H., 1979, Explaining Changing Patterns of International Production: in Defence of the Eclectic Theory, in *Oxford Bulletin of Economics and Statistics*, Vol. 41, No. 4, November.

Dunning, J.H., 1988, The Eclectic Paradigm of International Production: a Restatement and some Possible Extensions, *Journal of International Business Studies*, Vol. XIX No. 1, Spring.

Dunning, J.H. and Rugman, A.M., 1985, The Influence of Hymer's Dissertation on the Theory of FDI, *AEA Papers and Proceedings*, 229–32, May.

Dzabik, Z. and Smith, A., 1995, *Trade Performance and Trade Policy in Central and Eastern Europe*, London: Centre for Economic Policy Research.

Eichengreen, B. and Kohl, R., 1998a, The External Sector and Development in Eastern Europe: the Determinants of Differential Performance, *Journal of International Relations and Development*, Vol. 1, No. 1–2, July.

Eichengreen, B. and Kohl, R., 1998b, 'The External Sector, the State and Development in Eastern Europe', in J. Zysman and A. Schwartz (eds), op. cit.

Ellingstad, M., 1997, The Maquiladora Syndrome: Central European Prospects, *Europe–Asia Studies*, Vol. 49, No. 1.

Ellison, D.L., 1999, The Eastern Enlargement: a New or Multi-Speed Europe?, in B. Widmaier and W. Potratz (eds), op. cit.

Ernst, D., 1999, How Globalisation Reshapes the Geography of Innovation Systems – Reflections on Global Production Networks in Information Industries, mimeo.

Ernst, D., Ganniatsos T. and Mytelka, L.K. (eds), 1998, *Technological Capabilities and Export Success in Asia*, London: Routledge.

Erzan, R. and Holmes C., 1992, The Restrictiviness of the MFA on Eastern European Trade, Washington DC: The World Bank.

Estrin, S., Hughes, K. and Todd, S., 1997, *Foreign Direct Investment in Central and Eastern Europe: Multinationals in the Transition*, London: Pinter and The Royal Institute of International Affairs.

European Economy, 1994, *The Economic Interpenetration between the European Union and Eastern Europe*, No. 6.

Fagerberg, J. and Verspagen, B., 1996, Heading for Divergence? Regional Growth in Europe Reconsidered, *Journal of Common Market Studies*, 34, 431–48.

Faini, R. and Portes, R. (eds), 1995, *European Union Trade with Eastern Europe: Adjustment and Opportunities*, London: Centre for Economic Policy Research.

Fieleke, N., 1990 Commerce with the Newly Liberalizing Countries: Promised Land, Quicksand, or What?, *New England Economic Review*, May/June 1990, 19–33.

Finger, J.M., 1975, Tariff Provisions for Offshore Assembly and the Exports of Developing Countries, *Economic Journal*, Vol. 85, 365–71.

Finger, J.M., 1976. Trade and Domestic Effects of the Offshore Assembly Provision in the U.S. Tariff, *American Economic Review*, 598–611.

Flemming, J. and Rollo, J.M.C., 1992, *Trade, Payments and Adjustment in Central and Eastern Europe*, London: Royal Institute of International Affairs.

Forsgren, M. (ed.), 1992, *Managing Networks in International Business*, Philadelphia: Gordon and Breach.

Forstner, H. and Ballance, R., 1990, *Competing in a Global Economy: an Empirical Study on Specialization and Trade in Manufactures*, London: Unwin Hyman.

Freudenberg, M. and Lemoine, F., 1999, Central and Eastern European Countries in the International Division of Labour in Europe, *CEPII Documents de Travail*, No. 5, April.

Friis, L. and Murphy, A., 1999, The European Union and Central and Eastern Europe: Governance and Boundaries, *Journal of Common Market Studies*, Vol. 37, No. 2, June.

Friman, R.H., 1990, *Patchwork Protectionism – Textile Trade Policy in the US, Japan, and West Germany*, New York: Cornell University Press.

Frobel, F., Heinrichs J. and Kreye, O., 1980, *The New International Division of Labour*, Cambridge: Cambridge University Press.

Gacs, J. and Winckler, G., 1994, *International Trade and Restructuring in Eastern Europe*, Vienna: Physica-Verlag.

Gereffi, G. and Korzeniewicz, M., 1994, *Commodity Chains and Global Capitalism*, Westport: Greenwood Press.

Gerling, K. and Schmidt, K.D., 1998, Emerging Corporate Networks in Central-Eastern Europe Border Regions: Some Theoretical Arguments and Stylized Facts, *Kiel Working Paper*, No. 852, March.

Germidis, D., 1980, *International Subcontracting – a New Form of Investment*, Paris: OECD.

Giddy, I.H., 1978, The Demise of the Product Cycle Model of International Business Theory, *Columbia Journal of World Business*, XIII, 1, 90–7.

Giersch, H., 1979, *On the Economics of Intra-Industry Trade*, Tübingen: J.C.B. Mohr.

Gourevitch, P., 1986, *Politics in Hard Times – Comparative Responses to International Economic Crises*, Ithaca: Cornell University Press.

Grabbe, H. and Hughes, K., 1997, The Implications of Eastward Enlargement for EU Integration, Convergence and Competitiveness, paper presented at a TSER Workshop Technology, Economic Integration and Social Cohesion, MERIT.

Grabbe, H. and Hughes, K., 1998, Reform of the Structural Funds: Central and East European Perspectives, *European Planning Studies*, 6 (6), 665–76.

Graziani, G., 1994a, Trade Patterns and Comparative Advantages of Central Eastern Europe with EC countries, in J. Gacs and G. Winckler (eds), op. cit.

Graziani, G., 1994b, Italy's Manufacturing Trade with Eastern Europe – Specialization Patterns and Possible Impact of Liberalization on Italian Industry, in *European Economy*, op. cit.

Graziani, G., 1998, Globalization of Production in the Textile and Clothing Industry: the Case of Italian Foreign Direct Investment and Outward Processing Traffic, in J. Zysman and A. Schwartz (eds), op. cit.

Greenaway, D. (ed.), 1988, *Economic Development and International Trade*, London: Macmillan Press – now Palgrave.

Greenaway, D., 1991, New Trade Theories and Developing Countries, in V.N. Balasubramanyam and S. Lall (eds), *Current Issues in Development Economics*, London: Macmillan Press – now Palgrave.

Greenaway, D. and Milner, C., 1986, *The Economics of Intra-Industry Trade*, Oxford: Basil Blackwell.

Greenaway, D. and Winters, L.A. (eds), 1994, *Surveys in International Trade*, Oxford: Basil Blackwell.

Greenwood, J., Grote, J.R. and Ronit, K. (eds), 1992, *Organized Interests and the European Community*, London: Sage Publications.

Greenwood, J. and Ronit, K., 1994, Interest Groups in the European Community: Newly Emerging Dynamics and Forms, *West European Politics*, Vol. 17, No. 1, Jan, 31–52.

Grossman, G.H. and Helpman, E., 1991, *Innovation and Growth in the Global Economy*, Cambridge, Mass.: The MIT Press.

Grossman, G.M., 1992, *Imperfect Competition and International Trade*, Cambridge, Mass.: MIT Press.

Grubel, H.G. and Lloyd, P.J., 1975, *Intra-Industry Trade – the Theory and Measurements of International Trade in Differentiated Products*, London: Macmillan Press – now Palgrave.

Grunwald, J. and Flamm, K., 1985, *The Global Factory: Foreign Assembly in International Trade*, Washington DC: Brookings Institution.

Guerrieri, P., 1994,' International Trade Pattern, Structural Change and Technology in Major Latin American Countries, *Giornale degli Economisti e Annali di Economia*, Aprile–Giugno, 285–314.

Guerrieri, P., 1997, Trade Patterns, Foreign Direct Investment, and Industrial Restructuring in Central Eastern Europe, in J. Zysman and A. Schwartz (eds), op. cit.

Hall, P.A., 1986, *Governing the Economy – the Politics of State Intervention in Britain and France*, Cambridge: Polity Press.

Halpern, L., 1994, Comparative Advantage and Likely Trade Pattern of the CEECs, in R. Faini and R. Portes, op. cit.

Hamar, J., 1999, Policy Changes and the Altering Ways of Linking to the Global Corporate Networks – Hungarian Experiences with the OPT and MNCs, mimeo.

Hamilton, C.B. and Winters L.A., 1992, Opening up International Trade with Eastern Europe, in *Economic Policy*, 14, 78–116.

Hancké, B., 1997, Vorsprung, aber nicht länger (nur) durch Technik – Die schnelle Anpassung der deutschen Automobilindustrie an neue internationale Wettbewerbsbedingungen, in F. Naschold, *et al.* (Hrsg.), *Ökonomische Leistungsfähigkeit und institutionelle Innovation*, Berlin: Edition Sigma.

Harris, R.G., 1992, New Theories of International Trade and the Pattern of Global Specialisation, in G. van Liemt (ed.), *Industry on the Move: Causes and Consequences of International Relocation in the Manufacturing Industry*, Geneva: International Labour Office.

Hayes, J.P., 1993, *Making Trade Policy in the EC*, London: Macmillan Press – now Palgrave.

Helleiner, G.K., 1981, *Intra-firm Trade and the Developing Countries*, Oxford: Macmillan.

Herrigel, G., 2000, De-regionalization, Re-regionalization and the Transformation of Manufacturing Flexibility: Large Firms and Industrial District in Europe, in J. Dunning (ed.), *Regions, Globalization, and the Knowledge-based Economy*, Forthcoming, Oxford: Oxford University Press.

Hillman, A., 1982, Declining Industries and Political Support Protectionist Motives, *American Economic Review*, Dec., 72. 1180–7.

Hine, R.C., 1994, International Economic Integration, in D. Greenaway and L.A. Winters (eds), op. cit.

Hirsh, E., 1976, An International Trade and Investment Theory of the Firm, *Oxford Economic Papers*, Vol. 28, No. 2, 258–370, July.

Hix, S., 1994, The Study of the European Community: the Challenge to Comparative Politics, *West European Politics*, Vol. 17, No. 1, January, 1–30.

Hollingsworth, J.R., Schmitter, P.C. and Streeck, W. (eds), 1994, *Governing Capitalist Economies – Performances and Control of Economic Sectors*, New York: Oxford University Press.

Hölscher, J. *et al.* (eds), 1996, *Conditions of Economic Development in Central Eastern Europe*, Vol. 5, Economic Policy and Development Strategies in Central and Eastern Europe, Marburg: Metropolis-Verlag.

Hotopp, U. and Radosevic, S., 1999, The Product Structure of Central and Eastern European Trade: the Emerging Patterns of Change and Learning, *MOST-MOCT*, 2.

Houssiaux, J., 1957, Quasi-intégration et rôle des sous-traitants dans l'industrie, *Revue Economique*, No. 2, 221–47, Mars.

Hughes, G. and Hare, P., 1991, Competitiveness in Industrial Restructuring in Czechoslovakia, Hungary, and Poland, *The European Economy*, Special Edition No. 2.

Hughes, K., 1996, European Enlargement, Competitiveness and Integration, in K. Hughes (ed.), *Competitiveness, Subsidiarity and Industrial Policy*, London: Routledge.

Humbert, M., 1993, *European Firms Coping with Globalization*, London: Pinter.

Hymer, S., 1976, *The International Operations of National Firms: a Study of Direct Foreign Investment*, Cambridge, Mass.: MIT Press.

Inzelt, A.M., 1999, '. . .' in M. Myant, op. cit.

Jones, R.W., 1980, Comparative and Absolute Advantage, *Schweirische Zeitschrift fur Volkswirtschaft und Statistik*, 3, 235–60.

Julius, D., 1990, *Global Companies and Public Policy: The Growing Challenge of Foreign Direct Investment*, London: Pinter.

Kaminski, B., Wang, Z.K. and Winters, L.A., 1996, Export Reorientation in the Transition, *Economic Policy*, October.

Katzenstein, P.J., 1997, Germany and Mitteleuropa: an Introduction, in P.J. Katzenstein (ed.), *Mitteleuropa – Between Europe and Germany*, Providence: Berghahn Books.

Keohane, R.O. and Hoffmann, S., 1991, *The New European Community*, Boulder, CO: Westview Press.

Kesselman, M., 1992, How Should One Study Economic Policy-Making?, in *World Politics*, No. 44, July, 645–72.

Klodt, H., 1994, Perspectives on Comparative Advantage in East–West Trade, Paper presented at the WEL-Conference on Problems of Transformation Economies and of European Labour markets, held at the Zentrum für Europaische Wirtschaftsforschung, Mannheim, September 1st.

Kojima, K. and Terutomo, O., 1985, Toward a Theory of Industrial Restructuring and Dynamic Comparative Advantage, *Hitotsubashi Journal of Economics*, 26, 135–45.

Krueger, A.O., 1978, *Foreign Trade Regime and Economic Development: Liberalisation, Attempts, and Consequences*, Cambridge: NBER.

Krugman, P. (ed.), 1986, *Strategic Trade Policy and the New International Economics*, Cambridge, Mass.: The MIT Press.

Krugman, P., 1990, *Rethinking International Trade*, Cambridge: MIT Press.

Krugman, P. and Venakles, A., 1990, *Integration and the Competitiveness of Peripheral Industry*, London: Centre for Economic Policy Research.

Kurz, C. and Wittke, V., 1998, Using Industrial Capacities as a Way of Integrating the Central and East European Economies, in J. Zysman and A. Schwartz (eds), op. cit.

Lahille, E., 1995, *Au delà des délocalisations – Globalisation et internationalisation des firmes*, Paris: Economica.

Lall, S., 1980, Offshore Assembly in Developing Countries, *National Westminster Bank Quarterly Review*, April.

Landesmann, M., 1994, The Economic Interpenetration between the EC and Eastern Europe: Czechoslovakia, in *European Economy*, op. cit.

Landesmann, M., 1998, East–West Integration: Vertical Product Differentiation, Wages and Productivities Hierarchies, in J. Zysman and A. Schwartz (eds), op. cit.

Landsbury, M., Pain, N. and Smidkova, K., 1996, Foreign Direct Investment in Central Europe since 1990: an Econometric Study, *National Institute Economic Review*, No. 156.

Lankes, H-P. and Venables, A.J., 1996, Foreign Direct Investment in Economic Transition: the Changing Patterns of Investments, *Economics of Transition*, Vol. 4 (2).

Lassudrie-Duchêne, B., 1982, Décomposition Internationale des Processus Productifs et Autonomie Nationale, in H. Bourguinat (ed.), *Internationalisation et Autonomie de Décision*, Paris: Economica.

Lavigne, M., 1999, *The Economics of Transition – From Socialist Economy to Market Economy*, London: Macmillan Press – now Palgrave, 2nd edn.

Lawton, T.C., 1999, *European Industrial Policy and Competitiveness: Concepts and Instruments*, Basingstoke: Macmillan Press – now Palgrave.

Leamer, E.E., 1984, *Sources of International Comparative Advantage – Theory and Evidence*, Cambridge: The MIT Press.

Lee, J., 1986, Determinants of Offshore Production in Developing Countries, *Journal of Development Economics*, 20, 1–13.

Lemoine, F., 1995, La dynamique des exportations des PECO vers l'Union Europénne, *Economie Internationale*, No. 62, 2° trim.

Lemoine, F., 1996, Croissance Industrielle et dynamiques sectorielles en Europe Centrale, *Document de Travail CEPII*, No. 150.

Lemoine, F., 1998a, Integrating Central and Eastern Europe in the Regional Trade and Production Network, in J. Zysman and A. Schwartz (eds), op. cit.

Lemoine, F., 1998b, Trade Policy and Trade Patterns during Transition: China and Central European Countries Compared, in O. Bouin, F. Coricelli and F. Lemoine (eds), *Different Paths to a Market Economy*, Paris: OECD.

L'Observatoire Européen du Textile et de l'Habillement, 1993, *L'industrie des textiles et de l'habillement de la CE 1991/92: rapport factuel*, Paris: OETH.

Lorentzen, J., 1995, *Opening Up Hungary to the World Market: External Constraints and Opportunities*, Basingstoke: Macmillan Press – now Palgrave.

Lorentzen, J., 1998, Foreign Capital, Central Europe's Catch-up, and EU Enlargement: Policy Issues and Analytical Problems, *Journal of International Relations and Development*, Vol. 1, No. 1–2, July.

Lorentzen, J., Mollgard and Rojec, M., 1998, Globalisation in Emerging Markets: Does foreign Capital in Central Europe Promote Innovation?, *Journal of International Relations and Development*, Vol. 1, No. 1–2, July.

Lundvall, B.Å., 1988, Innovation as an Interactive Process: from User–Producer Interaction to the National System of Innovation, in G. Dosi, *et al.* (eds), *Technical Change and Economic Theory*, London: Pinter.

Lundvall, B.Å. (ed.), 1995, *National Systems of Innovation – Towards a Theory of Innovation and Interactive Learning*, London: Pinter, 2nd edn.

Majone, G., 1994, The Rise of the Regulatory State in Europe, *West European Politics*, Vol. 17, No. 3, July, 77–101.

Mannin, M., 1999, *Pushing back the Boundaries – the European Union and Central and Eastern Europe*, Manchester: Manchester University Press.

Maresceau, M., 1992, *The Political and Legal Framework of Trade Relations Between the European Community and Eastern Europe*, Dordrecht: Martinus Nijhoff.

Mariti, P. and Smiley, R.H., 1983, Co-operative Agreements and the Organization of Industry, *The Journal of Industrial Economics*, Col XXXI, No. 4, 437–51.

Marks, G. *et al.* 1996, *Governance in the European Union*, London: Sage Publications.

Martin, R., 1998, Central and Eastern Europe and the International Economy: the Limits to Globalisation, *Europe–Asia Studies*, Vol. 50, No. 1.

Maskell, P. and Malmberg, A., 1995, Localised Learning and Industrial Competitiveness, mimeo.

McLaughlin, A. and Greenwood, J., 1995, The Management of Interest Representation in the European Union, *Journal of Common Market Studies*, Vol. 33, No. 1, March.

McLaughlin, A., Jordan, G. and Maloney, W.A., 1993, Corporate Lobbying in the European Community, *Journal of Common Market Studies*, Vol. 31, No. 2, June.

Messerlin, P.A., 1992, The Association Agreements between the EC and Central Europe: Trade Liberalization vs Constitutional Failure, in J. Flemming and J.M.C. Rollo, op. cit.

Messerlin, P.A., 1993, The EC and Central Europe: the Missed Rendez-vous of 1992?, *Economics of Transition*, Vol. 1 (1), 89–109.

Messerlin, P., 1995, Central European Countries' Trade Laws in the Light of International Experience, in L.A. Winters (ed.), *Foundations of an Open Economy: Trade Laws and Institutions for Eastern Europe*, London: Centre for Economic Policy Research.

Messerlin, P.A., 1996, The MFN and Preferential Trade Policies of the CECs: Singapore and Geneva are on the Shortest Road to Brussels, Paris: Institut d'Etudes Politiques, mimeo.

Messerlin, P.A., 1996, The Re-emergence of Trade among the East-European and Baltic Countries: Commercial and Other Policy Issues, *Economic Bulletin for Europe*, Vol. 48, Geneva: UNECE.

Meyer, K., 1996, Business Operation of British and German Companies with the Economies in Transition, CIS Middle Europe Centre, London Business School Department Series No. 19.

Meyer, K., 1998, *Direct Investment in Transition*, Cheltenham: Edward Elgar.

Michalet, C.A., 1988, Les accords inter-firmes internationaux: un cadre pour l'analyse, in R. Arena *et al. Traité d'economie industrielle*, Paris: Economica.

Milner, C., 1990, Trade Liberalization and Specialization in Manufactured Goods, in A. Webbster and J.H. Dunning (eds), *Structural Changes in the World Economy*, New York: Routledge.

Milner, H.V., 1988, *Resisting Protection – Global Industries and the Politics of International Trade*, Princeton: Princeton University Press.

Moxon, R.W., 1974, Offshore Production in the LDCs: a Case Study of Multinationality in the Electronic Industry, Bull. No. 98–9, New York University Graduate School of Business Administration.

Moxon, R.W., 1984, Export Platform Foreign Investments in the Asia-Pacific Region, in R.W. Moxon, T.W. Roehl and J.F. Truitt (eds), *International Business Strategies in the Asia–Pacific Region: Environmental Changes and Corporate Responses*, Research in International Business and Finance, Vol. 4, part A, Greenwich and London: Jai Press.

Mutimer, D., 1992, and the Political Integration of Europe: Neofunctionalism Reconsidered, *Revue d'Intégration Européenne*, 1989, XIII, No. 1.

Myant, M., 1999, The Tigers of tomorrow? Structural Change and Economic Growth in East–Central Europe, in M. Myant (ed.), *Industrial Competitiveness in East–Central Europe*, Cheltenham: Edward Elgar.

Mytelka, L.K., 1987, Knowledge-Intensive Production and the Changing Internationalization Strategies of Multinational Firms, in J.A. Caporaso (ed.), *A Changing International Division of Labor*, Boulder, Co: Lynne Rienner Publishers.

Mytelka, L.K., 1991, Crisis, Technological Change and the Strategic Alliance, in L.K. Mytelka (ed.), *Strategic Partnerships – States, Firms, and International Competition*, London: Pinter.

Mytelka, L.K., 1991, Technological Change and the Global Relocation of Production in Textiles and Clothing, *Studies in Political Economy*, Oct., 109–43.

Mytelka, L.K., 1995a, Technological Capabilities: a Conceptual Framework, in D. Ernst *et al.* (eds), op. cit.

Mytelka, L.K., 1995b, Strategic Alliances and the Third World, mimeo.

Mytelka, L.K., 1998, Learning, Innovation, and Industrial Policy: some Lessons from Korea, in M. Storper, S.B. Thomadakis and L.J. Tsipouri (eds), *Latecomers in the Global Economy*, London: Routledge.

Mytelka, L.K., 1999a, *Competition, Innovation and Competitiveness in Developing Countries*, Paris: OECD.

Mytelka, L.K., 1999b, Locational Tournament for Foreign Direct Investments: Inward Investments into Europe in a Global World Economy, in N. Hood and S. Young (eds), *The Globalisation of Multinational Enterprise Activity and Economic Development*, London: Macmillan Press – now Palgrave.

Mytelka, L.K., 2000, Local Systems of Innovation in a Globalized World Economy, *Industry and Innovation*, June.

Mytelka, L.K., Farnelli, F. and Taye. T., 1999, Spatial Clusters and Export Growth in Developing Countries, International Trade Centre Executive Forum Proceeding Papers.

Naujoks, P. and Schmidt, K.D., 1994, Outward Processing in Central and Eastern European Transition Countries: Issues and Results from German Statistics, *Kiel Working Paper*, No. 631.

Neven, D., 1995, Trade Liberalisation with Eastern Nations: How Sensitive?, in R. Faini and R. Portes, op. cit.

Neven, D.J. and Roller, L.H., 1991, The Structure and Determinants of East–West Trade: a Preliminary Analysis of the Manufacturing Sector, in L.A. Winters and A. Venables (eds), *European Integration: Trade and Industry*, Cambridge: Cambridge University Press.

O'Cleireacain, S., 1990, Europe 1992, and Gaps in the EC's Common Commercial Policy, *Journal of Common Market Studies*, Vol. 28, No. 3, March, 201–17.

Oman, C., 1984, *New Forms of International Investment in Developing Countries*, Paris: OECD.

Oman, C., 1989, *The New Forms of Investment in Developing Country Industries*, Paris: OECD.

Oman, C., 1994, *Globalisation and Regionalisation: the Challenge for Developing Countries*, Paris: OECD.

Ostry, S., 1990, *Governments and Corporations in a Shrinking World – Trade and Innovation Policies in the US, Europe, and Japan*, New York: Council on Foreign Relations Press.

Panic, M., 1988, *National Management of the International Economy*, London: Macmillan Press – now Palgrave.

Pedler, R.H. and Van Schendelen, M.P.C.M., 1994, *Lobbying in the European Union – Companies, Trade Associations, and Issue Groups*, Aldershot: Dartmouth.

Pellegrin, J., 1997, Linking up with Western European Firms: On the Prospects of Outward Processing Traffic in Central Europe, in S. Baldone and F. Sdogati (eds), op. cit.

Piore, M. and Sabel, C., 1984, *The Second Industrial Divide – Possibilities for Prosperity*, New York: Basic Books.

Porter, M.E., 1985, *Competitive Advantage – Creating and Sustaining Superior Performance*, London: Macmillan Press – now Palgrave.

Porter, M.E., 1986, *Competition in Global Industries*, Boston, Mass: Harvard Business School Press.

Porter, M., 1990, *The Competitive Advantage of Nations*, London: Macmillan Press – now Palgrave.

Radosevic, S., 1998, The Transformation of National Systems of Innovation in Eastern Europe: Between Restructuring and Erosion, *Industrial and Corporate Change*, Vol. 7, No. 1.

Radosevic, S., 2000, Transformation of Science and Technology Systems into System of Innovation in Central and Eastern Europe: the Emerging Patterns of Recombination, Path-Dependency and Change, *Structural Change and Economic Dynamics*, forthcoming.

Rasiah, R., 1994, Flexible Production System and Local Machine Tools Subcontracting: Electronic Components Transnationals in Malaysia, *Cambridge Journal of Economics*, 18, 279–98.

Ravix, J.T., Charbit, C. and Romani, P.M., 1989, *Sous-traitance et intégration des processus productifs dans l'industrie europénne*, Rapport de Recherche DG XXIII, Bruxelles: Commission des Communautés Européennes.

Risse-Kappen, T., 1996, Exploring the Nature of the Beast: International Relations Theory and Comparative Policy Meet the European Union, *Journal of Common Market Studies*, Vol. 34, No. 1, March.

Rollo, J. and Smith, J., 1993, The Political Economy of Eastern Europe Trade with the European Community: Why So Sensitive, *Economic Policy*, 16 April.

Rollo, J.M.C., 1990, *The New Eastern Europe: Western Response*, London: RIIA.

Rugman, A.M., 1980, A New Theory of the Multinational Enterprise: Internationalisation versus Internalization, *Columbia Journal of World Business*, Spring 1980.

Ruigrok, W. and van Tulder, R., 1995, *The Logic of International Restructuring*, London: Routledge.

Rullière, J.L. and Torre, A., 1995, Les Formes de la cooperation inter-entreprises, *Revue d'Economie Industrielle*, Hors Série.

Sachwald, F. (ed.), 1993, *L'Europe et la Globalisation: Acquisition et Accords dans l'Industrie*, Paris: Masson.

Sachwald, F., 1994, Mondialisation: la concurrence Nord–Sud', in T. de Montbrial and P. Jacquet (eds), *RAMSES 95*, Paris: Dunod.

Sachwald, F. (ed.), 1994, *Les Défis de le Mondialisation, Innovations et Concurrence*, Paris: Masson.

Salavetz, A., 1999, 'Inter-firm Relationships and the Emerging Division of Labour between Developed Countries and Hungary: Empirical Evidence on Alternative

Transfer Channels for Technological and Managerial Know-how', in M. Fritsch, H. Brezinski (eds), *Innovation and Technical Change in Eastern Europe*, Cheltenham: Edward Elgar.

Sander, B., 1996, East–West Co-operation of Small and Medium Sized Enterprises: Evidence from the Berlin Region, mimeo.

Sander, B., 1997, Do Border Economies Generate Comparative Advantage for Small and Medium-Sized Enterprises? Evidence from the Maquiladora Industry, *Kiel Working Paper*, No. 806.

Scharpf, F.W., 1994, Community and Autonomy: Multi-level Policy-Making in the European Union, *Journal of European Public Policy*, 1: 2.

Schmidt, K.D., 1998, Emerging East–West Collaborative Networks: an Appraisal, *Kiel Working Paper*, No. 882, October.

Sharpston, M., 1975, International Sub-contracting, *Oxford Economic Paper*, 27, March.

Sinn, H.-W. and Weichenrieder, J., 1997, Foreign Direct Investment, Political Resentment and the Privatisation in Eastern Europe, *Economic Policy*, No. 24, April.

Snyder, F., 1999, Globalisation and Europeanisation as Friends and Rivals: European Law in Global Economic Networks, *EUI Working Papers*, LAW, No. 99/8.

Spinanger, D., 1992, The Impact on Employment and Income of Structural and Technological Changes in the Clothing Industry, in G. van Liemt (ed.), *Industry on the Move: Cause and Consequences of International Relocation in the Manufacturing Industry*, Geneva: International Labour Organization.

Stopford, J. and Strange, S. with J. Henley, 1991, *Rival States, Rival Firms – Competition for World Market shares*, Cambridge: Cambridge University Press.

Strange, S., 1985, Protectionism and World Politics, *International Organization*, Vol. 39, No. 2, Spring.

Strange, S., 1991a, An Eclectic Approach, in C.N. Murphy and R. Tooze (eds), *The New International Political Economy*, Boulder, Co: Lynne Rienner.

Strange, S., 1991b, Big Business and the State, *Millennium: Journal of International Studies*, Vol. 20, No. 2, Summer.

Strange, S., 1994a, Global Government and Global Opposition, in G. Parry (ed.), *Politics in an Interdependent World*, Aldershot: Edward Elgar.

Strange, S., 1994b, *States and Markets – an Introduction to International Political Economy*, London: Pinter Publishers, 2nd edn.

Strange, S., 1994c, Wake up, Krasner! The World has Changed, *Review of International Political Economy*, Vol. 1, No. 2, Summer.

Strange, S., 1995a, The Defective State, *Daedelus*, Vol. 24, Part 2, Spring.

Strange, S., 1995b, The Limits of Politics, *Government and Opposition*, Vol. 30, No. 3, Summer.

Strange, S., 1996, *The Retreat of the State – the Diffusion of Power in the World Economy*, Cambridge: Cambridge University Press.

Strange, S., 1998, Who are EU – Ambiguities in the Concept of Competitiveness, *Journal of Common Market Studies*, 36(1), 101–14.

Streeck, W., 1991, From National Corporatism to Transnational Pluralism: European Interest Politics and the Single Market, *Politics and Society*, 19 (2), 133–65.

Streeck, W. and Schmitter, P.C. (eds), 1985, *Private Interest Government: Beyond Market and State*, London: Sage.

Taylor, P., 1982, Intergovernmentalism in the European Communities in the 1970s: Patterns and Perspectives, *International Organization*, 36, 4, Autumn.

Tinbergen, J., 1954, *Centralisation and Decentralisation in Economic Policy*, Amsterdam: North Holland.

Torok, A., 1997, Spillovers from Abroad: a Sectorial Assessment of the Impacts of Foreign Direct Investment on Hungarian Industrial Development, in O.D.D. Soares *et al.* (eds), *Innovation and Technology Strategies and Policies*, Dordrecht: Kluwer.

Toyne, B., *et al.*, 1984, *The Global Textile Industry*, London: Allen & Unwin.

UNCTAD, 1995, *World Investment Report*, Geneva: United Nations.

UNCTAD, 1999, *World Investment Report*, Geneva: United Nations.

UNCTC, 1993, *World Investment Report – TNCs and Integrated International Production*, New York: United Nations.

UNECE, 1990, *Economic Survey 1989/90*, Geneva: United Nations.

UNECE, 1995, Outward Processing Trade between the European Union and the Associated Countries of Eastern Europe: the Case of Textiles and Clothing, *Economic Bulletin for Europe*, Vol. 47.

UNECE, 1997, *Economic Bulletin for Europe*, Vol. 49, Geneva: United Nations.

UNECE, 1998, *Economic Survey of Europe*, No. 3, Geneva: United Nations.

UNECE, 1999, *Economic Survey of Europe*, No. 1, Geneva: United Nations.

US Tariff Commission, 1980, Economic Factors Affecting the Use of Item 807 and 806.30 of the Tariff Schedules of the United States, TC Publication 339, Washington, DC: US Government Printing Office, September.

Vernon, R., 1966, International Investment and International Trade in the Product Cycle, *Quarterly Journal of Economics*, 80, 190–207.

Vernon, R., 1979, The Product Cycle Hypothesis in a New International Environment, *Oxford Bulletin of Economics and Statistics*, 41, 255–67.

Wallace, H. and Wallace, W. (eds), 1996, *Policy-Making in the European Union*, Oxford: Oxford University Press, 3rd edn.

Wallace, H., Wallace, W. and Webb, C., 1983, *Policy-Making in the European Community*, Chichester: John Wiley & Sons, 2nd edn.

Wallace, W. (ed.), 1990, *The Dynamics of European Integration*, London: The Royal Institute of International Affairs.

Webbster, A. and Dunning, J.H. (eds), 1990, *Structural Changes in the World Economy*, New York: Routledge.

Weston, A., Cable, V. and Hewitt, A., 1980, *The EEC's Generalised System of Preferences*, London: Overseas Development Institute.

Widmaier, B. and Potratz, W., 1999, *Framework for Industrial Policy in Central Eastern Europe*, Aldershot: Ashgate.

Wincott, D., 1995, Institutional Interaction and European Integration: Towards an Everyday Critique of Liberal Intergovernmentalism, *Journal of Common Market Studies*, Vol. 33, December.

Winters, L.A., 1992, *Trade Flows and Trade Policy after '1992'*, Cambridge: Cambridge University Press.

Womack, J.P., Jones, D.T. and Roos, D., 1990, *The Machine that Changed the World*, New York: Macmillan Press – now Palgrave.

Zysman, J. and Schwartz, A. (eds), 1998a, *Enlarging Europe: the Industrial Foundations of a New Political Reality*, Berkeley: IAS Publications.
Zysman, J. and Schwartz, A., 1998b, Reunifying Europe in an Emerging World Economy: Economic Heterogeneity, New Industrial Options, and Political Choices, *Journal of Common Market Studies*, Vol. 36, No. 3, September.

Appendix

A1   Panel of OPT firms interviewed in the Czech Republic and Hungary

Firms	Size	OPT proportion	Goods
OP Prostejov (Prague)	6000 employees	$\frac{3}{4}$ of exports; 50% production.	Men's trousers, jackets; women's tailleurs, skirts
Timo (Prague)	800 employees	10–12% production	Women's underwear, bras
ONA (Prostejov)	175 employees	50% production	Men's suits, coats
Fekon (Budapest)	1200 employees	90% production	Blouses, men's shirts
Elit (Budapest)	1200 employees	70% production	Mainly men's suits
Styl (Szombathely)	2100 employees	90% production	Women's/men's jackets
CKD-Elektrotechnika (Prague)	1000 employees, 100 in workshop	100%	Medical needles
ABB Elektro Praga (Prague)	1130 employees	high?	Electrical wall switches
Ateso (Prague)	3180 employees	very marginal	Car assembly
PAL (Prague)	4000 employees	3% total output	Assembly of motor
Choteborske Strojirny	5000 employees	5%	Metal drum for medical machines
CKD-Tatra (Prague)	1128 employees	3–5% production	Parts for car underframe
Tesla Karlin (Prague)	1050 employees	15% turn over	Man distribution frame
TOS Hostivar (Prague)	550 employees	30%	Grinding machines
Vilati (Budapest)	480 employees	95% production	Electr(on)ic components
VUOSO (Prague)	29–20 employees	10–20% production	Measuring systems
SVUS a.s.	200 employees	90% production	Medical drugs

Index